Bear Necessities

Bear Necessities

Rescue, Rehabilitation, Sanctuary, and Advocacy

Edited by

Lisa Kemmerer

BRILL

LEIDEN | BOSTON

This paperback was originally published in hardback under ISBN 978-90-04-29290-1.

Cover image: An Andean Bear and a Sun Bear, copyright of Lisa Kemmerer. The bear artwork was created by Rox Corbett.

Bear necessities : rescue, rehabilitation, sanctuary, and advocacy / edited by Lisa Kemmerer.
   pages cm
 Includes index.
  ISBN 978-90-04-29290-1 (hardback : alk. paper) -- ISBN 978-90-04-29309-0 (e-book) 1. Bears. 2. Wildlife rescue. 3. Animal welfare. 4. Endangered species. I. Kemmerer, Lisa, editor.
  QL737.C27B3945 2015
  599.78--dc23

        2015024971

ISBN 978-90-04-32838-9 (paperback, 2016)
ISBN 978-90-04-29290-1 (hardback, 2015)
ISBN 978-90-04-29309-0 (e-book, 2015)

Contents

PART IV
Bears and Beyond

List of Contributors

Lisa Kemmerer

is a philosopher-activist dedicated to working against powers of oppression, whether on behalf of the environment, nonhuman animals, or disempowered human beings. Her books include *In Search of Consistency: Ethics and Animals; Animals and World Religions; Sister Species: Women, Animals, and Social Justice; Call to Compassion: Reflections on Animal Advocacy and World Religions; Speaking Up for Animals: An Anthology of Women's Voices;* and *Primate People: Saving Nonhuman Primates through Education, Advocacy, and Sanctuary.* Kemmerer has hiked, biked, kayaked, backpacked, and traveled widely—including more than a year in Asia. She is currently associate professor of philosophy and religions at Montana State University Billings. You can see all of her books at lisakemmerer.com.

Victor Watkins

has worked on a variety of animal welfare issues for the World Society for the Protection of Animals (WSPA) over the past 30 years. Most of his efforts have been concentrated on wildlife protection, and he is currently WSPA's Wildlife Advisor. In 1992 Watkins initiated the world's first international bear protection campaign (called the Libearty Campaign), through which he developed the concept of forested bear sanctuaries, which enabled authorities worldwide to confiscate illegally held bears. He is the author of *Bear Sanctuary* (www.bearsanctuary.com), rich with stories (and photos) from Libearty Bear Sanctuary in Romania.

Amy Corrigan

is Director of Education and Cruelty-Free Living Campaigns and Zoo Animal Welfare Researcher for ACRES (Animal Concerns Research & Education Society), a Singapore-based animal protection charity (http://www.acres.org.sg), where she has worked since 2005. ACRES, which runs campaigns both in Singapore and throughout Asia to improve animal welfare and work towards the eradication of animal abuse, is currently working to establish a bear rescue centre in Lao PDR. Previously, Amy spent three years in Thailand as Director of the Wildlife Friends of Thailand Rescue Centre, working with victims of the exotic pet trade and the tourism industry.

Kassie Siegel

Director of the Center for Biological Diversity's Climate Law Institute, is a graduate of the University of California Berkeley School of Law, and campaigns for the protection of plants and animals imperiled by climate change and for the reduction of greenhouse gas pollution. Together with Brendan Cummings, she wrote and litigated the legal petition that resulted in Endangered Species Act protection for the polar bear in 2008.

Brendan Cummings

is Senior Counsel at the Center for Biological Diversity, where he focuses on litigation for the protection of endangered species. Originally from Los Angeles, Cummings is a graduate of the University of California Berkeley School of Law. He currently lives in Joshua Tree, California.

Jill Robinson

British-born Jill Robinson (MBE, Dr. med. vet. h.c.) is founder and CEO of Animals Asia Foundation in Hong Kong (www.animalsasia.org). In 1993, as a consultant for the International Fund for Animal Welfare, Jill visited a bear farm in southern China, undercover, and found endangered Asiatic black bears in cages so small they could not stand or turn around, with rusty, filthy catheters—leaking bile—protruding from their bellies. On that day, Jill made it her mission to end the trade in bear bile for traditional medicines. In partnership with the authorities, Animals Asia has built sanctuaries and rescued hundreds of bears in China and Vietnam, and continues to work to close down the bear bile industry.

Siew Te Wong

Malaysian wildlife biologist Siew Te Wong, born in Penang, Malaysia, has been studying and working on behalf of sun bear conservation since 1998. He completed his B. Sc. and M. Sc. at the University of Montana, in the United States. He has been a fellow with the Flying Elephants Foundation, and was co-chair of the Sun Bear Expert Team with the International Union for Conservation of Nature Species Survival Commission (IUCN/SSC) Bear Specialist Group. He is currently a member of three IUCN/SSC Specialist Groups, and is the CEO of the Bornean Sun Bear Conservation Centre (www.bsbcc.org.my), which he founded in 2008 in Sabah, Malaysian Borneo.

Christina Lapis

Born and raised in Brasov, Romania, Christina Lapis studied foreign trade at University of Bucharest, then worked as an editor for a literature magazine, and took a job in tourism, until she immigrated to Germany, where she met her French husband. The couple relocated to Romania after the revolution, and created Liberty Bear Sanctuary (www.milioanedeprieteni.org). Lapis' has always been sensitive to the suffering of nonhuman animals. Faith is central to her love and care for all creatures. Lapis is Christian and a vegan who believes it is wrong to kill or manipulate God's creatures.

Charlotte Lorraine Cressey

is an animal rights activist and educator, Chopra-Center Certified Meditation Instructor, creator of Earth Energy Yoga® (www.CharlotteCressey.com), feminist, student of Women and Gender Studies at University of Massachusetts, Dartmouth, lover of life, and enthusiast for the many benefits of a vegan lifestyle. Her concern for animals began at three years old, when she refused to eat meat after learning that it had once a been a living being. She has six years of experience volunteering with wild animals at Wildlife Rescue and Rehabilitation in Illinois. Cressey believes in the revolutionary power of love and challenges the tendency to believe that cruelty is natural in the world. Through her presentations, meditation, and yoga classes she assists people in unearthing the infinite wellspring of joy, love, compassion, and wisdom within. She views veganism, meditation, and yoga as part of a larger goal to create a peaceful, harmonious existence for humans, animals, and the Earth.

Sarah M. Bexell

Born in Minnesota (U.S.), Sarah M. Bexell has worked for wildlife conservation for twenty-two years, and for giant pandas for thirteen years. She works both at the Institute for Human-Animal Connection at the University of Denver (http://www.humananimalconnection.org/index.htm) and at the Chengdu Research Base of Giant Panda Breeding (Panda Base, www.panda.org.cn, established in 1987). Bexell lives half of each year in China, where she designs conservation interventions through education, training staff, grant writing, and facilitating international collaboration. Co-author of Giant Pandas: Born Survivors (Penguin Books, 2012), Bexell not only loves pandas, but all beings, and has therefore been vegetarian since 1994 and vegan since 2004.

Fakhar-i-Abbas

Pakistani wildlife biologist Fakhar-i-Abbas received a doctorate from University of Punjab and did postdoctoral work at Wright State University in Ohio. Motivated by faith, Fakhar-i-Abbas is an avid writer and spokesperson for nonhuman animals. He has written 85 biology research articles, encouraged protection of native flora and fauna at thousands of schools, and has spoken on behalf of conservation and animal rights in more than 5000 mosques. He also founded the Bioresource Research Centre, and with the financial support of World Society for the Protection of Animals, coordinated the founding of

Pakistan's "Kund Bear Sanctuary." Fakhar-i-Abbas has been instrumental in rescuing 62 bears, closing down 90 percent of Pakistan's bear baiting competitions, and hopes to continue until every last remaining bear is rescued.

Dalma Zsalakó
Hungarian zoologist Dalma Zsalakó holds a zoology degree from the University
of Leicester (UK) and a Masters degree in conservation from the University of
East Anglia (UK). She worked for the Andean Bear Project in Ecuador (renamed
Andean Bear Foundation) before being hired by Santa Martha Rescue Centre,
where she tended a variety of native South American animals, including
Andean bears. After two and a half years in Ecuador, she took a position as Bear
Manager with Animals Asia Foundation at their Chengdu sanctuary (China),
looking after Asiatic black bears rescued from bile farms.

Kerry Fugett
American Biologist Kerry Fugett earned a degree in Physiology and Neuro-
science from University of California, San Diego. She transitioned into environmental systems during her study abroad program in Equatorial Guinea,
where she studied habitat distribution of frogs on Bioko Island. After gradua-
tion, she joined a research group studying invasive wasps in Hawaii National
Park. Desiring to work overseas again, Kerry took a job in 2011 as volunteer
coordinator for the Andean Bear Foundation in Ecuador: For 8 months she
coordinated volunteers monitoring collared Andean bears in the Intag region
of Ecuador, and helped with rehabilitation and release.

Simona Kobel
Growing up in Switzerland, Simona Kobel worried that much-loved plants and
animals might go extinct. Always fascinated by nature, she earned a degree in
biology, then volunteered with the Andean Bear Conservation Project (http://
www.andeanbear.ort) in 2009. For three months Kobel hiked the cloud forest
and climbed among Andean peaks (2000 and 3000 meters/ 6500 and 9800 feet)
in the Intag region of Ecuador, helping to collar bears and collect data (by radio
telemetry and triangulation) on Andean bear home ranges, habitat use, and
activity patterns.

Chris Darimont
Evolutionary ecologist Chris Darimont has strong personal, scholarly, and
practical interests in Animal Welfare. As a Science Director for the Raincoast
Conservation Foundation and Assistant Professor and Hakai-Raincoast
Conservation Scholar at the University of Victoria, Canada, his research focuses

on sensitive carnivores, like wolves and bears, who suffer because of humans, both through persecution and competition (for land and food). Chris has received fellowships and awards from the Natural Science and Engineering Research Council of Canada, International Fund for Animal Welfare, the Animal Welfare Institute, and Earth Day Canada.

Kyle Artelle

is a Raincoast biologist interested in the interaction between ecological processes of functioning ecosystems and the human social and political realms. His academic and environmental awards include Saanich Environmental Award, Environment Canada Science Horizons Internship Grant, Millennium Excellence Award, and Natural Science and Engineering Research Council of Canada awards (including two Undergraduate Student Research awards and the Alexander Graham Bell Canada Graduate Scholarship). He is currently a PhD student at Simon Fraser University, studying the behavioral and ecological responses of bears to anthropogenic and natural fluctuations in food abundances.

Heather Bryan

is a Raincoast biologist and PhD Candidate in the Faculty of Veterinary Medicine at the University of Calgary. She applies non-invasive research methods to study wildlife diseases in order to understand how environmental changes affect wildlife health. One of Heather's many passions is to share her infectious enthusiasm for ecology with youth through workshops designed to inspire young people to study science and conservation. She has been recognized for her academic and outreach achievements by Wings Worldquest and has received two National Science and Engineering Council Industrial Postgraduate Scholarships, a Queen Elizabeth II Scholarship, an Ecosystem and Public Health Scholarship, and a Let's Talk Science Coordinator Award.

Chris Genovali

has served as Executive Director for the Raincoast Conservation Foundation for twelve years. His articles on Canadian wildlife and conservation have appeared throughout Canada and internationally (Globe & Mail, Vancouver Sun, Victoria Times Colonist, The Ecologist, Seattle Post-Intelligencer, Vancouver Province, Edmonton Journal, etc, and online: Huffington Post, Common Dreams, Truthout, Counterpunch, The Tyee, etc.). Chris has also had the opportunity to be a radio and television spokesperson on the Canadian Broadcast Corporation's US National Public Radio, BBC radio, BBC television, Channel 4 UK, the Knowledge Network, and CBC News Vancouver.

Misty MacDuffee

is a biologist with Raincoast's Wild Salmon Program. She has spent more than 15 years working in BC's coastal watersheds, advocating for the protection of salmon-based ecosystems. Her work centres around salmon population health, the influence of salmon diets on brown bears, assessing and implementing sustainable fisheries, and the appropriateness of traditional fisheries models to accomplish the objectives of Canada's Wild Salmon Policy. MacDuffee is a conservation representative on the federal Integrated Harvest Planning Committee and a member of the Steering Committee for Rivers-Smith Inlet Salmon Ecosystem Protection Society. She advocates for fisheries reform, incorporating the needs of salmon- dependent predators into management.

Paul Paquet

is an internationally recognized authority on mammalian carnivores, especially wolves, with research experience in several regions of the world. He worked for many years as a biologist for the Canadian Wildlife Service. He now serves as Senior Scientist with the Raincoast Conservation Foundation, as an Adjunct Professor in the Geography Department at the University of Victoria, and as an international consultant and lecturer. Paquet was one of the architects of the World Wide Fund for Nature and the European Union's Large Carnivore Initiative for Europe. He also holds positions at the Universities of Calgary, Manitoba, and New Brunswick, where his current research focuses on the effects of human activities on the survival of large carnivores, and the conservation of these highly endangered species.

Mick Webb

A lifetime animal lover, it was only natural that Mick Webb would gravitate to an organisation (www.NorthShoreBears.ca) formed to help prevent the unnecessary killing of local bears. Born in England, he immigrated to Canada in 1975, where he now lives in North Vancouver, British Columbia, with his wife Brenda, and their fox terrier, Reggie. Webb loves all dogs, but holds a special fondness for terriers; he belongs to a fox terrier rescue group in Washington State. Now retired, he enjoys long woodland walks with his dog, writing, and indulging his love of motorcycles.

Ann Bryant

Raised in Minnesota, Ann Bryant is the founder and executive director of Lake Tahoe's 15-year-old BEAR League, a 1500 member, volunteer-based NGO that promotes, through education, "People Living in Harmony with Bears." Bryant

Majored in Philosophy in the hopes of coming to understand some of life's many mysteries, but instead realized that the Natural World, including nonhuman animals, hold much of what she was looking for, and are willing to share their answers if we open our minds and listen. A vegetarian since childhood, Bryant has always related well with animals, especially wildlife.

Tara Zuardo

Wildlife attorney with the Animal Welfare Institute (www.awionline.org), coordinates policy and legal reforms on wildlife conservation issues. Zuardo obtained a Bachelor degree from the University of California, Berkeley, and a J.D. and certificate in Environmental and Natural Resources Law with an emphasis in Animal Law from Lewis & Clark Law School. Zuardo has published wildlife law articles in Animal Law, and worked on animal welfare policy and legal reform projects for a handful of organizations, including the International Fund for Animal Welfare, In Defense of Animals, and the Golden Gate Audubon Society.

Anna Beech

served as the Director of Communications for Panda Mountain from 2013–2014. During this time, Anna assisted with a variety of education programs and supported the development of a panda habitat restoration program with stakeholders in Sichuan Province including universities, research institutes and related government departments. Currently, Anna serves as a Policy and Strategy Adviser at C40 Cities Climate Leadership Group, undertaking research to support the C40's East Asia expansion strategy.

Marc Brody

Conservationist Marc Brody received a National Geographic grant for giant panda habitat restoration in China. As senior advisor to the Wolong Nature Reserve (in Sichuan, China), Marc founded Panda Mountain (http://www.pandamountain.org), an NGO managing integrated habitat conservation and sustainability initiatives for indigenous villagers at Wolong. For 20 years, Marc has also managed the U.S.-China Environmental Fund, an environmental NGO in China. When not working in Wolong, Marc is actively restoring an oak savanna and upland prairie around his home near Madison, Wisconsin.

Thomas Regele

received his Ph.D. in Romance Languages from the University of Oregon in 2005. As Assistant Professor of Spanish at Montana State University-Billings, his research interests focus on articulations of state, nation, individual, and society. More recently, he is researching myths and traditions of indigenous Mayan cosmologies as viewed through the lens of psychoanalysis, particularly indigenous perceptions of and reactions to manifestations of the non-corporeal or spiritual.

Daniel Kirjner

is a vegan-feminist activist and doctoral student at University of Brasília in Brazil. His research focuses on links between the construction of masculinity and the glorification of violence against animals and women in contemporary capitalist societies. Since 2011, Daniel has offered presentations about the connections between feminism and animal liberation in Brazil and the United States. Recently, his articles have been accepted for publication in Brazil, Australia, and the U.S. Kirjner works to heighten awareness of the importance of feminism for changing predatory male behavior in Western cultures, and focuses on learning about, questioning, and deconstructing masculinity in his own life.

Dana Medoro

Associate Professor of American Literature at the University of Manitoba, is Chair of the Farm Animal Welfare Committee with the Winnipeg Humane Society and a member of its Board of Directors. She has been working on behalf of animals for over a decade, primarily campaigning against the use of intensive-confinement systems in industrialized animal agriculture.

Introduction

Lisa Kemmerer

Wilderness and Bears

It was deep dusk, time to bed down, but I had not seen a suitable camping site for more than an hour. This was prime camping area … except for the bear signs. I could see gigantic piles of bear scat strewn across the narrow spit. Still, I pulled up and made camp, stuffing odiferous items into bear barrels and stashing them more than 100 meters (330 ft.) from my campsite. I also cooked and ate dinner 100 meters from the tent—and 100 meters from the food stash—then crawled into my sleeping bag. I placed a can of bear spray by my head, where I could find it quickly in a pinch, and fell peacefully to sleep.

I awoke sometime in the night to the wuff-snuffling and rustle of heavy-weights. Despite their close proximity, I was more fascinated than frightened: Brown bears were going about their lives just outside my tent—just one meter (3 ft.) from my right shoulder. I had heard about brown bears ripping into tents and mauling people for no apparent reason, but I had been among bears long enough to know that they were more eager to avoid me than I was to avoid them. I had seen dozens of black and brown bears across decades of outdoor adventures—always with a sense of wonder—and only briefly before they disappeared from sight. Just once they held ground, when I pulled ashore to investigate a whale carcass buzzing with bear activity. Though curious, I moved on. The carrion was their prize—and I knew they would defend it.

On this particular night, I wasn't going anywhere. Too tired to fight sleep, I drifted off to the wuff-snuffling of bears outside my tent.

Brown bears add an additional layer to any wilderness experience. Good judgment is critical, and knowing how to camp is essential (both for ourselves and for bears)—but nothing assures us that we will avoid a chance encounter with one of these powerful citizens of the wilderness. No matter how cautious we are, we might startle a bear near a stream or come too near a carrion stash, triggering aggression. Among brown bears, we sleep knowing that someone might kill and consume us during the night, and that we are largely defenseless against such an attack. However remote the possibility, this knowledge is humbling and enriching. Brown bears remind us what it means to be animals—part of the natural world.

© KONINKLIJKE BRILL NV, LEIDEN, 2015 | DOI 10.1163/9789004293090_002

Humans and Bears

Bears provide an opportunity for self-reflection. Bears and humans share habitat and essential behaviors, and the physical resemblance between bears and humans can be "striking, and somewhat frightening" (Nelson 175). Both bears and humans occupy a wide range of ecosystems. Both are opportunistic omnivores, consuming a large variety of foods. Both are among just a handful of species that live on land but also swim and climb (but cannot fly). Females are significantly smaller than males. Bears and humans both have frontal, binocular vision. The lips of bears, like human lips, are free of the gums. As with humans, bear forearms rotate in a full circle, and their front forelimbs have two bones—radius and ulna (G. Brown 47). Both species have soles on the bottoms of their feet, and five toes. Their hind feet leave prints that look remarkably like human footprints, and are similarly employed: Heels on the back paws of bears touch down first, followed by the entire sole, all of which is weight-bearing (Dolson 85; Wood 98). Like our hands, their forepaws are dexterous—they can "pick pine nuts from cones, and unscrew jar lids"; bears are able to open a variety of "bear-proof" lids (G. Brown 74, 98). Both bears and humans are able to stand upright. Both sit on their tailbones, settling for a rest on logs, stumps, and rocks.

Humans and bears both defend offspring fiercely: Male bears usually defer to females with cubs "because they know that she will defend them to the death" (Domico and Newman 16; Wood 54). Bears and humans both snore. Both reprimand young for misbehaving—a smack with an open paw tells a cub to modify behaviors (G. Brown 48; Wood 56). Both we and they demonstrate affection, have strong memories, and are relatively intelligent. Both are playful, curious, and wily (G. Brown 136–37, 98, 97, 130–131). We are even susceptible to some of the same maladies, including arthritis, cataracts, tuberculosis, bronchopneumonia, and dental cavities (G. Brown 91–92).

Bears and Human Cultures

With so many obvious and intriguing similarities, it is reasonable to assume that our age-old fascination with bears stems, at least in part, from seeing ourselves in these distinctive beings. Indeed, across continents and time people have given bears special mention. Ancient cultures have pulled bears into their circle with terms of endearment such as "man bear," "wise man," "sacred man," "elder brother," "uncle," "great grandmother/father," and "four-legged human" (G. Brown 25–28). Humans have named both cities and children after bears: Place-names such as those of Bern and Berlin, and personal names such as

Bernard and Robert, stem from native words for "bear" (Dolson 149). Humans have focused ceremonies and rituals around bears, and have recreated bears in drawings, paintings, and sculptures. Ancient people recounted innumerable myths about bears and bear-human relations—still today we create and share stories about bears.

Artifacts from ancient human civilizations include the bones of bears and artistic depictions of bears, suggesting that bears were important both ritually and for worship (Gill 116). Bear remains have frequently been found in burial sites. Xi'an's ancient Chinese tombs hold the skulls of very large giant pandas (Domico and Newman 125). Ancient people in the Swiss Alps manipulated leg bones through the cheek arches of bear skulls, and filled stone chests with groupings of carefully placed bear skulls (*Ursus splaeus*) (Gill 116; Domico and Newman 5)). Bear images and bear remains were stashed in funerary sites in what is now England. Sometimes Celtic people decorated their dead with beartooth necklaces or left images of bears in graves; they also laid kings to rest on bear skins (Green 42, 54, 52, 217).

Bears were extremely important to cultures of early North America. In the northwest, the Kwakiutl (coastal British Columbia) frequently carved bears on totem poles (Wood 89). In the southeast, people placed objects ceremonially alongside the bones of both the Florida cave bear (*Tremarctos floridans*) and the giant short-faced bear. Sioux peoples (Minnesota and Dakotas, into Iowa and Nebraska) had bear visions, bear rituals, bear dreamers, and bear medicine men (DeMallie 40–41). Pawnee people (Nebraska and northern Kansas) revered bear shamans, Ute (Utah, Nevada, Colorado, and Arizona) engaged in a bear dance, and the Omaha (Nebraska and Kansas) danced in imitation of bears—a dance reserved for those believed to be blessed by supernatural brown bears (Lowie 164, 177, 184).

It is easy to identify bear imagery in petroglyphs, pictograms, and rough paintings left by earlier peoples across Europe. A particularly intriguing bronze sculpture from Bern, Switzerland, depicts a big-headed, very large bear facing the Patron of Bears, a tidy, slim, robed woman seated with what looks to be a bowl of fruit. An inscription on the image dedicates the art to Celtic bear-goddess, Artio (steming from "artos" which means "bear"). She was likely viewed as having a close affinity with bears, assuring their continued existence as well as the success of the hunt, and serving as an intermediary between humans and bears (Green 217–18). Standing in front of a dead tree and stretching forward toward the woman, mouth slightly opened, perhaps the bear hopes to taste some fruit. (see figure 0.1)

Many ancient myths feature bears. In North American mythology, no other animal "assumed such a widespread and honored position" as did bears

FIGURE 0.1 *Artio, Celtic goddess with bear, bronze, 200 CE, sketch by Lisa Kemmerer*

(Wood 8). Mythology of the Modoc people (Southwestern Oregon) recounts how a grizzly bear and a Sky spirit gave birth to the first human beings (Erdoes 85–7). Among Athapaskans (Alaska and NW Canada) myths explain how Bear held (and thereby controlled) all-important Fire, which was inevitably stolen (and dispersed) by other animals (Campbell 277). Hero legends of the Seneca, Iroquois, and Delaware (in and around New York) tell of a large and fierce bear (Nya-Gwahe)—bones of an immense, extinct, short-faced bear have been unearthed in this region—a bear roughly twice the size of the largest contemporary bear and likely the largest mammalian carnivore ever to walk the earth (Wood 5). A Scandinavian myth teaches that men can take on the attributes of bears by putting on a bear-skin shirt that will turn ordinary men into fierce warriors (Dolson 152). The word "berserk," literally meaning "bear shirt," initially referred to such a fierce warrior ("Berserk"). Myths of the Blackfoot (Montana and Alberta, US/Canada border) tell of a sacred bear-spear used for battle and for curing the sick, gifted to the people by a gentle-eyed Great Bear (Spence 189).

Awareness of inter-species similarities between humans and bears seems particularly evident in North American myths that tell of bears and humans who become partners, creating children who cannot be distinguished from other human beings and who live compatibly among both bears and humans. The Haida people (coastal British Columbia) tell of a young woman, kidnapped by bears and wed to a bear, who gives birth to two boys. She and her boys are eventually brought back to the mother's village, where they live among humans for the rest of their days (Erdoes 419–423). Blackfeet myths recount a maiden enraging her family by choosing to marry a grizzly instead of a man. Her father kills her bear-husband, and through the "agency of her husband's supernatural power," the young wife becomes a fierce bear to avenge his death—tearing through her people's camp, killing even her own father and mother (Spence183). A Cherokee myth tells of a man who moves in with bears and learns to live as they live, even growing thick body hair—though he continues to walk upright. When hunters killed his bear friend, he returns to his human family, but dies soon after because he "still had a bear's nature and could not live like a man" (D. Brown 22).

We continue to create and share stories about bears through the printed word and animated media. Relatively few English-speakers reach adulthood without hearing the children's story, *Goldilocks and the Three Bears*. First published in the early 19th century, the origins of this story have been lost to time. The version that most of us know is about a curious little girl named Goldilocks, who stumbles onto a bear's home in the woods when the bear family is out for a morning walk. She barges into their home and rudely samples porridge, chairs, and beds—always preferring those of the baby bear. Goldilocks gobbles up all of his porridge, breaks his chair, and falls peacefully to sleep in his little bed, where she awakens to find the bear family looking down at her. Terrified, she flees (Dolson 156).

Walt Morey's children's novel, *Gentle Ben* (1965), features a friendship between a boy (Mark) and a bear (Gentle Ben), and their many shared adventures. The location of Morey's story was moved from Alaska to Florida, and a brown bear was replaced with a captive American black bear (an orphan named Bruno) in order to create the television series, *Gentle Ben,* which aired 56 episodes in just two seasons (1967–1969), and the film *Gentle Giant* (1967). In 2002 and 2003, remakes of *Gentle Ben* were shaped into two made-for-TV movies ("Gentle," *My Time*; "Gentle," *Wikipedia*; "Grizzly").

The inspiration for A.A. Milne's delightfully bumbling honey-colored bear, Pooh, was a very real bear. In 1914, Captain Harry Colebourn, a veterinarian who was caring for army horses in Quebec, bought a cub (for $20, from a hunter who had shot the cub's mother) at a train stop in Manitoba. Colebourn hand-raised the cub, whom he named Winnipeg. When his brigade shipped to France, he gave the young bear to London Zoo, where she was an instant hit. It was there that Milne met Winnipeg, who inspired both *Winnie-the-Pooh* (1926) and *House at Pooh Corner* (1928). Winnipeg died in 1934, but Pooh is alive and well in the hearts and minds of millions of Milne's readers as well as those who are familiar with this humble honey-loving bear by way of animated media (G. Brown 234; Dolson 168).

Smokey, a fictional bear whose name was given to a real bear, was fabricated by the U.S. forest service in 1944, for educational purposes. This stout bear holds a shovel, wears blue jeans fastened with a black belt, and has "Smokey" written on his tan ranger's hat. In 1950, when a burned cub was rescued from a tree in a forest fire in New Mexico, the rescued bear was dubbed the living Smokey. After his burns healed, he was housed in a Washington DC zoo until he died in 1976. The educational image of Smokey Bear lives on—"the longest-running public service campaign in history"—teaching yet another generation that "only you can prevent forest fires" (Dolson 145; G. Brown 234–35).

Yogi Bear, "the most popular television cartoon creation of TV's early years," Debuted in 1961 as a cartoon starring a bear named Yogi, who wore only a white collar, green tie, and green hat (Dolson 86). He often spoke in rhymes, and his favorite pastime was stealing "pic-a-nic" baskets from park visitors. Dressed in a light blue tutu/skirt and yellow scarf, his girlfriend, Cindy Bear, disapproved of Yogi's thieving ways, as did his pint-sized sidekick, Boo-Boo Bear. Boo-Boo, wearing only a blue bow tie, served as Yogi's conscience, urging Yogi to follow park rules and leave "pic-a-nic" baskets alone. *Yogi Bear* was popular enough to be turned into a host of animated television shows, movies, comic books, video games, and a 2010 live-action 3-D animated film, *Yogi Bear*.

Stuffed bears are perhaps the most pervasive evidence of our fascination with bears. The first "teddy bear" was sold in Morris and Rose Michtom's shop in New York City in 1902. Morris Michtom saw a Clifford Berryman cartoon in the *Washington Post* that portrayed Roosevelt's refusal to shoot a bear, though the bear had been clubbed and restrained specifically for the success and pleasure of the president's hunt. The *Washington Post* bear was patterned after a koala cub, despite the fact that the actual bear—roped and ready to be killed—was an adult American black bear, who weighed about 100 kg (220 lbs.). On seeing this cartoon bear, Michtom asked his wife, Rose, to design a toy replica. She did, and she also asked the president for permission to call the toy a "Teddy" bear, which he reluctantly granted (G. Brown 233–34; Dolson 74).

So it was that Michael Bond saw a lonely-looking teddy bear on a shelf in a store near London's Paddington Station on Christmas Eve, 1956, and took the bear home for his wife. The stuffed bear inspired Bond to write *A Bear Called*

Paddington, which became the first in a long series of extremely popular children's stories featuring a well-meaning, polite immigrant, who loves marmalade sandwiches ... and just happens to be a bear. Bond's books tell how Paddington Bear arrived from Peru with a note pinned on his coat (like so many children left in London's railway stations after the war), how he was adopted by the Browns, and of the young bear's adventures and mishaps in his new home. The stories highlight Paddington's remarkable ability to get into trouble, offset by his determination to "get things right." Bond's books have been translated into "30 languages across 70 titles" and have "sold more than 30 million copies worldwide" ("Paddington").

From ancient myth to contemporary stories adapted for cinema, humans create and recreate stories about bears and bear-human relations. Images of bears grace the graves of long dead peoples, while contemporary children around the world fall asleep cuddling stuffed and tattered teddy bears. Our fascination with bears appears to be as old as human civilization, and shows no sign of fading.

Hunting Bears

Despite the allure of bears, and our perceived affinities, humans have hunted these large mammals for centuries. Perhaps because of a felt kinship with bears, killing them often required elaborate rituals. For example, the Northern Saulteaux (Ojibwa) viewed American black bears as kin, as capable of understanding both what was said and why certain things were done—both when alive and after death. Hunters apologized before killing a bear, and begged the victim not to become angry about being killed. Saulteaux were obligated to only kill bears with a club and knife, and once dead, they dressed bears in finery. The bear's body was then divided, and there were strict rules as to which members of the community would eat prescribed portions of the body. When finished, the skull, muzzle skin, and ears were left as an offering on a pole, along with tobacco and decorative ribbons, in the hope of successful future bear hunts. They believed that bears only came to hunters when sent by the chief of bears—and only if previously hunted bears delivered a favorable report (Gill 117, 119). Similarly, Naskapi (Labrador Peninsula) hunters apologized before killing a bear, and placed an offering of tobacco in the bear's mouth after death (Gill 115).

Among the indigenous Ainu of Japan, the Asiatic black bear was considered a god. When a mother bear was killed and her young cub captured, the orphan was brought to the village with pomp and celebration, and placed with a human family to play with human children, and to be nursed by a human mother alongside her biological children. When the cub's sharp claws became dangerous, the orphan was caged. A couple of years later, the bear would be taken out and paraded around, poked with arrows to induce fury, pinned down and pierced in the heart with an arrow (Campbell 335–37). Counterintuitively, the purpose of the prolonged ritual was to ask the "divine bear being" to bring a favorable report back to the gods—to report how well he or she had been treated by the Ainu—in the hope that more bears might be sent to be killed, providing both food and skins (Campbell 336–37).

Bear flesh and fur were important to many earlier communities. The Cree (Eastern Canada) overtly referred to the American black bear as "black food" (G. Brown 25). Bears were also killed out of fear. When describing a successful brown bear hunt, the Koyukon (northern North America) would often say, "We got rid of that one" (Nelson 186). Though they killed bears, earlier peoples lacked sophisticated weaponry and were spread too thin to decimate bear populations. Within recorded history—in some instances within living memory—bears were plentiful in vast forested regions and wide-open spaces of Europe, Asia, and the Americas. This is no longer the case. A handful of brown bear subspecies, including California golden brown bears, Mexican grizzlies, and Atlas brown bears, survived into contemporary times only to be blasted into oblivion by modern weapons.

The California brown bear—still the official state animal—stands proud on California's flag, is central to the names of two state university sports teams (California Golden Bears of UC Berkeley, UCLA Bruins of UC Los Angeles), and is the mascot (Scottie the Bear) for a third university (UC Riverside). But the last known California brown bear was shot in 1922 for the sake of a bear rug, probably long ago sent to the dump. (Domico and Newman 63).

Mexican grizzlies were last seen in the 1960s. This smallish (360 kg/800 lbs) bear grazed on greens, fruits, and insects, and with the arrival of animal agriculture, the occasional lamb or calf. Consequently, farmers and ranchers shot, poisoned, and trapped this silvery brown bear into oblivion ("Mexican"). "[R]egarded by farmers as a pest and by ordinary people as dangerous," they were ultimately exterminated "due to cattle ranching in both the United States and Mexico" ("Brown"; "Mexican").

The only bear to survive until recent times in Africa, another smallish bear who fed on nuts and roots in the Atlas Mountains of Morocco, Tunisia, and Algeria, was driven to extinction less than 150 years ago. When the Roman Empire expanded into Africa, thousands of Atlas bears were pitted against criminals to entertain the elite. Emperor Caligula once saw 400 of these beautiful reddish-orange-brown bears to their deaths in a single day; Emperor

Gordian squandered one thousand precious bears in just one blood-sport orgy (Domico and Newman 144). Apparently, the killing continued after the Romans retreated: The last sighting of an Atlas bear was in the 1870s.

Bear hunting and trapping continue to be permitted in many nations, including the U.S. and Canada. In contemporary times, the ratio of bears to humans is precipitously slanted in favor of humans, and our killing methods have become much more deadly. The world's bears have little chance against modern weapons in a world where roads provide ready access to once secluded habitat.

Bears and Wilderness

Bears are ecologically important. They balance rodent and insect populations, fertilize riparian lands, and "plant" seeds—just one pile of scat can carry upwards of 300 seeds. After passing through a bear, seeds are considerably more likely to germinate: raspberries twice as likely, chokeberries thrice as likely, and dogwood a whopping seven times more likely (Wood 73). While digging for roots and grubs, bears loosen the earth, helping new seeds take root; they feed scavengers such as eagles and seagulls, wolves and foxes, who hover nearby in hopes of securing leftovers (Wood 77). Bears kill sick and wounded wildlife, helping to maintain healthy populations, and they reduce the spread of disease by consuming carrion (G. Brown 173).

Bears also offer hope for medical breakthroughs: If we come to understand bear dormancy—how some bears are inactive for months without loss of bone mass and without any incapacitating loss of muscle structure—we might better tend bedridden humans (Wood 36). This must be done, of course, without confining, controlling, or otherwise mistreating bears—they are not here for our purposes.

The bears of the world are flagship species, species that capture our imaginations and our hearts, species that are therefore more likely to gain our attention—and our protection. In the process, we protect habitat, thereby securing the futures of myriad other living beings. The Yangtze River dolphin (baiji) and the western black rhino—both recently declared extinct—did not move us to much-needed change. Perhaps bears can.

This anthology has one clear purpose: Heighten awareness regarding the precarious plight of the world's bears with the explicit hope of helping to bring change. It is my hope that readers—that you—will become part of the change that is necessary if we are to secure a future for bears. In so doing, we secure the futures of many species currently threatened by human habits and lifestyles.

It is my hope that you will support individuals and organizations that help bears, and that you will make necessary lifestyle changes to protect bears and their habitat.

Authors

Many authors in this anthology are busy activists; some know English only as a second (or third) language. In most instances, I work extensively with authors to create lucid essays, sometimes co-authoring in order to bring important ideas, experiences, and understandings to press.

I   *Bear Basics*

Essays in the first section introduce bear species and some of the key problems that harm these bears and threaten dwindling bear populations. The first essay introduces the world's eight bear species. Next, **Victor Watkins** takes us to Greece, Turkey, Pakistan, and China, describing "dancing" bears, bear baiting, and the bear bile industry, and describing the creation of the world's first bear sanctuary. After working at a wildlife sanctuary in Thailand, **Amy Corrigan** settled in Singapore, where she works to free bears from dank pits in zoos and unconscionable bile farms throughout Southeast Asia. Closing the first section, working at the Center for Biological Diversity, **Kassie Siegel** and **Brendan Cummings** explore politics and policies of climate change, the Arctic, and polar bears.

II   *A World of Trouble*

In the second section, authors describe specific problems facing particular bear species in certain areas of the world. Founder and CEO of Animals Asia Foundation, **Jill Robinson** explains the bear bile market, and what this industry does to the health and lives of endangered Asiatic black bears such as Franzi, who spent 22 years in the bile industry. **Siew Te Wong** and I explore the large ecological role of the pint-sized sun bear, the work of the Bornean Sun Bear Conservation Centre, and the rehabilitation of a tiny cub named Mary. **Cristina Lapis** tells of her work at Romania's Libearty Sanctuary Zărneşti on behalf of Eastern Europe's disappearing brown bears. **Charlotte Cressey** describes American black bear rescue, rehabilitation, and release. **Sarah M. Bexell** describes her work with giant pandas, on whose behalf she presses for much-needed change. Pakistani wildlife biologist **Fakhar -i- Abbas** describes the history and practice of bear baiting, and the joy of tending rescued bears at Kund Bear Sanctuary. In the next essay, I explain how Wildlife sos (wsos) closed down India's dancing bear industry and set the standard for sloth bear veterinary care around the world. **Dalma Zsalakó** relays her adventures on the steep slopes of the Andes Mountains, while **Kerry Fugett, Simona Kobel,** and I explain why Andean bears are at risk and describe the work of Ecuador's Andean Bear Foundation.

III   *Policy*
The third section examines polices that affect bears, starting with six members of British Columbia's **Raincoast Conservation Foundation,** who describe how typical fisheries management policies harm ecosystems and coastal brown bears, and how this organization has brought change through informed advocacy. Also in British Columbia, **Mick Webb** looks back on grassroots actions that successfully created a community where people and bears coexist peacefully. My essay offers a window onto the convoluted relationships between U.S. government wildlife agencies and wildlife rehabilitation. **Ann Bryant** explains how a bear turned her down a path that ultimately brought big changes for black bears in California's Lake Tahoe region, and **Tara Zuardo** describes how her work as a lawyer reshaped her understanding of U.S. courts and problems facing the nation's Endangered wildlife. In the last policy essay, **Anna Beech** and **Marc Brody** describe China's state-of-the-art captive breeding program, and life for pandas on Panda Mountain.

IV   *Bears and Beyond*
Opening the closing section, I highlight critical ways in which our personal daily choices affect the survival of the world's bears. **Tom Regele** juxtaposes earlier indigenous views of the Andean bear with those of Catholics who conquered South America to explore the role of mental conceptions in determining the fate of species. Sociologist **Daniel Kirjner** and I compare Erwing Goffman's explanation of Total Institutions both with animal exploitation and with animal sanctuaries, highlighting the necessity and the tragedy of a Cambodian bear sanctuary. In the final essay, **Dana Medoro** leafs through the writings of such diverse masters as William Faulkner, Jacques Derrida, and Lewis Carroll to explore how we envision our place in the world, and how this understanding shapes our interactions with cats and oysters and bears.

Bears and Wilderness

Humans breed prolifically, consume voraciously, and aggressively pursue wildlife with deadly weapons. Our consumption habits create climate change.

As our numbers grow, we increasingly invade and destroy habitat, isolating dwindling wildlife populations, threatening innumerable species—including bears. Despite the dire predicament of bears, many European communities resist re-introduction of brown bears in nearby forested regions out of fear—though their homes are built where bears recently roamed. People living in and around the Andes shoot bears to prevent them from eating maize—planted in fields that only recently replaced critical bear habitat. Around the world, poachers follow newly created logging roads into once remote forests in order to hunt down bears, in order to exchange bear gallbladders and paws for cash. In the U.S., an influx and proliferation of humanity has extirpated brown bears from most of their previous range, and vastly reduced all bear species. In regions now bereft of brown bears, we have extirpated one of very few species that was strong and fierce enough to remind us that we are no more essential to the unfolding of this planet than the Yangtze River dolphin or the western black rhino.

When I leave the cloistered and pampered world of human civilization to hoist backpack or paddles, family and friends never fail to caution me regarding bears. I am careful, but I am much more concerned about the welfare of bears than I am about the remote possibility that a bear might harm me. And I am much more focused on the importance of protecting bears—both for their sake and for our own. Bears heighten my senses and humble me with the knowledge that, once stripped of the artifice of human civilization, I am just another edible animal. In the presence of bears, we can be reminded of things too often overlooked in our busy, cosmopolitan lives, things that are vitally important with regard to the earth's future. It is important for human beings, increasingly urban, to stand outside of our human-centered, human-dominated, plastic and pavement world to explore our personal limitations and frailties, to better see our damaging power, unjustified arrogance, and ultimate irrelevance.

References

"Berserk." *Online Etymology Dictionary.* Accessed Dec. 15, 2012. <http://www.etymonline.com/index.php?term=berserk>.
"Brown Bear." *Wikipedia.* Accessed Dec. 15, 2012. <http://en.wikipedia.org/wiki/Brown_bear>.
Brown, Dee. *Folktales of the Native American: Retold for our Times.* NY: Henry Holt, 1979.
Brown, Gary. *Great Bear Almanac: A Comprehensive Guide to the Bears of the World,* Second Edition. CT: Lyons Press, 2009.
Campbell, Joseph. *Primitive Mythology: The Masks of God.* NY: Penguin, 1987.

DeMallie, Raymond J. "Lakota Belief and Ritual in the Nineteenth Century." *Sioux Indian Religion*. Ed. Raymond J DeMallie and Douglas R. Parks. Norman: U. of Oklahoma, 1987. 25–43.

Dolson, Sylvia. *Bear-ology: Fascinating Bear Facts, Tales & Trivia*. Masonville: PixyJack Press, 2009.

Domico, Terry and Mark Newman. *Bears of the World*. NY: Facts on File, 1988.

Erdoes, Richard, and Alfonso Ortiz, ed. *American Indian Myths and Legends*. New York: Pantheon, 1984.

"Gentle Ben." *Wikipedia*. Accessed Nov. 13, 2012. <http://en.wikipedia.org/wiki/Gentle_Ben>.

"Gentle Ben." *My Time Well-Wasted*. Accessed Nov. 13, 2012. <http://www.mytimewell-wasted.com/primetime/pt1019.php>.

Gill, Sam D. *Native American Religions, an Introduction*. Belmont: Wadsworth, 1982.

Green, Miranda. *Animals in Celtic Life and Myth*. NY: Routledge, 1992.

"Grizzly and Wild Bears." *TVAcres.com*. Accessed Nov. 13, 2012. <http://www.tvacres.com/bears_grizzly_gentle.htm>.

Lowie, Robert H. *Indians of the Plains*. Garden City, NY: Natural History Press, 1954.

"Mexican Grizzly Bear was Last Seen in 1964." *Supergreenme*. Accessed Dec. 15, 2012. <http://www.supergreenme.com/go-green-environment-eco:Mexican-Grizzly-Bear-Was-Last-Seen-In-1964>.

Nelson, Richard K. *Make Prayers to the Raven: A Koyukon View of the Northern Forest*. Chicago: U. Chicago Press, 1983.

"Paddington Bear." *Wikipedia*. Accessed Nov. 27, 2012. <http://en.wikipedia.org/wiki/Paddington_Bear>.

Spence, Lewis. *North American Indians: Myths and Legends*. London: Studio, 1985.

Wood, Daniel. *Bears*. Vancouver, Canada: Whitecap, 2005.

PART I

Bear Basics

∴

CHAPTER 1

Bear Basics

Lisa Kemmerer

From the unkempt, insect-sucking sloth bear to the round-headed, bamboo-munching panda, living bears are as diverse as their fictional counterparts. In fact, there has been considerable debate as to which species are rightly included in the bear family: Giant pandas were erroneously classified in the raccoon family and sloth bears were placed among the sloths, while Koala "bears" were mistakenly classified with bears, though they are now recognized as marsupials (Macdonald 587). Based on DNA analysis, most experts recognize eight extant bear species (*Ursidae* family):

- giant panda (*Ailuropoda melanoleuca*)
- Andean (spectacled bear, *Tremarctos ornatus*)
- sloth (*Ursus ursinus* or *Melursus ursinus*)
- sun (Malay or Malayan, *Ursus malayanus* or *Helarctos malayanus*)
- Asiatic black (moon bear, *Ursus thibetanus* or *Selenarctos thibetanus*)
- American black (*Ursus americanus*)
- brown (*Ursus arctos*)
- polar (*Ursus maritimus*)

Coming into the World

The earliest bear ancestor, Dawn bear (*Ursavus elemensis*, a long-tailed carnivore "about the size of a fox terrier"), lived in subtropical Europe about 20 million years ago (Miocene era) (Macdonald 575; Domico and Newman 3; G. Brown 2). Giant pandas, the oldest living bear species and the only bears with 42 chromosomes, emerged about 20 million years ago (Craighead 19). Of the North American short-faced bears (*Arctodus simus*), abundant about 15 million years ago, only the Andean bear remains. Andean bears are the second oldest bear evolutionary branch, and the only bear species with 52 chromosomes (Craighead 19). In contrast, *Homo sapiens* emerged about 500,000 years ago, evolving to modern humans (*Homo sapiens sapiens*) just 200,000 years ago. Roughly 10,000 years ago, European cave bears (*Ursus spleaeus*) disappeared, leaving piles of bones in caves from Spain to the Caspian Sea (Craighead 17; Domico and Newman 4–5).

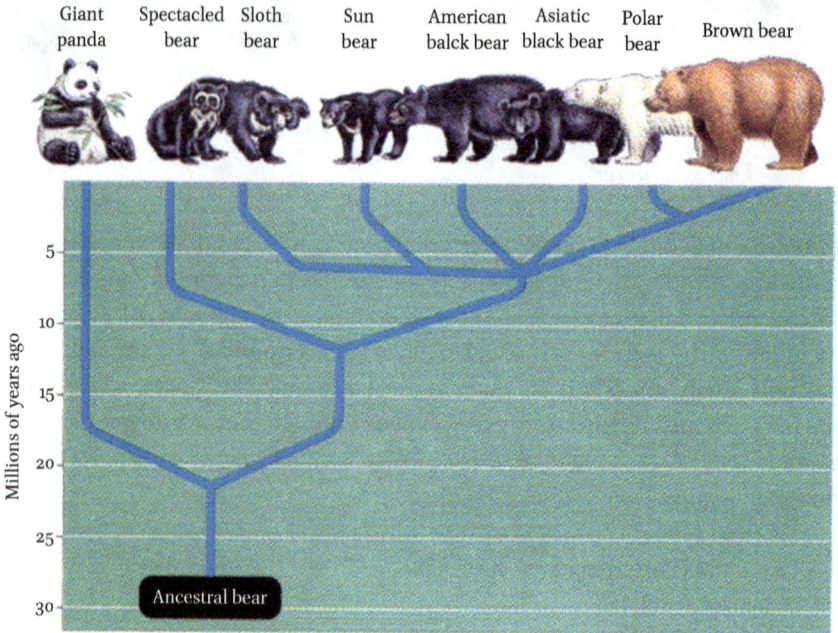

| Giant panda | Spectacled bear | Sloth bear | Sun bear | American balck bear | Asiatic black bear | Polar bear | Brown bear |

FIGURE 1.1 *Evolution Chart* from Antranik.org, reprinted with permission

The remaining six bear species (excluding giant pandas and Andean bears) have 74 chromosomes, emerged from a common ancestor between 4 and 8 million years ago, and are classified as *Ursinae* (sometimes called "true bears") (Craighead 13, 14, 19). Eurasian bears (*Ursus etruscus*) flourished about 6 million years ago, and are the ancestors of today's black, brown, and polar bears (Domico and Newman 4; Craighead 14; Brown 5). Polar bears branched from the brown bear line in the last millennium, are most closely related to northeastern Siberian brown bears, and likely evolved in Northern Asia (Craighead 21, 17). (Figure 1.1)

Between 1.5 and 3.5 million years ago, first black and then brown bears migrated across the Bering Sea land bridge to the Americas. American black bears became a distinct species 2 million years ago (Domico and Newman 5; Craighead 14). In Asia, black bears also evolved, developing into three distinct species:

- sloth bears (likely isolated on the Indian subcontinent, diverging around 8 million years ago),
- sun bears (likely isolated on the Malay Peninsula about 5 million years ago),
- Asiatic black bears (probably isolated on the Tibetan Plateau or in the Himalayas more generally, also about 5 million years ago) (Craighead 17; Brown 3).

What about Bears

Bears have long thrived in a world that is rarely constant—they are among the most adaptable species on the planet (Wood 2, 59). Bears range across four of the earths' continents (North and South America, Europe, and Asia) and nearly 60 countries, largely in the Northern hemisphere. They occupy a wide range of ecosystems, including prairies and grasslands, tundra, alpine slopes, the icy Arctic, and a particularly wide variety of forests. India and China provide habitat for the greatest variety of bear species—four. Both nations have Asiatic black, brown, and sloth bears. Additionally, sun bears live in India and pandas live in China. Canada and The United States each harbor American black, brown, and polar bears. Similarly, Russia has Asiatic black, brown, and polar bears. Brown bears occupy a thick swath of land from the Western tip of Scandinavia to the Eastern tip of Russia and across Alaska and Canada to the Hudson Bay, while polar bears live only in the Arctic and Andean bears only occupy a thin strip of land that runs through the Andes (Craighead 25). Panda, sun, sloth, and Asiatic black bears dwell exclusively in Asia. Australia, Antarctica, and Africa do not have wild bear populations, though brown bears roamed the very northwestern edge of Africa until fairly recently (G. Brown 36).

The Latin word for "bear" is "*ursus*"; the Greek word for bear is "*arctos*." "Bear" stems from Old English, has roots in Germanic languages, and means "the brown one" (Websters 181; G. Brown 184). Bear fur includes three basic colors: black, white, and brown. Brown comes in many shades, including yellowish (honey), reddish (cinnamon), or dark brown (chocolate), while "white" can also be cream, tannish, or tend toward yellow or orange. Additionally, there is tremendous color variation within bear species that are named after a single color, such as American black bears, who can be chocolate, cinnamon, tan, honey, cream, silver, white, or bluish-white. Finally, many "black" bears (Andean, sloth, sun, Asiatic, and American black bears) have white, cream, orange, or tan chest and/or face markings (G. Brown 66–70).

Most bear species look larger than they are thanks to their thick fur, but some species are, in fact, relatively small among "large" mammals: The biggest bear species weigh about twenty times what the smaller bear species weigh (G. Brown 57, 60) (Table 1.1). Bears have relatively short tails, legs, and necks, and short front legs in relation to hind legs. They have comparatively large heads with rounded ears and smallish eyes (G. Brown 47–48). Bears have long, strong claws that do not retract, and they walk with toes pointed inward, projecting a bow-legged appearance (G. Brown 47). Most bear species are diurnal (active during the day) but many have adapted to avoid human beings, feeding at night (G. Brown 176). Bears depend fundamentally on their keen sense of smell, though

TABLE 1.1   *Weight and Size Chart*

	Male: normal weight ranges kgs/lbs	Male: average height at shoulder m/ft	sex weight difference	heaviest on record kg/lbs
sun	27–65/60–143	0.7/2.3	10–45%	66/145
sloth	80–145/176–320	0.6–0.9/2–3	slight	175/385
Asiatic black	60–200/132–441	0.7–1/2.3–3.3	slight	200/440
Andean	100–175/220–386	0.7–0.9/2.3–3	30%	200/440
giant panda	100–150/220–330	0.7–0.8/2.3–2.8	10%	150/330
American black	60–225/130–500	0.7–1/2–3.3	33%	426/940
brown	135–545/300–1200	0.9–1.5/3–4.9	40–50%	1134/2,500
polar	400–600/880–1320	up to 1.6/5.3	45%	1002/2,210

(Macdonald 578, 580, 585, 587, 589; Stirling 164; Brown 57, 61; Domico and Newman 91, 107–8, 113, 123)

they have color vision and excellent night vision (Macdonald 574; G. Brown 82). They communicate largely through scents, but also with body language and a variety of vocalizations (Craighead 38). When among their own kind, bears tend to create a social hierarchy, which helps to keep the peace (Wood 63; Macdonald 582). Cubs stay with their mothers for an average of two years— long enough to learn where and how to forage (Craighead 29, 33). In the wild, bears generally live between 20 and 30 years, and roughly ten years longer in captivity (Wood 20; Macdonald 577, 580, 585, 589). Their teeth continue to grow throughout their lifetime, such that a bear's age can be determined by tooth analysis (Domico and Newman 7). Though bears might appear cumbersome, most bear species are quick and powerful—even graceful.

With their long teeth and claws, bears are easily mistaken for hunters, but their bulky bodies are built for strength and power, not speed, "evidenced by their thick limbs, massive shoulders, and short backs" (Dolson 43). Skeletal structures indicate that bear ancestors were much more carnivorous than their contemporary descendants. Comparing contemporary bear skulls with those of their ancestors reveals molars that have adapted for grinding vegetation, becoming flatter and wider over time, becoming flatter and wider, like our own teeth (Macdonald 575; Wood 29). Bears are classified as carnivores—the earth's largest carnivores—though they are omnivores. Among today's bears, only polar bears hunt to satisfy most of their caloric needs (G. Brown 82).

Bears spend most of their waking hours foraging. They depend on specific food staples, many of which are seasonal (G. Brown 166). Some species live almost exclusively on greens, berries, fruits, roots, tubers, and nuts, while others supplement fruits and vegetation with larvae, grubs, termites, ants, and a variety of other insects; some seek out fish, crabs, crayfish, frogs, rodents, lizards, and small birds (Wood 5). Certain bear species eat flesh only at certain times, such as when fish are spawning. Most bears readily consume carrion, and larger brown bears can overpower wolves and mountain lions to steal their kill (G. Brown 167). Testifying to their legendary sweet tooth, locals have called bears "honey bear" (sun, sloth, and Asiatic black), "honey paw" (American black and brown bears), and "little-mother of honey" (brown bears) (G. Brown 25–28).

Bears tend to be solitary—well dispersed to reduce the likelihood of food shortages—though females are often accompanied by cubs, and both males and females gather around rich food sources. Witnesses have reported as many as 100 polar bears around a whale carcass, and as many as sixty bears congregating to fish for salmon at McNeil falls (Alaska, southwest of Anchorage) (Domico and Newman 73, 55; Wood 61). Bears also share space for a period of time to court and mate, though mothers raise young alone, staying with cubs one to three years, sometimes sharing territory with adult daughters.

Implantation of fertilized eggs is delayed from spring until autumn in every bear species except the sun bear (G. Brown 137). If the prospective mother does not gain enough weight coming into winter, the fertilized egg will be reabsorbed, allowing a struggling bear to avoid pregnancy, preserving her energy for survival in tough times, and preventing cubs from being born only to suffer and die prematurely (Craighead 30; G. Brown 137–38). If the mother does establish the requisite fat reserves, her embryo attaches to the uterine wall in the autumn (with longer delays for bears living farther north), at which time the fetus begins to develop (Wood 38). Among the earth's many and varied animals, only bears are born during their mother's dormancy (Wood 38).

Denning is likely an evolutionary adaptation to seasonal food shortages and inclement weather (Schwartz, Miller, and Haroldson 566). A denning bear's metabolism might drop 50 percent, heart rate 80 percent, but temperature only a few degrees. Some bears lose 40 percent of their body weight while denning (Wood 57). Dormancy/denning/hibernation varies depending on how far north a bear lives. Northern bears (Asiatic black, American black, brown, and polar bears) remain dormant as long as seven months and spend the majority of their lives in dens, during which time they do not eat, drink, urinate, or defecate (Wood 57, G. Brown 154; Domico and Newman 11–12; Schwartz, Miller, Haroldson 567). Depending on the latitude, bears emerge from winter dens anytime between February (in southern areas) and June (in the Arctic) (Wood

40). The longest recorded dormancy was that of an American black bear in Alaska, who denned for 8 months (Wood 57). In southern habitats, where food can be accessed year-round, bears do not generally enter a period of dormancy (Wood 36).

Gestation is short, and bear cubs are born helpless—tiny, naked, toothless, and blind (Craighead 30; Wood 34, 38). Dormant mothers awaken intermittently to check and clean up after their cubs, and draw their young close to a nipple (Wood 38). Their mother's milk is rich in fat—between 32 and 48 percent—containing about three times as much energy and ten times as much fat as our nursing milk (Wood 46; Craighead 30). Among North American bears, the richest milk is that of polar bears, followed by brown and then black bears (Craighead 30). Newborns squirm, sleep, and suckle. Like human infants, cubs suck on whatever they can put to their mouths, including toes (Wood 53). In relation to their final weight, offspring weigh much less than the newborns of other mammals. Birth during dormancy protects these tiny, vulnerable beings while they begin to grow. Even so, mortality rates are high: The first six months claim one third of American black bear cubs, while the first year claims half of brown and polar bear cubs (Wood 40).

Giant Panda (Ailuropoda melanoleuca)

Giant pandas, separated from the rest of the *Ursidae* family for more than 20 million years, are the only extant bear species in the bear subfamily *Ailuropodainae*, genus *Ailuropoda*, and they harbor a handful of unique characteristics (Domico and Newman 124). Most bears have round pupils, but giant panda pupils are vertical slits, like a cat's pupils, inspiring both their Latin name, *Ailuropoda melanoleuca*, which translates as "black and white cat-foot," and nicknames such as "giant cat bear" and "catlike bear" (Domico and Newman 123; G. Brown 21–22). They have a comparatively long tail, unique vocalizations (akin to bleating), stark color contrast, and a large, round heads. Perhaps their most unusual feature is an enlarged wrist bone capable of moving independently. This bone effectively creates an "opposable thumb," helping pandas to hold and eat bamboo (Domico and Newman 124).

Giant pandas are quite shy and restrained, and are the least athletic among bears. They can and do climb trees, especially when young, but are poor climbers and are more terrestrial than most other bear species. Except when young and playful, or fleeing enemies, giant pandas stay close to the ground, and they do not care much for water (Stonehouse 36; G. Brown 130, 165).

The German name for the giant panda translates as "bamboo bear" (G. Brown 26). These bears depend almost exclusively on bamboo for sustenance, with bamboo comprising 99 percent of their diet. Thirty-five bamboo species are essential to the panda's survival, though these rolly polly bears consume more than 60 bamboo species. They spend as much as 14 hours a day foraging, consuming 12–38 kg (26–84 lbs) of bamboo—"up to 40 percent of their body weight" ("Ailuropoda"; Macdonald 586). The Giant panda's strong jaws, adapted for chewing fibrous plant matter, are the reason for the panda's distinctive (and very large) round head.

Giant pandas live in a tiny area of fragmented habitat in the isolated mountains of south-central China (G. Brown 284). Instead of denning, they descend to lower elevations when the weather turns cold. Their fur is thick and woolly, insulating them against a damp, high-altitude climate (Macdonald 587). There are two subspecies, the more numerous Sichuan pandas sport a black and white coat and live predominantly in Sichuan Province. The brown and white Qinling panda lives only in the Qinling Mountains of Shaanxi Province at 1300–3000 meters (4000–10,000 ft.). Both bears have a cream to white band around their mid-section, with dark, starkly contrasting eye-patches, ears, and limbs (including feet and shoulders)—perfect camouflage in their snowy, rugged habitat.

Panda home ranges can be as small as 4 km² (1.5 m²) or as large as 30 km² (12 m²) (Macdonald 587). Female pandas share ranges, defending only a smaller plot as private territory (G. Brown 165). When ready to give birth, they create nests on the ground, in caves, or in hollow trees or stumps. At birth, pandas are very tiny—just 0.1 percent of what their mother weighs (compared with human newborns at 5 percent) (Macdonald 586). Pandas can live about thirty years in captivity, but usually only survive about twenty years in the wild (Macdonald 585, 587).

Perhaps as many as 1600 giant pandas remain, or perhaps as few as 1000 (G. Brown 284; Macdonald 587). "The threat to pandas comes from humans": Expanding human populations have reduced and fragmented panda habitat, forcing bears from subtropical lowlands into higher altitudes (Macdonald 587). "There are now only about 25 'islands' of panda habitat left; two thirds of these support fewer than 50 pandas. This means that about 16 of these isolated populations will soon go extinct unless more habitat is restored" (Craighead 106). Giant pandas are the only bear species listed as Endangered on the IUCN Red List. Fortunately, more than 50 percent of the giant panda's remaining habitat is now protected, and there are 33 giant panda reserves. There are also clear laws Protecting pandas against poaching and strict sentences for legal infringements. Until 1997, poaching was punishable by death, and several poachers were executed (Macdonald 586; "Ailuropoda").

Andean or Spectacled Bear (Tremarctos ornatus)

Tremarctos ornatus describes a tremendous bear with an ornate design. Andean bears have black or brown fur (sometimes reddish-brown) and variable cream-colored markings on their faces, throats, and chests, often sporting white circles or semi-circles around their eyes—their most common local name is "spectacled bear" (G. Brown 25). Though the second-largest land mammal in South America (second only to the tapir), the Andean bear is actually mid-sized among bears, becoming smaller as larger bears are hunted from the population (Craighead 97).

Andean bears are the only South American bear, and the only surviving short-nosed bear (subfamily *Tremarctinae*), having branched from the rest of the *Ursidae* family about 13 million years ago (Craighead 97; Domico and Newman 107). Whereas most bears have fourteen pairs of ribs, Andean bears have only thirteen (Domico and Newman 107). Like giant pandas, Andean bears create nests for birthing (under large rocks or trees), their jaws are comparatively large and strong, and they eat almost nothing but plant matter, depending largely on fruits, when available, and a family of tropical plants called bromeliads, which constitute 50 percent of their diet. (One of their local names is "bromeliad-eating bear") (G. Brown 169). They also enjoy cacti, grubs, berries, grasses, honey, and rich sap that lies just underneath tree bark (Craighead 97; "Andean").

Andean bears live in a wide variety of habitats, including rainforests, dry forests, steppe lands, inland deserts, and coastal scrub deserts. They have been sighted at elevations as high as 4,200 meters (13,800 ft.), and perhaps wander snowlines yet higher (Domico and Newman 107; Craighead 97). Able to find food year-round, Andean bears need not den. They are good swimmers and excellent tree climbers, spending considerable time in the forest canopy (G. Brown 127, 129). Quite shy, they readily scramble up trees to escape danger, as well as to eat, nap, or sleep. When their favorite fruits are in season, they build sleeping platforms with leaves and branches in fruit-bearing trees, where they rest between feeding sessions (Domico and Newman 110; Craighead 98).

We know comparatively little about Andean bears. There are no recognized subspecies, and very little information on reproduction or cub growth and development (G. Brown 165, 142, 144, 140, 79). It is probable that as few as 2000 Andean bears remain in the wild, and their numbers are expected to continue to decline ("Tremarctos"; Domico and Newman 107). Humans are their greatest threat, especially through habitat loss, which exposes Andean bears to the guns of farmers, ranchers, and poachers (Craighead 98).

Sloth Bear (Melursus ursinus)

Sloth bears were next to begin their separate evolutionary journey. *Melursus ursinus* means "little black bear," but sloth bears are mid-sized among bear species. Their most noticeable (and charming) characteristic is their unkempt, shaggy, rangy appearance. They have a long, heavy coat of unruly black fur, especially thick on the back of the neck, but shorter on legs, underline, and muzzle (G. Brown 55). Sloth bears also have noticeably long, shaggy fur on their ears and, like pandas, have longer tails in relation to body size. They sometimes sport a cream-colored "U," "V," or "Y" on their chests, and often have a brown or cream muzzle. Uniquely, sloth bear cubs (most often two) ride crosswise on their mother's backs, clinging to her long fur. This allows the mother to forage with very young cubs, and to flee danger, simultaneously carrying her young to safety (Craighead 95, 92).

Many of this disheveled-looking bear's most unique features stem from insect-eating tendencies (Macdonald 589; Craighead 92). Sloth bears have unusually large paws in relation to body size, and distinctly curved, long claws with which to dig for ants and termites—they can smell grubs 1 meter (3 ft.) underground (G. Brown 77, 172). Sloth bears have only 40 teeth—two less than other bear species, leaving a gap in the front of their mouths—and long lips, for which they have been called "lip bear" (Craighead 91, G. Brown 28). Sloth bears dig into termite dens, close their nostrils, blow debris away, protrude their limber lips to create a straw-like effect, then suck termites into their mouth through the gap in their teeth (Craighead 91; Domico and Newman 101). They can be heard blowing and sucking termites from 200 meters (650 ft.) distant (Domico and Newman 104). Like other bears, they also enjoy seasonal fruits, seeds, berries, and flowers, but they are not hunters, and even carrion holds little to no interest (G. Brown 55, 172). Sloth bears have a sweet tooth, and will endure the stings of hoards of bees to raid honey from hives—*Melursus* translates as "honey bear" (Macdonald 589).

Their long, sickle-shaped digging claws allow sloth bears to hang upside down from tree limbs, a habit that misled scientists, who initially categorize these bears as sloths (G. Brown 55). But they are much faster than sloths—they can outrun dogs as they hop and scramble over branches and brush across rough terrain. They are comfortable swimmers and exceptional climbers—though they do not climb trees when threatened, likely because tigers, their primary nonhuman enemies, also climb trees (Stonehouse 30; G. Brown 127, 130; Domico and Newman 103).

Now limited to the Indian subcontinent, there are two recognized sloth bear subspecies: the Sri Lankan sloth bear and the Indian sloth bear. Both live in increasingly fragmented lowland forests in a subtropical, monsoon climate (Macdonald 589). Their home ranges vary widely, from 2 km² (less than 1 m²) to about 100 km² (40 m²), depending on food availability ("Melursus"). Until recently, these shaggy bears also lived in Bangladesh, but have not been sighted there since the 1990s ("Melursus"). Numbers continue to decline, and there are likely only 7000 and 10,000 sloth bears remaining in the wild (Domico and Newman 101).

Sun Bear (*Malay or Malayan bear*, Helarctos malayanus)

Sun bears prefer dense, lowland tropical rainforests, and are often called Malay or Malayan bears because the center of their habitat is the Malay Peninsula—*Helarctos malayanus* translates as "Malaysian sun bear." Unfortunately, they have become somewhat rare in Malaysia, and are believed to be extinct in Bangladesh (Brown 33). They have fared somewhat better in Thailand, Laos, and Myanmar.

Sun bears are the smallest and lightest of bears (though stocky). They are noticeably bow legged even among bears, with powerful front legs, large paws, and long, sharp, sickle-shaped claws for digging roots and insects and climbing trees. Cubs climb more easily than they walk. Sun bears often create nests in trees, where they nap high in a forest canopy, lying on their tummies. Though they seem to prefer to climb, they are also excellent swimmers (G. Brown 160, 55, 78, 127, 130; Craighead 86).

Their fur is dark brown or coal-black, thick, and considerably shorter than the fur of other bears, with a cream to orange colored "U" or bib-shaped patch on the chest (Craighead 86; Macdonald 588). They are named for this cream-colored patch, which can remind onlookers of the rising sun. Their muzzles are light in color, ranging from grey through cream to orange. Sun bear ears are smaller in relation to body-size than those of other bears, while their heads are comparatively larger—broader and heavier. Their forest enemies are snakes and big cats (tigers and leopards). They emit loud growls or barks as they rush at enemies and intruders (Craighead 86).

Sun bears have comically long tongues, suited for collecting honey and insects. They subsist on fruits (especially figs), greens, and a variety of insects (including termites, ants, beetle larvae, and bee larvae). They also eat small animals such as lizards, birds, and rodents ("Helarctos"; Brown 173). In their equatorial habitat, food is available year-round, and they have no need to den. Consequently, there is no need for delayed egg implantation, and sun bears are the only member of the *Ursidae* family that mates and gives birth throughout the year (G. Brown 55, 135).

There are two sun bear subspecies, the sun bear and the smaller Borneo sun bear. Borneo, one of Earth's largest islands and home to one of the world's oldest rainforests, is governed by three separate nations (Indonesia, Malaysia, and Brunei), complicating efforts to protect the Borneo subspecies. Along with Andean bears, sun bears have been "sadly overlooked" by scholars (Domico and Newman 91). As a result, information is not readily available regarding their range, how long they live in the wild, how a mother bear cares for or nurses her young, or the stages of cub development (G. Brown 165, 94, 151, 149, 145).

Asiatic Black Bear (*moon, Asian, Himalayan, or Tibetan black bear,* Selenarctos thibetanus *or more recently,* Ursus thibetanus)

Asiatic black bears have comparatively large ears set far apart on relatively round heads (Domico and Newman 113). Their fur is shiny black, with a thick ruff around their necks (like the sloth bear), making them look larger than they are. Asiatic black bears have a brown or tan muzzle with a white chin, and distinctive cream-colored markings on their chests, as if wearing a bandana or a crescent moon necklace (with the moon resting on its rounded edge), lending both their common name, "moon bear," and their Latin name, which translates as "Tibetan moon bear."

Asiatic black bears are good swimmers, excellent climbers, and most often live in forests, either broad-leafed or coniferous, from sea level up to and beyond 4,000 meters (13,000 ft.). Their range varies from less than 1 km² in Russia to more than 180 km² (70 m²) in Japan (Craighead 80–81; "Ursus"; G. Brown 165). Smaller Asiatic black bears are sometimes killed by tigers or other bears, especially brown bears. Facing such fierce predators, it is not surprising that Asiatic black bears can be dangerous when startled, or if they feel threatened. Females den before giving birth, but Asiatic black bears in warmer habitats do not otherwise den—they simply descend to lower elevations when the weather turns cold (Domico and Newman 118).

Like most bear species, their food sources are seasonal and largely plant based. They eat succulent shoots, wildflowers, and tender leaves in springtime, insects (such as termites and beetle larvae) and fruits in the summer, and nuts in autumn, including "acorns, beechnuts, walnuts, chestnuts, hazelnuts, or stone pine seeds," which help build fat reserves for cooler temperatures and/or dormancy ("Ursus"). Asiatic black bears also eat carrion, and if the opportunity presents itself, kill and eat vulnerable or smaller animals, such as rodents ("*Ursus*: Asiatic"). When seeking fruits and nuts, Asiatic black bears climb trees and spend much time aloft, sometimes creating tree nests, leading to the moniker "he who likes to sit high" (Macdonald 588; G. Brown 26).

There are seven recognized subspecies, including isolated populations in Japan and Taiwan, and a smaller reddish-brown bear, the Baluchistan bear, remaining in only a few fragmented areas of Pakistan and Iran. Asiatic black bears continue to decline throughout most of their range; the "Baluchi" bear is "one of the world's rarest mammals" (Craighead 79; "Baluchistan"; G. Brown 21, 51, 282; Macdonald 588). Japan is the only nation where it is legal to hunt

Asiatic black bears (Macdonald 588). In late spring, Japan's black bears feed on tender sap underneath the bark of trees, and they are therefore vigorously hunted on behalf of timber industries, killing 2,000 to 3,000 bears annually (Domico and Newman 116; G. Brown 174). Countries such as Vietnam offer no protection or regulations for Asiatic black bears, and hunters sell bear body parts for traditional Chinese medicines, scoring several hundreds of dollars for just one paw or one gallbladder (G. Brown 51, 282, 283): "In Asia, a bowl of bear paw soup sells for u.s. $800 and a single gram of bear gall bladder for u.s. $50 ($1800 an ounce)" (Wood 8).

American Black Bear (Ursus americanus)

Ironically, American "black" bears have more color variation than any other animal classed as a carnivore (Wood 69; Rogers 157). While nine of every ten are black, they can also be various shades of brown (chocolate, cinnamon, and honey), blond, yellow, silver, or white (G. Brown 66; Craighead 64; Domico and Newman 19, 22). In Yosemite National Park (CA), more than 90 percent of American black bears are brown, cinnamon, tan, or blonde (G. Brown 67). British Columbia's rare and protected Kermode bear carries a recessive gene whereby 10 percent of offspring are white, cream, orange, gold, or gray ("Kermode"; G. Brown 23).

American black bears thrive in a variety of habitats, including tundra, prairies, forests—even urban environments (G. Brown 49; Rogers 157). These agile bears are excellent tree climbers, strong swimmers, and they can sprint up to 30 mph (50 kmph) (Wood 43, 69; G. Brown 120, 124, 127; Rogers 159). In southern states, American black bears crawl into a hole and remain lethargic for a short period during the cold season. Further north, they enter into a deeper, longer period of dormancy (sometimes 7 months, with the record being 8 months in Alaska) (Macdonald 584). These bears are territorial: Females defend markedly less territory than males, whose ranges overlap with those of females and average about 80 km² (50 m²) but can be as large as 800 km² (500 m²). Their wandering ways have led to monikers such as "gap crosser," "ridge runner," and "spirit of the forest" (Rogers 158; Macdonald 576; G. Brown 165, 25).

American black bears are creatures of habit (easily food conditioned) and determined scavengers. They can open screw-top jars and manipulate door latches, and they quickly learn how to open well-designed "bear-proof" lids with their remarkably dexterous forepaws (earning such colorful tags as "happy hooligan") (G. Brown 49, 25). Before denning in the fall, in a state of excessive hunger called hyperphagia, American black bears sometimes gain as much as 13 kg (30 lbs) per week (Wood 15; 70). They tend to prefer forest meadows, where they graze near protective trees (Domico and Newman 19). Predominantly grazers (at least 85 percent), they eat vast quantities of grasses and weeds, and can eat "tens of thousands of nuts or berries in a day" (Wood 70; Pelton 550–551; Macdonald 584). Insects constitute the bulk of an American black bear's animal intake, though they also eat carrion (Pelton 550–551).

Threats to American black bears include hunting and trapping, poaching, automobiles, and the U.S. government's Predator Control Program (Pelton 552). Hunters kill more than 40,000 American black bears annually, sometimes eliminating 20 percent of a local population (Macdonald 585). More than 80 percent of the Pacific Northwest's hunted black bears are killed on behalf of forestry interests (despite studies showing that trees can be protected simply by providing hungry bears with alternative food sources). In the course of their careers, some paid hunters personally kill upwards of 1000 bears (Wood 70; G. Brown 174; Domico and Newman 33–34).

American black bears are intelligent; they are smaller, more numerous, and more widespread than other bears of North America (Pelton 551; Craighead 63). North America houses 600,000–800,000 American black bears, who occupy only about 62 percent of their original range, persisting in only 32 U.S. states (Wood 12, 5; Pelton 547; Macdonald 584, 585).

There is much disagreement regarding subspecies.[1] Somewhere between 15 and 18 subspecies are generally recognized, including those based on color variations (cinnamon, glacier, and kermode) and regional populations (such as Mexican, Kenai, Newfoundland, and Vancouver) (Craighead 22, 63–64; G. Brown 19; Rogers 160). The Louisiana subspecies (*Ursus americanus luteolus*), dwindling in the bayous of Mississippi and Louisiana, is listed as Threatened by the U.S. Endangered Species Act. American black bears in Florida (*Ursus americanus floridanus*) and other southern regions, as well as the rare glacier (*Ursus americanus emmonsii*) and Kermode (*Ursus americanus kermodei*) bears of Alaska and British Columbia, are also at risk (Rogers 160; Pelton 547; Macdonald 585).

---

1   To be protected, a subspecies must be officially recognized, so identifying subspecies is critical, controversial, and unnecessarily difficult (Craighead 37). In addition to genetics and anatomy, "geographical, dietary, [and] behavioral" variations must be taken into account, and whether or not a particular population is isolated (G. Brown 19). There are only two distinct types of DNA, for example, among 15 or 16 commonly recognized American black bear subspecies, distinguished by such details as their range or color (Craighead 22; G. Brown 19). Brown bear protection is hindered by the fact that there are "as many subspecies as there are disagreements as to what is a 'valid' subspecies" (Brown 19). An early (1918) authority on brown bears identified 86 subspecies (one-third of which were in Alaska) (Domico and Newman 38). Since then, up to 56 subspecies have been proposed for recognition—only fifteen are somewhat widely recognized (Craighead 34; Brown 20).

Brown Bear (Ursus arctos)

Brown bears are the most widespread bear species, spanning three continents (Macdonald 576). Until recently, there were fifteen or sixteen generally recognized extant brown bear subspecies, ranging in color from light blond to black, including the Himalayan, Carpathian, Hokkaido, Marsican, grizzly, and Kodiak brown bears (G. Brown 20; Churcher 163). Recent DNA analysis suggests only five subspecies (Schwartz, Miller, and Haroldson 556).

As with every other bear species (and species more generally), humans are the number one cause of dwindling populations, largely through "excessive human-caused mortality and habitat loss" (Schwartz, Miller, and Haroldson 571, 576). In Europe, brown bears

> disappeared from Denmark as long as 5,000 years ago. Over the rest of Europe they survived much longer, but died out as forests were replaced by farmland. The last British bears disappeared from southern forests just over 1,000 years ago. The last German bears survived in the forests of Bavaria until 1836. The Swiss killed the last of their bears in about 1904. A few remained in the French Alps until 1937. (Stonehouse 13)

Today only "remnant populations" of less than twenty-five individuals live in Spain, France, Italy, and Greece (Macdonald 579).

Brown bears have also been extirpated from much of their earlier range in North America. They were hunted from California by 1922, Oregon by 1933, and by 1935 were extirpated from the southwest (Domico and Newman 63). By 1975, hunters eliminated 31 of 37 U.S. bear populations (Schwartz, Miller, Haroldson 558). Extirpated from 98–99 percent of their range across the contiguous United States, only a remnant population remains in the Rocky Mountains and along the U.S.-Canada border: now Only "five isolated populations survive, totaling about 1000 individuals," now federally protected as a Threatened species under the Endangered Species Act (Schwartz, Miller, Haroldson 558, 575, 572; Macdonald 579). Alaska and parts of Canada provide something of a safe haven for North America's 58,000 remaining brown bears (32,700 bears in Alaska, 25,300 in Canada), and brown bear viewing has become a lucrative business—more lucrative than bear hunting, adding nearly $30 million to the economy annually (Schwartz, Miller, Haroldson 575 572).

Adult brown bears are poor climbers, but "strong and skillful" swimmers; some can sprint 55–66 kmph (35–40 mph)—the fastest of bears (Schwartz, Miller, Haroldson 559; G. Brown 130, 127, 124). A hump of muscle over their shoulders helps them to dig up foods such as roots, grubs, and ground squirrels (G. Brown 51; Wood 75, 81). Their claws can be an intimidating eight centimeters (3 in.)

long (Schwartz, Miller, Haroldson 558). They sometimes kill very young or disabled ungulates, including caribou, elk, musk ox, and moose. Where available, brown bears have a taste for fish, and can down ten full-length salmon in one hour (Wood 76–77). Nonetheless, even where meaty sources of sustenance are sometimes available, greens are the brown bear's mainstay—weeds, sedges, and grasses (Schwartz, Miller, Haroldson 568). Like most other bear species, brown bears also consume berries and bugs: The Syrian brown bear lives almost exclusively on plants, as do Japan's brown bears (almost 99 percent vegetable matter) (G. Brown 169–70; Domico and Newman 39–40, 42). Before denning, a brown bear can consume 41 kg (90 lbs) of food daily, and develop 20 centimeters (8 in.) of fat (Domico and Newman 39–40).

Pregnant females in northern regions den for about 7 months (G. Brown 154); only brown bears in Turkey and Iran do not den (Domico and Newman 47). Brown bears are large among land mammals, lending to nicknames such as "dog of God" and "broadfoot." The heaviest bears (those from coastal North America) weigh a remarkable 1134 kg (2,500 lbs) (G. Brown 61, 57). Other subspecies are comparatively small, such as the Syrian brown bear, weighing only about 140 kg (300 lbs) (G. Brown 57; Stonehouse 12).

Brown bears can be dangerous when startled, or if they feel threatened. On average, six people are mauled in North America over the course of a year (Wood 25). Seeing a fresh brown bear footprint, or catching a glimpse of this bear's massive countenance, can quicken one's heartbeat and broaden one's step, earning them common names such as "step-widener" (Lapp), but brown bears are certainly not innately dangerous, as evidenced by local names such as "unaggressive giant" (G. Brown 26).

Polar Bear (Ursus maritimus)

Polar bears evolved from brown bears and are genetically similar enough to interbreed in captivity, creating fertile offspring (Domico and Newman 65; G. Brown 140–141). Their Latin name, *Ursus maritimus,* translates as "sea bear." As marine mammals, polar bears are uniquely adapted to Arctic ice and water (Craighead 57). They swim nearly 10 kmph (6 mph), and up to 95 km (65 m) without rest (G. Brown 127; Craighead 58; Domico and Newman 69). They swim underwater with their ears flat against their heads, nostrils closed, and eyes opened for hunting. The polar bear's "forepaws are large and oarlike"; their front legs provide power while their hind end works only as a rudder (Macdonald 580). Cubs, who do not have enough fat reserves to stay warm in icy waters, ride on their mother's back if she needs to swim (Amstrup 598; Wood 98; Domico and Newman 77).

Polar bears live only in the Arctic Circle; their range is determined by sea ice. There are roughly 25,000 polar bears remaining; more than half live in Canada (Macdonald 580; Wood 10; "Ursus maritimus"). Largest of the world's bear species, polar bear males average just over 1.5 meters (5 ft.) at the shoulder; standing on their hind legs, they can reach to a height of 4 meters (13 ft.) (Macdonald 580; G. Brown 61, Stonehouse 20). Compared with other bear species, polar bears have long necks and small heads, and the longest and largest canine teeth (Domico and Newman 66; G. Brown 73). Their skin is black (including a black tongue), and they generally have black claws (Amstrup 589). They live into their early thirties in the wild, and more than forty years in captivity (Stirling 164; G. Brown 94).

Polar bears can climb ice walls and sprint up to 56 kmph (35 mph), but are "relatively inefficient walkers" (G. Brown 124, 130; Amstrup 598). They migrate (walking and swimming) as much as 1000 km, following the ice as seasons change, and they travel many miles to hunt: One bear walked from Alaska to Greenland; in the course of three hundred and sixty-five days, one collared bear journeyed nearly 600,000 km^2 (Amstrup 587, 590, 593). Locals call the polar bear "nanook" ("nanuk") or "eternal vagabond" and "nomad of the Arctic" (G. Brown 28). Despite their wandering ways, polar bears frequent familiar territories with known food sources, and expectant mothers repeatedly return to the same area to den (Stonehouse 22–23; Wood 27). Polar bears who den on drifting ice travel many miles while denning, and scientists do not understand how, on waking, these bears are able to find their way back across miles of snow and ice to their home range (Amstrup 596).

While other bear species den when food is scarce, polar bears den to protect vulnerable newborns (Amstrup 592, 595). During this time mothers are without food or water for 4–8 months, emerging with cubs that are roughly 3 months old (Macdonald 580; Amstrup 598, 595; Amstrup 595).

Most carnivorous among bears, polar bears tend to look on every other animal (including humans) as prey (Craighead 58). Their stomachs can hold a remarkable 70 kg (150lbs) of food (Domico and Newman 66). Unlike any other known species, if food becomes scarce, polar bears enter a metabolic state similar to that of hibernation *at any time of year*, helping them through lean times (Amstrup 598; Domico and Newman 75). They can smell a seal breathing-hole through 1 meter (3 ft.) of ice from a kilometer (0.6 m.) distant (Macdonald 580; Wood 30; Domico and Newman 73). Seals are their primary source of food, but polar bears will also kill and consume belugas, walruses, and sea birds, and scrounge for seaweed, clams, crabs, and a variety of fish. Like most bears, they feast on carrion. Polar bears, while more carnivorous than other bears, are omnivores who forage for greenery and berries during the summer (Amstrup 592; Domico and Newman 74; Wood 105).

Protecting Bears

Each bear species is listed by the Convention on International Trade in Endangered Species (CITES): American black, brown, and polar bears are listed under Appendix II, while each of the remaining five bear species—at greater risk—are listed under Appendix I. A pending proposal, if passed, will move the polar bear to Appendix I. The International Union for Conservation of Nature (IUCN) Red Data List (animals vulnerable to extinction) labels polar, Andean, Asiatic, sloth, and sun bears as Vulnerable, and giant pandas, the rarest of bears, as Endangered— defined as vulnerable to and in danger of extinction (G. Brown 281–85).

In light of ever-increasing human populations, shrinking habitat, and climate change, bears are likely to continue to dwindle. Because bear species travel across international borders, successful efforts to protect bears will need to be international. The world's eight bear species will only survive if we work together to protect bears and their habitat, while simultaneously curbing our growth and consumption.

References

"Ailuropoda melanoleuca" *IUCN Red List of Threatened Species.* Accessed Oct. 5, 2012. <http://www.iucnredlist.org/details/712/0>

Amstrup, Steven C. "Polar Bear: *Ursus maritimus.*" *Wild Mammals of North America: Biology, Management, and Conservation,* 2nd edition. Ed. George A Feldhamer, Bruce C. Thompson, and Joseph A. Chapman. Baltimore: Johns Hopkins U. P., 2003. 587–610.

"Andean Bears." *San Diego Zoo: Zoo Blogs.* Accessed Oct. 18, 2012. <http://blogs.sandiego zoo.org/tag/spectacled-bear/>

"Baluchistan Black Bear." *Bears of the World.* Accessed Dec. 9, 2012. <http://www.bear softheworld.net/baluchistan_black_bears.asp>

"Bear Classification." *Bears of the World.* Accessed Dec. 15, 2012. <http://www.bearsoft heworld.net/bear_classification.asp>

Brown, Gary. *Great Bear Almanac: A Comprehensive Guide to the Bears of the World,* Second Edition. CT: Lyons Press, 2009.

Churcher, C.S. "Grizzly or Brown Bear: *Ursus arctos.*" *The Smithsonian Book of North American Mammals.* Ed. Don E. Wilson and Sue Ruff. Washington: Smithsonian Institute Press, 1999. 160–163.

Craighead, Lance. *Bears of the World.* Stillwater MN: Voyageur, 2000.

Dolson, Sylvia. *Bear-ology: Fascinating Bear Facts, Tales & Trivia.* Masonville: PixyJack Press, 2009.

Domico, Terry and Mark Newman. *Bears of the World.* NY: Facts on File, 1988.

"Helarctos malayanus." *IUCN Red List of Threatened Species.* Accessed Nov. 28, 2012. <http://www.iucnredlist.org/details/9760/0>

"Kermode Bears." *Bears of the World.* Accessed Dec. 9, 2012. <http://www.bearsoftheworld.net/kermode_bears.asp>

Macdonald, David W., ed. *The Encyclopedia of Mammals.* Oxford U. Press, 2009. 574–588.

"Melursus ursinus." *IUCN Red List of Threatened Species.* Accessed Nov. 23, 2012. <http://www.iucnredlist.org/details/13143/0>

Pelton, Michael R. "Black Bear: *Ursus americanus.*" *Wild Mammals of North America: Biology, Management, and Conservation,* 2nd edition. Ed. George A Feldhamer, Bruce C. Thompson, and Joseph A. Chapman. Baltimore: Johns Hopkins U. P., 2003. 547–555.

Rogers, L. L. "American Black Bear: *Ursus americanus.*" *The Smithsonian Book of North American Mammals.* Ed. Don E. Wilson and Sue Ruff. Washington: Smithsonian Institute Press, 1999. 157–160.

Schwartz, Charles C., Sterling D. Miller, Mark A. Haroldson. "Grizzly Bear: *Ursus arctos.*" *Wild Mammals of North America: Biology, Management, and Conservation,* 2nd edition. Ed. George A Feldhamer, Bruce C. Thompson, and Joseph A. Chapman. Baltimore: Johns Hopkins U. P., 2003. 556–586.

Stirling, I. "Polar Bear: *Ursus maritimus.*" *The Smithsonian Book of North American Mammals.* Ed. Don E. Wilson and Sue Ruff. Washington: Smithsonian Institute Press, 1999. 163–164.

Stonehouse, Bernard. *A Visual Introduction to Bears.* NY: Checkmark, 1998.

"Tremarctos ornatus." *IUCN Red List of Threatened Species.* Accessed Nov. 5, 2012 <http://www.iucnredlist.org/details/22066/0>

"Ursus maritimus." *IUCN Red List of Threatened Species.* Accessed Dec. 19, 2012. <http://www.iucnredlist.org/details/22823/0>

"Ursus thibetanus." *IUCN Red List of Threatened Species.* Accessed Nov. 29, 2012. <http://www.iucnredlist.org/details/22824/0>

"*Ursus thibetanus*: Asiatic Black Bear." *Animal Diversity Web.* Accessed Nov. 29, 2012. <http://animaldiversity.ummz.umich.edu/site/accounts/information/Ursus_thibetanus.html>

Webster's Encyclopedic Unabridged Dictionary of the English Language. NY, Random, 1996.

Wood, Daniel. *Bears.* Vancouver, Canada: Whitecap, 2005.

CHAPTER 2

Bear-Aware for Twenty Years

Victor Watkins

I have worked for the World Society for the Protection of Animals (WSPA, recently renamed World Animal Protection, WAP) for more than thirty years. My work initially involved every aspect of international animal welfare: stray animal control, farmed animal welfare, wildlife trade, and disaster relief (for animals caught in natural and man-made disasters such as earthquakes, floods, and volcanic eruptions). But my main interest was always wildlife, and much of my time working with WSPA has focussed on wildlife protection.

In the late 1980's I became WSPA's Wildlife Director. At that time there were a number of wildlife groups creating awareness and raising funds to save and protect endangered species, so there were many popular wildlife protection campaigns to "save" the whale, seal, rhino, elephant, dolphin, tiger, and so on. It was during this time that I became aware that bears were not yet on the popular radar—and that they should have been. At the time there was very little awareness of the factors that threatened bears in the wild, or of the horrific suffering that captive bears around the world faced. As WSPA's wildlife director, I received news from a variety of dependable sources that exposed serious, ongoing threats to bears, both from habitat loss (due to the rapid expansion of human populations) and exploitation (for "entertainment," and because of an insidious demand for bear body parts).

From tourists relaying reports of gypsies who dragged tethered bears along city streets, I learned that European brown bears were suffering in Greece and Turkey, exploited as "dancing bears" for tourist dollars. Sadly, there were many ignorant (or indifferent) tourists willing to drop money in a hat in front of a dancing bear, or to pay for a souvenir snapshot of a bear, making this form of exploitation and abuse a lucrative enterprise. Gypsies sometimes managed to collect the equivalent of $100 an hour at the expense of these miserable bears.

The first undeniable and alarming evidence of these problems reached me in 1990, when WSPA co-funded an investigation into the Asian trade in bears and bear parts (undertaken by bear specialists Chris Servheen and Judy Mills). This report showed, for the first time, evidence of a variety of bear bile farms in Asia, where bear bile was—and still is—harvested for traditional Asian medicines. Bile farms in nations across Asia incarcerate thousands of Asiatic black bears for the duration of their lives in cages so small that bears often cannot turn around or sit up. On Chinese bear farms, bile is extracted from a living

© KONINKLIJKE BRILL NV, LEIDEN, 2015 | DOI 10.1163/9789004293090_004

bear's gall bladder via a crude tube inserted through the animal's abdomen; the bile is later dried and used in medicines. In Vietnam, caged bears are tranquilised before their bile is removed with a syringe. In South Korea farmed bears are killed to obtain their gall bladder, which is then sold to the pharmaceutical industry.

Because of this booming Asian trade in bear bile, poachers hunt bears all over the world—just for their gall bladders—which are removed and sold to Asia, or to Asian medicine shops in Europe and America. Brown bears in America, spectacled bears in South America, and even polar bears in the Arctic are killed for this lucrative trade in a thriving market for a "wonder drug" that has been hyped up by Asian pharmaceutical industries, many of whom hold stakes in lucrative bear farms. Those invested in bear bile farms promote bile products in as many ways as they can—wines, eye drops, teas, shampoos, as well as a myriad of medicines—all of which lead to more and more bears kept in cages.

Bears have also been exploited all over the world in circuses, zoos, and private collections. Although a growing number of zoos are keeping bears in a more enriched environment, the sad truth is that the majority (thousands) of zoos, circuses, and private collectors around the world, do not provide bears (or other animals in their care), with adequate enrichment, thwarting their natural behaviours.

Dimitri

As horrifying evidence of the plight of bears around the world trickled in, I felt that WSPA had to do something on their behalf. After months of research, WSPA launched a World Campaign for Bears—Libearty—in London, in February of 1992. The Libearty Campaign immediately grabbed public interest and (ever-essential) public support, enabling WSPA to investigate and begin to lobby on behalf of bears around the world .... So it was that I found myself in a gypsy camp in Greece in April of 1992.

Dimitri, an old European brown bear (likely more than 30 years old) chained in a small shed in a gypsy's camp in northern Greece, was the first bear that I came across while investigating "dancing" bears. His owner dragged the decrepit bear out of the shed, tugging at the chain that ran through Dimitri's nose. The old bear looked weary, his face held an expression of fear and exhaustion. His small round ears were flattened against his head in anticipation of pain. His long, creamy brown fur was matted with mud. His large paws looked torn and calloused from a lifetime of standing on concrete, and he was completely blind—possibly from malnutrition. It was clear that this bear was very sick—he was literally dying on his feet. Despite his deplorable condition, the gypsy made him stand on his hind legs and shuffle his feet for me as if I were a tourist.

Dimitri would have been caught in the forests of northern Greece as a young cub. In order to catch such cubs, hunters shoot their mothers. The hunter who shot Dimitri's mother sold him to a gypsy community that trained and kept him for the rest of his life. Generations of gypsies have forced captive bears like Dimitri to "dance"—to stand on their hind paws, shifting their weight back and forth—solely to solicit money from passers-by.

Training a 200 kilo (440 pound) wild animal with sharp teeth and quick claws is not easy, so people resort to brute force. A heavy chain was placed around Dimitri's neck to secure him for a lifetime. Then, to control Dimitri, metal chains were put through piercings in his lips and nose. (Scars told us that these chains had been torn from his lips and nose more than once, leaving jagged, gaping wounds.) To make him "dance," the young Dimitri was forced to stand on a hot metal plate, and/or his legs were beaten to force him to lift them off the ground. Needless to say, such training would have caused immense physical and mental suffering.

Creating Sanctuaries with WSPA

Unfortunately, I could not rescue Dimitri at that time—I had nowhere to place this tired, sick old bear. Sanctuaries must be in place if we are to confiscate dancing bears like Dimitri. Consequently, creating sanctuaries was central to the Libearty Campaign—sanctuaries designed and funded by WSPA, but owned and managed by a local authority or local NGO. With this goal in mind, WSPA developed the first bear sanctuary design, and supported the construction of bear sanctuaries throughout the 1990's in countries as diverse as Greece, Turkey, Thailand, India, and Pakistan. Other animal advocacy organizations have joined in the process, creating sanctuaries for bears in China, Cambodia, Indonesia, Germany, Bulgaria, and also in the U.S. and Canada.

Before WSPA designed and built the first large forested bear sanctuary, enabling bears to be legally confiscated and cared for on a long-term basis, there were a few bear rescue and rehabilitation projects underway in North America, but these facilities took in orphans, cared for them, then released them back to the wild. They were not designed to provide lifetime care, which requires large, natural enclosures complete with grasses. brush, trees and pools. "Rehabilitation centres" aim to provide shelter, care, and to rehabilitate animals in need, with the goal of releasing them back into their natural environment, which is often possible for younger animals but unlikely for bears who have been caged for long periods, or who suffer broken teeth and claws as a result of biting cage bars and living on concrete for many years. "Sanctuaries" provide lifetime or long-term shelter and care for animals in need.

Bear sanctuaries are designed with one or more large natural forested enclosures, at least three hectares (7 acres) and sometimes closer to 8 hectares (19 acres), each surrounded by tall fences enforced with electric wires. Bear sanctuaries provide bears with trees for climbing, pools for swimming, and plenty of earth for digging. Because their enclosures are much smaller than their normal wild habitat, sanctuary staff provide food daily, mainly in the form of fruits and vegetables. But the bears also forage for food in the vegetation that grows in their ample enclosures, including nuts, berries, roots, shoots, and anything else they can find. Sanctuary bears even hibernate in their forested enclosures. It is wonderful to see bears who were rescued from appalling captive conditions, roaming an expanse of forest on their own terms, among their own kind, in a bear sanctuary.

Greece—Remembering Dimitri

While I could do nothing for Dimitri at the time, I did not forget him. Months later, WSPA formed an alliance with a newly developed Greek environmental group, Arcturos, to confiscate "dancing" bears in Greece. Together, WSPA and Arcturos established a veterinary rescue centre in Greece, and built the world's first bear sanctuary in the forests of northern Greece in the spring of 1993. Then, with the support and help of the Greek government and local police, we searched gypsy camps to locate and confiscate captive brown bears.

As we searched across Greece, I watched hopefully for Dimitri. I wanted to offer him a place of sanctuary, a retirement from the horror of life as a dancing bear. At last we found him, but he was in a terrible state. His eyes were weeping sockets; his teeth had rotted and were falling out of his abscessed mouth. He was extremely weak, and his body was nothing but a frail bag of bones. Though our veterinarian examined Dimitri, there was little that could be done apart from putting him peacefully to sleep.

I was saddened that I could not save Dimitri—that I could not offer him even one month of dignity and peace in a sanctuary. Nonetheless, his sorry life and drawn-out death strengthened my resolve. In fact, Dimitri inspired all of us who knew him in our efforts to end the practice of using "dancing" bears. Thankfully, and to the credit of the Greek authorities and the Greek people, we were successful.

Turkey—A Rainy Rescue

Later that same year the Turkish government supported a WSPA campaign against captive bears similar to the one we ran in Greece. Marginalized gypsy communities settled in camps outside the city of Istanbul had been keeping European brown bears chained to trees in popular parks in central Istanbul for decades. Each day gypsies unchained the bears and led them onto and across busy streets in search of families enjoying an afternoon walk, or businessmen eating lunch on nearby park benches, or more commonly in later years, the gypsies targeted foreign tourists. When they found a likely target, they forced the bears to "dance" on their hind legs, while the gypsies solicited coins from onlookers, or tried to persuade passers-by to pay to have their photo taken with a bear.

In 1993 I organized the rescue of a dozen such brown bears chained in parks in central Istanbul. The night of the rescue was made difficult by a torrential downpour. The bears, as always, looked miserable: Long, shaggy coats matted against malnourished bodies, dark eyes mirroring the misery and suffering of their daily existence. Some of the bears were huge. But, chained and distraught as they were, they looked small—pitiful shadows of their wild counterparts. When we approached each chained bear, he or she shrank back in fear, ears flattened back—probably expecting to be beaten. Forced to live on dry bread, with occasional bits of rotten fruit, the bears were severely malnourished; several had developed cataracts, and were blind. Nonetheless, they were forced onto the streets each day to earn their keep.

For eight long hours our team of vets and police worked to tranquilise, cut away chains, and carry each bear to transport cages. The transport cages were loaded onto trucks, and the bears travelled for six hours to reach the new Karacabey Bear Sanctuary in mountains above the city of Bursa, in Turkey.

Visiting Rescued Bears in a Turkish Sanctuary

I did not know what to expect when I returned to visit the bears at Karacabey some months later. I could scarcely recognize them as the same bears we had rescued from chains on the streets of Istanbul in a downpour. With a proper bear's diet they had put on a great deal of weight—they seemed much bigger, with glossy coats and bright eyes. They spent their days climbing trees, swimming in water pools, and wandering through the lush forest enclosures in search of new treats—a buried root here and an apple there. It was clear that these bears were content—even happy. I watched them splash in their pools, chase each other, or engage in mock-fights with visible pleasure.

When I was developing the concept of bear sanctuaries, I was repeatedly told by "experts" that bears put together into an enclosed area would fight continuously, but it was clear that these sanctuary bears found comfort and fulfilment in shared company. There was a hierarchy, and dominant bears wandered around like Lords, with others keeping a respectful distance. But many of the bears had formed small groups within the larger group and frequently played together.

Karacabey Bear Sanctuary has since taken in more than fifty bears, and Turkey's cruel trade in dancing bears was quickly eradicated. Rescues are stressful and difficult, but long-term rewards are ample.

Libearty—Romanian Refuge for Rescued bears

Most recently (beginning in 2005), I worked with a Romanian animal protection group to create a bear sanctuary in the heart of Transylvania, in Romania. The new Romanian sanctuary, whose construction was funded by WSPA, is owned and managed by Milioane de Prieteni (Association for the Protection of Animals, founded in 1997 by Cristina and Roger Lapis). Cristina Lapis, executive director of Milioane de Prieteni and an amazing advocate for bears, proudly named the new facility the Libearty Bear Sanctuary. She has persuaded Romanian authorities to place a nation-wide ban on keeping captive bears (which was common until 2006, when the Libearty Sanctuary was founded). She has also worked hard to create public awareness regarding the plight of Romania's bears: Romanian school children visit her sanctuary throughout the summer months, and teachers now provide lessons on bear protection and other animal welfare issues—unheard of before the founding of the Libearty Sanctuary. Also as a consequence of Cristina's diligent outreach, caged bears are much more likely to be reported to authorities—and confiscated.

Bear Baiting in Pakistan

Sanctuaries are central to rescuing bears, whether bears exploited for begging in the streets in Turkey and Greece, or bears forced to fight dogs in remote villages of Pakistan. Bear baiting, pitting dogs against tethered bears, was apparently a favourite pastime of King Henry VIII and Elizabeth I, and was a common form of entertainment in 16th and 17th century Europe. Although bear baiting disappeared from Europe by the mid-19th century, this bloody sport continued among influential local Landlords in Pakistan, who proudly pitted their fighting dogs against captive, tethered Asiatic black bears, in competition with the dogs bred and kept by other Landlords.

In 1993, Libearty investigations uncovered this grisly sport thriving in remote areas of Pakistan. Local townsfolk gathered to watch, and hundreds of tethered bears were forced into vicious battles against powerful dogs. At first the Pakistan government denied any knowledge of these cruel events—which were illegal, at least in the law books. In response, WSPA presented the authorities with a detailed document describing where each event took place, complete with photos and video recordings of bear baiting events. Faced with such evidence, it was clear that wildlife protection laws were being blatantly broken, and the Pakistan government was forced to act, supporting our work. As a result, bear baiting events have been drastically reduced, and it is possible to foresee a time when these cruel matches are eradicated altogether.

Again, to rescue these badly wounded bears, Pakistan needed a bear sanctuary. WSPA worked with Dr. Fakhar-i-Abbas at the Bioresource Research Centre (BRC, a local NGO) to build a bear sanctuary in northern Pakistan, completed in 2000. Once the sanctuary was in place, we were ready to go to work. So in July 2001 I joined a rescue team to rescue Rustam, an Asiatic black bear, whose face was terribly bruised and swollen from the teeth of fighting dogs. Rustam was quite young (around 8 years old), but he was a big bear: When he stood up on his hind legs he was taller than I, and probably weighed twice as much. His fur was coal black with the usual large white crescent on his chest, which gives this species their common name, "moon bears." His shaggy long fur and round ears gave him the appearance of a huge, real-life teddy bear, and I was surprised by his calm nature. Even though he had been severely mistreated by humans, and though he must have suffered greatly in the many baiting fights he endured, he showed no signs of aggression.

Rustam did, however, show a keen interest in the fruit we had brought to tempt him into our transport cage. After a few sweet apricots, he confidently followed his nose—and the apricots—into our cage, and was carried to a waiting vehicle. It took 24 hours to drive Rustam from the south of Pakistan to the Kund Bear Sanctuary in Pakistan's North West Frontier Province, where he spent his first few days sitting in a cool water pool, perhaps relaxing for the first time in his life.

Bear Farming in Asia

Unlike bear baiting, bear farming is a legal business in China and South Korea. For centuries, in some Asian countries, Asiatic black bears have been hunted for their bile and gall bladders, which are used for traditional Asian medicines. In the 1980s, China started farming bears—catching bears from the wild, caging them, and extracting their bile via tubes inserted into their gall bladders.

There are probably more than 12,000 Asiatic black bears enslaved on bile farms in China. Despite the fact that there are many herbal and synthetic alternatives, bear bile is promoted for economic gain. Furthermore, China produces far more bear bile than is needed to meet medicinal demand, so bear bile is made into tonics, wine, teas, shampoos, and other products for which this ingredient is not the least bit essential. The number of bears in farms is likely to increase because Chinese authorities support this industry due to enormous profits garnered, and maintain close relations with wealthy, powerful businessmen who have invested in this enterprise.

For twenty years animal protection groups have campaigned against the appalling treatment of wild bears on China's bile farms, but the government has endorsed the expansion. As a result, more bears are being bred on these farms, and Asiatic black bears are also illegally caught from the wild and sold to bear bile farms. China's bear bile products are even sold via television and the internet, which has increased the demand for this stunningly cruel product, and also increased the likelihood that bears will be poached from the wild in any country where bear populations are still found.

Vietnamese and South Korean governments are currently phasing out bear farming, and are likely to close down all bear bile farms within a few years. China's bile farms, however, are still going strong, and Animals Asia Foundation set up a bear sanctuary in China in 2001 (The China Bear Rescue Centre), to provide a permanent safe-haven for bears rescued from these bile farms— usually from farms that have been shut down by authorities for failure to comply with government regulations.

Bears in Zoos and Circuses

While exploiting bears for bile or entertainment ("dancing" or fighting) is clearly cruel, zoos, circuses, and private collectors too often slip under the wire—we fail to recognize that these institutions can and do inflict psychological and physical distress on caged animals, and bears in zoos and circuses are too often viewed as expendable. This should not be taken lightly.

Wild bears climb, dig in the earth, and travel many kilometres a day in search of a variety of foods. When caged, they are usually denied most of their natural behaviors,. In the absence of freedom, and access to their natural habitat, bears ought to be provided with "enrichments," including foraging scenarios to help them occupy their intelligent minds and strong bodies. But bears in zoos are rarely provided with such enrichments. In zoos around the world I have witnessed atrocious examples of startling cruelty to bears kept in small, rusted cages on crumbling concrete, without even a tree branch or blade of grass or patch of earth. Bears in these zoos pace relentlessly and exhibit unnatural, stereotypic behaviours, endlessly expressing frustration and stress without relief. I have even seen bears in zoos fight, ripping chunks of flesh from each other— while zoo visitors enjoy the show and zoo management remains oblivious or un-interested in the welfare of animals in their care.

Animals in zoos are frequently bred simply because babies draw the paying public. But babies soon lose their cute appeal and often become "surplus" zoo bears, euthanized to create space for the next round of cute cubs. In some cases, "surplus" bears are sold to circuses, to poorer zoos in undeveloped countries, or even to private collectors dealing in "exotic pets."

Zoos, in general, still have a long way to go to meet the needs of their captive animals. Fortunately, in a growing number of zoos who are members of National Zoo Associations, there is an increasing awareness of the need to prioritize the welfare of the animals in their care. If you visit zoos, ask the curator how many bears have been bred over the past decade, and where those bears have gone. While they are not likely to tell you if the zoo has sold or euthanized bears, it is important to ask such questions in order to remind zoos of public concerns regarding captive wildlife. Better yet, check to be sure zoos are providing animals with adequate space and enrichment, and if they are not, please do not visit. Instead, send an e-mail suggesting that they improve conditions for captive animals so that you will be willing to visit next time around.

In contrast with zoos, there are no good circuses that exploit wild animals. Circuses generally keep bears in very small cages between shows and when they are transported from town to town, or across international borders (in so-called "Beast-Wagons"). Not only are wild animals in circuses strictly confined, they are also subjected to cruel training methods: They are forced, usually by physical punishment, to perform unnatural "tricks" such as riding bicycles and balancing on balls. Anyone who would find such unnatural and demeaning acts "entertaining" has never paused to consider the bear's point of view. Please do not ever visit any circus that exploits wild animals.

Conclusion

When I joined WSPA's staff over thirty years ago, we did not know that bears were suffering and dying as "dancing" bears, on bile farms, or in bear baiting matches. We were not aware of the extent of suffering bears had to endure in badly managed zoos, or how often bears are trapped in circus acts and kept in tiny cages throughout their lives. At that time, bear sanctuaries did not exist anywhere in the world. There are now bear sanctuaries in roughly twenty-five countries, and thousands of bears have been rescued. Thanks to these sanctuaries—as well as dedicated organizations and innumerable supporters—bear baiting has been nearly eradicated, along with "dancing" bears. But we have a long way to go: Thousands of bears continue to suffer on bile farms, and in circuses and poorly managed zoos. We continue to work to protect wild bear populations, especially against poaching for body parts for Traditional Asian Medicines. I hope that this book will bring more widespread awareness of the serious issues endangering and harming bears, and that readers like you will do what it takes to bring change on their behalf.

CHAPTER 3

Making a Difference for Bears in Asia

Amy Corrigan

No matter where I travel, I often see teddy bears on sale, and children clutching these icons of childhood. Many of us grow up with teddy bears as our earliest companions, an unshakable source of childhood comfort. Despite this early love for stuffed bears, real flesh-and-blood bears are some of the most abused beings on the planet: They are killed for the "delicacy" of bear paw soup, they are exploited as walking medicine cabinets, they are kept in deplorable conditions at many zoos, they are turned into clowns by circuses and animal shows, they are crammed into pits where they must beg and fight for scraps of food, they are made to fight teams of trained dogs, they are forced to dance in the streets, and cubs are stolen from their mothers and sold into the pet trade. It is shameful how little regard we have for real bears in contrast with our youthful love for teddy bears.

My passion for bears started while working at Wildlife Friends Foundation of Thailand (WFFT), a wildlife rescue centre, between 2002 and 2005. At WFFT, Malayan sun bears rescued from the pet trade and tourism, and Asiatic black bears rescued from wildlife traders, find sanctuary—a second chance at life. It was there that I met two young Malayan sun bears who had been rescued from an elephant park—Peanuts, with a deformed mouth, and Poppy, with stunted legs. Both bears looked like they had just been sprayed with hair gloss—they had that beautiful, glossy fur of sun bears, with a glorious glint of dark chestnut when glimpsed at an angle to the sun. Their little faces struck me as dog-like, and their wrinkled foreheads made them look permanently puzzled, a response that seemed reasonable in light of their past. These two bears had spent years tied to a platform where tourists could be photographed standing next to them. Yet despite mistreatment and poor care, the personalities of these gorgeous bears shined through. Poppy was calm and placid, with one of the most gentle faces I have ever seen. Peanuts, in contrast, was a boisterous bundle of energy. Had he been a schoolboy, he would have been the class clown.

Working at WFFT offered fascinating insights into the lives of Malayan sun bears and Asiatic black bears. I was constantly amazed at their ability to bounce back from human-inflicted horrors. Many WFFT bears were cubs, so I became "bear mum." Pooh, another Malayan sun bear at WFFT, was rescued from life as a "pet." She spent her youth tethered on a small chain, walking in repetitive circles day after day. I helped nurse Bouncer, an Asiatic black bear

© KONINKLIJKE BRILL NV, LEIDEN, 2015 | DOI 10.1163/9789004293090_005

cub, back to health after he had his leg amputated—his leg rotted after he was caught in a leghold trap. With his large round ears and fuzzy fur, Bouncer looked like the typical cartoon bear cub, except that his soulful (often frightened) eyes made him look much older. He was incredibly fearful, letting out sharp barks of alarm whenever we were nearby. In time, Bouncer learned to trust us, and it was a pleasure to watch the look of wild-eyed fear disappear from his face. It was heart breaking to see these tiny bears without their mothers. We did what we could provide the best bear upbringing possible among humans; I was the best bear-mum that I could be. Some of my happiest memories at WFFT stem from walking cubs daily into the forest, encouraging them to climb trees and do all the things that bears are supposed to do, meanwhile watching them grow into confident little individuals, each with his or her own personality.

When I moved from Thailand to Singapore to work for ACRES (Animal Concerns Research & Education Society) in 2005, I was shocked to discover polar bears housed at the Singapore Zoo in an open-air enclosure. Clearly polar bears do not belong in the tropics, yet someone decided to bring Sheba, a young female polar bear, to the Singapore zoo in 1978; two others followed, both of whom died. When I arrived in Singapore there were two bears at the zoo—Sheba and her grown-up male cub, Inuka. These two majestic polar bears looked extraordinarily out of place in their tiny open-air enclosure—and they looked miserably hot. I tried to imagine what it might feel like to walk around in a thick fur coat, with a host of other physical adaptations to Arctic climates, in Singapore's hot, humid environment—it was hard to imagine that kind of perpetual, discomfort.

ACRES works to improve the welfare of animals in Asian zoos. Whereas at WFFT most of my work was hands-on, directly helping orphaned, injured, or displaced bears, at ACRES I delved into research, investigation, education, and campaigns on behalf of animals, including bears. ACRES conducts scientific investigations and detailed surveys into the welfare of zoo animals and, most importantly, collaborates with other NGOs (including WSPA, Love Wildlife Foundation, and several Malaysian organizations), as well as with government authorities, zoos (and zoo associations), to improve conditions and standards for captive wild animals. For example, an ACRES study demonstrated that Singapore's polar bears displayed clear signs of heat stress most of the time, along with pronounced stereotypic behaviours—odd, repetitive, behaviours caused by stress and boredom, indicating that their needs are not being met. We worked together with the zoo to improve living conditions for Sheba and Inuka, and to phase out their polar bear exhibit. The zoo followed some of our recommendations, and in 2006 the Singapore zoo announced that, after Sheba and Inuka had lived out their full lives—or as full as their lives could be in such unnatural conditions—they would no longer house Arctic animals. Still, Inuka is fairly young, and he would be much better off in a modernized zoo and/or a cooler climate. We continue to advocate for his relocation, though Sheba is too old to be moved. As long as there are polar bears in Singapore, we will advocate for improvements. As I write, a new improved temperature-controlled enclosure is finally being constructed. At least Singapore's polar bears will be given a significantly better living environment, and perhaps when Sheba passes they will send Inuka to a more suitable climate.

I soon realised that Sheba and Inuka were just the closest and therefore the most visible victims of compromised welfare in Asian zoos. We began detailed surveys of the welfare of animals in zoos across Malaysia and Thailand, and discovered that bears often draw the short straw when it comes to quality enclosures. In both countries we found scores of bears, mainly Malayan sun bears—but also Asiatic black bears and sometimes brown bears—kept in wholly substandard conditions. These bears are typically kept in a small cage or pit with a concrete floor, usually with no private areas to escape from the probing eyes of humanity. "Enrichment" has not yet come to these zoos, and "furniture" is often restricted to a branch or two. Many bears have nothing in their enclosure except their very own selves. Consequently, bears commonly engage in stereotypic behaviours, especially pacing up and down or in circles, often with repetitive neck-twisting. Alternatively, bears lie motionless for hours on end, in a state that has been described as "learned helplessness," in which they seem to have simply given up on life. When we could, we offered bears in barren enclosures leaves, branches, sticks, and rocks. We carried backpacks loaded with bags of peanuts and raisins to scatter inside their enclosures—a slight distraction from the tedium of their monotonous lives. At least for a moment, we could make the lives of zoo bears a little bit better, and for those of us working at ACRES, the happiness of individual bears matters.

Some of the saddest-looking bears we saw were five Malayan sun bears imprisoned in small, dark, damp, dungeon-like cages in Malaysia's Saleng Zoo. One of these bears somehow got hold of a broken piece of pipe, and the bear was playing with that pipe as if it were the best toy in the world—it was probably the only stimulation she or he had come across in months, maybe years. We campaigned with other activists for something to be done about this horrible excuse for a zoo. Thankfully, to Malaysia's great credit, Saleng Zoo was closed down by the authorities in June of 2011.

Unfortunately Saleng Zoo was just one of many substandard zoos in the area, and the animals at Saleng Zoo were just a few among many we have found suffering in zoos throughout the region. In one Malaysian zoo we found tiny sun bear cub, not more than a few months old, in a rusty little cage hidden down one of the zoo's back alleys. He or she was sitting on a wet, cracked floor, surrounded by soggy rice that had been thrown into the cage. There was no sign that the bear was being fed special milk formula—an absolute essential for such a tiny cub, still of nursing age. Flies and rats flew and scurried around the cage, delighted by the rotting rice. He had no water, no shelter, no toys, and worst of all, no mother. I wished I could open the cage and take him away with me to raise him or her as as an orphan bear should be raised, not only with the basic necessities, but with plenty of entertainment, including contact with peers. But I could not, and so I wonder, was he tossed into the barren pit-style enclosures with adult bears, who already had barely enough space to move? Did he die of some disease or malnutrition? ... or was he killed? ACRES has learned that several zoos in the region may sell body parts from wild animals. Was this little bear sold to a bile farmer, or killed for the price of paws and gallbladder? ACRES also learned that zoos in the area may sell wildlife into the pet industry. The misery of that little bear still haunts me, and I hope that whatever happened, his suffering was either short or in some way alleviated.

One of our most difficult tasks is to watch animal shows, and make a note if animals are expected to perform unnatural tricks. Circus-style animal shows contravene the WAZA (World Association of Zoos and Aquariums) Code of Ethics and Animal Welfare (set by the zoo industry itself), which states that animal presentations should "not demean or trivialize the animals in any way." Unfortunately, when we watch (or film) animal shows we see Malayan sun bears or Asiatic black bears riding bicycles, pushing themselves around on scooters, balancing on balls—you name it, if bears are not supposed to do it, they are probably made to do it somewhere in a zoo, circus, or bear park for the sake of human entertainment. One of my saddest moments was watching a man train a young Malayan sun bear to ride a bicycle at Danga Bay Petting Zoo in Johor, Malaysia. The bear's paws were tied to the handlebars and pedals. Every time he faltered, he crashed to the ground. When he fell, the bicycle crushed his lower leg and forepaw, and the trainer beat the bear's face with a stick. It is difficult to keep one's composure and pretend to be a happy tourist, clapping with delight while animals are abused and humiliated. But under-cover ACRES employees must mask emotions to remain undercover. Only if we are focussed and determined can we hold up long enough to gain the information and footage we need to bring change.

When not being "trained" or exploited in a degrading circus-style animal show, these large animals are kept in tiny, barren cages. With nothing else to do, they pace. Most people who attend these horrible events probably do not know that they are paying for such misery with their entrance tickets, so informing people about the unseen cruelty behind such circus-style animal entertainment is a very important part of our work at ACRES.

But it's not all bad news for bears in zoos in Asia. Some zoos, such as Songkhla Zoo in Thailand, have made tremendous strides to provide captive bears with large, enriched habitats, with many natural features. It was wonderful to see the Malayan sun bears and Asiatic black bears at Songkhla Zoo playing, climbing, and foraging—being bears. While bears are always best in the wild, some cannot be released, in which case enriched quarters that simulate natural environments, like those at Songkhla Zoo, are best. Numerous non-profit bear sanctuaries now also provide bears that cannot be released back into the wild with permanent homes, complete with pools, wooded areas, grasses, and brush. Many of these facilities also help to educate people about bears.

ACRES continues to work to improve the welfare of captive wildlife, including bears, and has also developed education programs: When citizens are aware that bears and other animals suffer in zoos and circus-style animal shows, they support change, and there is strength in numbers. ACRES is also working to end the bear bile trade and bear farming (largely Asiatic black bears, but also Malayan sun bears). There are no bear farms in Singapore— bear farms only exist in a handful of countries, including China, Vietnam, Korea, and Lao PDR (Lao People's Democratic Republic, formerly Laos), but wherever they exist, the suffering of bears is prolonged and intense.

An undercover bear farm investigation in China revealed that Singapore is a primary market for bear bile medicines, despite the fact that the sale or possession of bear products, including bear-derived medicines, is illegal in Singapore. So ACRES took action to curb Singapore's illegal trade in bear-derived medicines, thereby curtailing demand in one of bear bile's biggest illegal markets. To do this we had to prove to Singapore's authorities that trade in bear parts was a local problem, at which point authorities could take action to clamp down and prosecute offenders. So 2001, just after ACRES was founded, we began our first undercover investigation: We posed as customers in Traditional Chinese Medicine (TCM) shops to see if we could purchase bear bile medicines or gallbladders. We were offered (but *never* bought) every imaginable bear-derived medicine, from bear bile pills and powder to whole gallbladders—a staggering 73.5% of randomly-selected shops sold bear bile medicines and/or bear gallbladders. We filmed our interactions with hidden cameras and promptly presented our findings to the authorities. Prosecutions soon followed—we even managed to nab one of Singapore's main bear bile importers.

While stopping the supply is helpful, nothing ends trade like dried-up demand. ACRES wanted the citizens of Singapore—potential consumers of bear-derived medicines—to understand the cruelty of bear farming in the hope that they would stop buying bear products, or never buy them in the first place. Over the past ten years, through public roadshows (tabling/postering), leafleting, and presentations, ACRES informed thousands of Singaporeans about the cruelty of the bear bile industry. In the process, we found that many people did not know the ugly truths of bear farming, and that on learning about these horrific practices, many people told us that they would *never* take bear medicines again.

ACRES also works with the TCM (Traditional Chinese Medicine) community in Singapore to eradicate trade in bear parts. Toward this end, ACRES created STOC (Singapore TCM Organizations Committee): TCM companies and shops can pledge never to sell products derived from bears (and also tigers and rhinoceroses), and in return, ACRES offers them a label to place in their shop window declaring that they are "Endangered-Species Friendly." Over 300 Singapore shops now proudly display this label, and we continue to urge yet more shops to take the pledge. We also encourage consumers to patronise *only* shops sporting the ACRES and STOC label when looking for medicines.

To see if we were making progress, we conducted a second undercover investigation of illegal bear body parts/medicine sales in Singapore in 2006. When we visited TCM shops, armed with undercover cameras, we were pleased to find that the number of shops selling bear bile medicines and/or gallbladders had dropped dramatically, to just 20 percent. This was, indeed, a sign of progress! And this was accomplished in just five years! But there is yet much work to be done if we are to wipe out trade in bear parts and bear-derived medicines in Singapore. Until there are *no* shops, companies, or individuals selling bear bile medicines and gallbladders in Singapore, we will continue undercover investigations and educational campaigns, and promote shops that carry ACRES and STOC labels.

While those of us at ACRES knew that bile farms were ugly, we never really understood the miseries of these farms until we visited one in Lao PDR. We were mortified by the horror of what we had previously only read about or seen on videos. The bear farm that we visited held row on row of helpless Asiatic black bears in tiny cages with open wounds in their abdomens, created and kept open to drain bile. Some cages held cubs, probably captured from the wild (which means their mothers were likely killed in the process). We knew that these cubs would spend the rest of their lives in small cages, with permanent holes stabbed into their soft bodies, so that bile could be extracted day after week after month after year.

Each of these individual bears had his or her own history of sorrow and loss, pain and forgotten hopes. We found one young female Asiatic black bear, like many bears on bile farms, who had become very sick. She was so ill that she had stopped eating. Instead of caring for this exhausted bear, the farmers simply put her cage outside, with her in it, and left her there to die. Despite the fact that she was a large bear, filling most of the cage, she looked frail, lying in a steel cage with her life ebbing. Perhaps she was relieved to at last be on the verge of escaping her barred prison of pain and exploitation. As we stood by helplessly, she reached out and touched our hands. Her paw felt powerful, yet incredibly gentle. My colleague, Louis, stroked the top of her large paw, putting his fingers into her thick, coarse fur—fur that was designed to survive all weather conditions in the thick forests of Asia. Her curled claws were overgrown and shiny—she had not climbed a tree or touched the earth for many years. Despite her pain and deprivation at the hands of humanity, she showed no sign of aggression. We talked to her, hoping in some small way to provide her with a just a moment that might be different from the rest of her life, and to say sorry for what our species had done to her. She died the next day, free at last.

She touched our hands and reached our hearts, and in her memory we at ACRES have vowed to do all we can to free as many bears as possible from bile farms. ACRES is now working with the authorities to establish a bear rescue centre in Lao PDR (for Asiatic black bears and possibly Malayan sun bears) for rescued bears, complete with an education centre, a means of bringing lasting change.

With education, change is possible. For example, Europe's bear pits are mostly gone, and bear baiting has been outlawed in most EU countries. The tireless efforts of groups such as Wildlife SOS and IAR (International Animal Rescue) have put an end to the practice of keeping "dancing" sloth bears in India, and they have developed sanctuaries where these rescued bears can live out the remainder of their lives in peace and comfort. Animals Asia is also doing a fantastic job rescuing bears from bile farms in China and Vietnam. There are many worthy individuals and organizations helping to bring change for bears—and other exploited, suffering nonhuman animals—but it is important to remember that change does not come free or easy: Changes are won by the work of dedicated activists with the support of generous members and donors.

Sadly, there are still thousands of bears suffering all over the world: In substandard zoos, in circuses, in bear parks, in homes, in restaurants, in markets, on the streets, in bile farms, and in forests where they are trapped in painful steel-jawed traps. I urge you to support organisations that help bears and other nonhuman animals, and to do your part to help bring change: Never engage in any activity that harms bears or that supports people who exploit and thereby harm bears, and never buy bear-derived products. You can also give the bears a voice—speak up when you see cruelty, alert authorities and NGOs, and help prevent and raise awareness about animal exploitation and suffering. And you can write letters, both to companies involved in animal abuse, telling them how you feel about these activities and their company, and to newspapers, exposing companies that exploit animals and helping to educate others. You can also post information about animal exploitation on Facebook and write about what you have learned in your blog.

I've always been fascinated by bears; it is my dream to one day see a bear in the wild, without taint of human interference—a wholly free and natural bear. I may never get to see such a bear, but as one person with a voice, I will work to bring change for bears and other animals: I pledge to spend the rest of my days, in whatever ways I am able, working to make the world a better place for *all* living beings.

CHAPTER 4

Polar Bears: Watching Extinction in Real Time

Kassie Siegel, Brendan Cummings

Sometimes extinction confronts us in the form of a black and white picture, such as that of Martha, the last passenger pigeon, who died in 1914, alone in a cage in the Cincinnati Zoo. Passenger pigeons were already extinct in the wild, so one single individual—Martha—signaled the loss of a species. Other times, extinction comes in the form of simple nothingness. One day the last individual disappears, without humans even knowing what they have caused, or what has been lost.

A few months ago, on a back-stage museum visit, we held the skin of a passenger pigeon and touched the pelt of the last California golden brown bear known to have been killed. Gone for close to a century now, these animals no longer exist in living memory, and can only be experienced in word, painting, photo, or at rare moments, through an aging skin locked in the back room of a museum.

Though sometimes represented by an artifact—some bit of remains—extinction is, in truth, a void. This void is usually acknowledged only grudgingly—after intensive, but ultimately futile searches and long waiting periods fed by denial. Scientists recently scoured the fractured forests of Vietnam for the country's last Javan rhinoceros, and the wilds of Cameroon in hopes of finding a handful of remaining Western black rhinos. In both cases, they came up empty; in 2011, with no hope left, both rhinoceros subspecies were declared extinct.

We have become familiar with extinction. The dodo bird caught us by surprise, but we knew the rhinoceros was in danger—we watched the rhino slip away. Similarly, on the shores of Hudson Bay in Manitoba, Canada, extinction seems imminent.

Wapusk National Park

Access to Wapusk National Park is tightly controlled. Tourists travel in vehicles that amount to oversized school buses jacked up on jumbo tires. From this steel-coated vantage point, safely beyond the reach of their inquisitive paws and hungry jaws, human beings watch these great white hunters on the shore of the Hudson Bay. Around the world, people treasure polar bears, though most only know these bears through photos and film. To witness polar bears in their natural habitat is nothing short of enthralling.

In November, 2011 we took our fourth trip to Wapusk National Park, the first having been in 2007. Along with scientists and educators, we entered the park on a teched-out Tundra Buggy run by Polar Bears International. Affectionately labeled "Buggy One," this vehicle serves as a platform for educational webcasting, blogging, and for interviews concerning polar bears and climate change. At night, Buggy One docks at a mobile tourist lodge that is set up on the tundra for just a few weeks each year—those few weeks when the bears cluster on the shores of Hudson Bay, waiting for the water to freeze so they can once again roam the sea-ice realm where they hunt, mate, and raise their young.

Polar bears live only in the Northern hemisphere, in areas where sea ice remains for a substantial portion of the year. In parts of the Arctic, mother polar bears give birth to cubs in caves excavated in the snow on top of drifting pack ice, emerging from the den in the springtime hundreds of miles from where they fell asleep in the fall. These great bears require ice for all of their most basic, essential behaviors, from travelling to finding mates to hunting —seals form the core of a polar bear's diet, and they can only hunt seals successfully on ice.

On our first evening, as we ate dinner around a folding table in Buggy One, the almost-full moon rose in yellow glory over the open, rippling waters of Hudson Bay. It was a lovely sight. But knowledge sometimes destroys beauty. We knew that the moon should be rising over ice, not open water. It was mid-November, and there was virtually no ice on the bay. Nighttime temperatures remained above freezing, and because polar bears are creatures of the ice, unable to maintain their body weight on land, we were filled with dread for what these eerily warm conditions would bring. Global warming has lengthened the ice-free season in this area over the past few decades, and polar bears have subsequently declined in numbers. When the ice-free period extends too long, bears become thinner, less healthy, and eventually starve.

Climate Change

Rangers in national parks could not prevent the last rhinos in Vietnam and Cameroon from being hunted to extinction. They tried. With well-armed guards packing polished heat, they tried. But human greed and selfishness are not easy to push back. The quest for profits and long life—long life for wealthy humans, not for rhinoceros—could not be overcome even to preserve a species. Polar bears in Canada's Wapusk National Park are not primarily imperiled by poaching, but by human consumption. We are the problem, and we must be the solution. A shift in human values—or at least a shift in our behavior—is essential if we are to have a future complete with polar bears.

Though they are ice-dependent, the polar bear's sea-ice habitat is rapidly melting. Sea ice at the top of the world grows each winter and shrinks to an annual low at the end of each summer. Both the maximum winter extent and minimum summer extent of sea ice have been declining since satellite data measurement began in 1979. Climate scientists have called the Arctic "the Earth's early warning system" because the Arctic is warming about twice as fast of the rest of the globe. Summer sea ice shows the sharpest decline, hitting a new record low of 1.32 million square miles (3.41 million square kilometers) of sea ice in 2012. The Arctic has already lost an area of ice about two-thirds the size of the contiguous United States.

Because sea ice is essential for their survival, scientists have long predicted that climate change would be disastrous for polar bears. In 2004, leading polar bear scientists published a paper describing the observable effects of climate change on polar bear populations, and predicted their extinction if sea ice continues along current declining trends. That same year, a major research effort (the Arctic Climate Impact Assessment) predicted that summer Arctic ice pack would either be completely gone or greatly reduced by the end of the century. The future for polar bears looked grim, even though complete sea-ice loss was estimated to be at least a century away—enough time for the world to come to grips with the problems at hand, and address greenhouse gas emissions.

Unfortunately, melting in the Arctic has accelerated, and the polar bear's plight has worsened much faster than was anticipated in 2004. Disappearance of summer sea ice is no longer viewed as an end-of-century phenomenon, but as something likely to occur within the next twenty years, possibly even sooner. Not surprisingly, of the world's 19 polar bear populations, a whopping eight are now classified as declining. Because they are largely unstudied, seven of the remaining groups are listed as undetermined. Only three polar bear populations are considered stable, and one very small population has increased, thanks to the implementation of strong hunting restrictions. How long can polar bears hold on as the ice melts?

Western Hudson Bay polar bears, those protected in Wapusk National Park, have lived for thousands of years in the Bay's biologically rich seasonal ice ecosystem, and were once among the largest and most fecund of polar bear populations. But earlier ice melt in the spring and delayed freezing in the fall have taken their toll—Wapusk's bears are dwindling. Between 1987 and 2004 the sea-ice season diminished by an average of three weeks, and the polar bear population declined by 22 percent, dropping from about 1200 to only 935 individuals. Scientists studying bears in Hudson Bay project that sea-ice season in this region will be so short within the next several decades that polar bears will be unable to reproduce: Western Hudson Bay polar bears, like the California grizzly, will no longer exist. There will be polar bears farther north, but in areas where these massive mammals die out, it is impossible to comprehend what we have destroyed.

Polar bears are at risk throughout their entire range. Leading climate and polar bear scientists examined the future status of polar bears in a warming Arctic in 2007, and concluded that more than two-thirds of the world's polar bears will be gone by mid-century. The "good news" was that they predict that some high Arctic polar bears may survive through the end of the century. Even so, the probability of extinction is greater than 40 percent by 2100. These researchers, aware of the shortcomings of previous predictions, warned that their study likely understates climate changes that lie ahead, and the bears' resultant peril.

Climate change moves like a tanker in the ocean—it cannot easily be reversed or even shifted. It takes several decades to experience most of the warming effects from a molecule of carbon dioxide. Consequently, based on greenhouse gases that have already been emitted, we are currently committed to roughly a doubling of the earth's warming. In other words, even if greenhouse emissions were magically halted right now—completely—the planet would still continue to warm for decades. Because of this "climate commitment," it may already be too late to save polar bears in the Western Hudson Bay. But even if we have already failed the bears of Churchill, it is not too late to save polar bears elsewhere. If we commit to *rapid* reductions in greenhouse gases, we can slow, and ultimately reverse, ice-melt. But deep pollution reductions need to start *immediately*.

In some ways it is fortunate for polar bears that the actions we need to take to save them are the same actions required to save ourselves. The Arctic is critical to the earth's climate system—it is the Earth's air conditioner—or perhaps a bit more like a sunhat. Arctic landscapes reflect most of the sun's energy back into space, but as climate change melts the ice, the Arctic's reflective effect is lost, and warming accelerates. In addition, the Arctic is critical because permafrost stores vast amounts of greenhouse gases. As climate change thaws permafrost, these gases are released into the atmosphere, further accelerating planetary warming. Thus the impact of Arctic meltdown is huge and affects every inch of the planet. Slowing and reversing the warming of the Arctic is an essential part of solving the climate crisis globally. If we don't save polar bears, we can't save ourselves.

Acknowledging a Problem, Taking Action

Early in 2005, as the Kyoto Protocol went into effect—absent the participation of the United States—we filed a legal petition with the U.S. government to protect polar bears under the U.S. Endangered Species Act. The Bush administration denied climate change, and was generally hostile toward the protection of endangered species. Nevertheless, thanks to the polar bear's irresistible charisma, the process of petitioning to list polar bears as an Endangered Species captured the world's attention. At that time we wondered, could an imperiled Arctic icon force the Bush administration to acknowledge the threat of climate change?

Two lawsuits and three years later, the verdict was in: Yes! The Endangered Species Act requires that decisions regarding wild populations be made solely on the basis of science, without regard to political maneuvering. The strength of scientific evidence combined with an unprecedented public interest in protecting polar bears (including supporting comments from three quarters of a million people), forced the Bush administration into a corner: While the oil men in power did not want to list the bear as endangered, refusal to do so would be challenged, and a federal court would then decide whether the Bush administration could rationally conclude that climate change did not imperil polar bears. On May 15, 2008, with a court order in place that forced a verdict, the Bush administration "chose" to do the right thing. Government officials acknowledged that the polar bear was a threatened species—the first species to be listed under the Endangered Species Act solely due to the threat of climate change.

As the saying goes, acknowledging a problem is the first step toward a solution. Compelling the U.S. government to admit that unchecked climate change would drive polar bears to extinction was an important step, but the critical work lies ahead—we must implement policies that will actually save the polar bear from extinction.

We cannot save polar bears without very deep and rapid greenhouse gas reductions. The irony of our country's apathy and inaction (despite a clear threat from climate change), is that we have the strongest and most successful domestic environmental laws in the world—including the Endangered Species Act. But such laws do little good when our leaders do not implement them, and we do not force them to do so. It is a common misconception that because climate change is a "new" threat, our existing environmental laws do not provide solutions. To the contrary, existing laws can carry us far down the emissions-reduction road. The Endangered Species Act can help reduce greenhouse pollution just as it has helped reduce pesticides, mercury, and other pollutants that threatened now-recovered species such as bald eagles. The Clean Air Act can also be deployed to help reduce greenhouse gas emissions—economy wide. Solutions to the climate crisis are within our reach, but this is a democracy, and *we* must demand them. We must demand, with urgent conviction, that elected officials take action and call out those who deny climate science, whether our civic leaders or our loved ones. Additionally, we must reduce our personal carbon footprint. All that we seem to lack is the collective and individual will to make these essential changes. Polar bears are worthy of the extraordinary effort and considerable change necessary if we are to reverse global climate change and save the species.

Ugly Realities

Our language has a tendency to mask the ugliness and pain of extinction. What does it mean for a species to fall into decline, or disappear altogether?

In 2011, in Churchill, a severely emaciated bear simply dropped and died of starvation. In November, 2010, a polar bear cub starved to death on film, falling into seizures because his or her mother was too depleted to provide milk. Recently, polar bears consumed spilled, fermented grain that had been piled on the outskirts of Churchill for decades: The skinniest bears imaginable, ribs painfully visible, rooted in the dirt to consume this insufficient and inappropriate food source. Polar bears in Wapusk National Park are smaller and lighter than they used to be, fewer cubs survive, adults die of starvation much more frequently, and the population is declining. These bears are on a course to be the first population to disappear, but they will not be the last. In every area where summer ice has been reduced by climate change, polar bears face a similar fate. Global warming is not an abstract phenomenon for these bears, but a deadly reality. Starvation is ugly, and polar bears are just one of many species affected.

Count humans among those affected. According to the Global Humanitarian Forum, more than three hundred thousand people (and counting) are already dying each year because of climate change. Entire island nations—the Carteret Islands (one of the most low-lying of all Pacific Island nations), Tuvalu, the Marshall Islands, and the Maldives—face evacuation and displacement. As always, most of the victims are in the "developing" world, while the "developed" world is the primary source of the problem. And of course there are the polar bears.

Creating a Future for Polar Bears

Despite the dire situation for bears in the Hudson Bay, over the next several days, the bears worked their magic. One day several males approached quite close and were play-fighting, wrestling and rolling on the ground, looking fierce and majestic one moment, then teddy-bear-cute the next. At times we even forgot the very real possibility of polar bear extinction, so lost were we in the sound of their footsteps, the rhythm of their breathing, and the wonder of their massive bodies, so magnificently adapted for life in the frigid North.

FIGURE 4.1 *Polar Bear*

When we left Wapusk National Park after several days of webcasting, media interviews, and intense blogging, our sense of grief was sharper than it had been previously. We were deeply saddened by the tragic reality of climate change: It is probably already too late to save these particular polar bears from a slow and miserable death culminating in their extirpation from this vast area of their natural range.

Watching bears out on the tundra in Wapusk National Park is magical. When bears are in sight, visitors can easily forget sorrows that lie ahead, and become lost in the sound of padded feet on crunchy snow, the huff-huff of breath, and the visible strength of their massive bodies. These great beasts have evolved to live in the frigid North—and they can live nowhere else. Will we do what it takes to save polar bears—and millions of other species, including human beings—from gross suffering and possible extinction?

PART II

A World of Problems

..

CHAPTER 5

Franzi: Beloved Ambassador for Bears on Bile Farms

Jill Robinson

Wednesday, October 7, 2009: As I peel Franzi her last grapes, I remember when I fell in love with her for the first time. It was on December 6, 2002; we had just closed down another brutal bear farm, but there was no time to celebrate. We were looking at the tiniest bear cringing in the corner of the tiniest cage we had ever seen. This little bear had given up hope—and small wonder, with her catalogue of injuries and abuses—she had clearly suffered for years. A hole in her abdomen poured with bile and pus and an abscess the size of a golf-ball throbbed with pain under her chin. She had been declawed, detoothed, and demoralized. Franzi was just one of many victims of China's bear bile industry.

It took me about three seconds to fall in love with Franzi, to cry for her sorrowful eyes, which darted away from mine, afraid that this new person would hurt her as much as the last. On that day, she both won and broke my heart.

Loving Franzi

Franzi was one of 19 Asiatic black bears (also called "moon bears" because of the beautiful yellow crescents on their chests) confiscated from a bile farm, and transported to our Moon Bear Rescue Centre outside the capital of Sichuan, Chengdu. She had been milked daily for her bile for many years.

Bear bile is used by some traditional Chinese medicine practitioners as a remedy for "heat-related" conditions affecting organs such as the eyes and liver, even though many practitioners know that herbal alternatives are cheaper, just as effective, and cruelty-free. There are also many affordable synthetic options. Nonetheless, bear bile products are still used to treat everything from hangovers to impotence, and are even touted as a cure for cancer.

Franzi had been a slave to this unnecessary trade for more than two decades. Standing before us, she was a perfect and tragic example of "stress dwarfism": she had a normal bear-shaped head, but a crudely stunted body because she had been squashed in a cage just 18 inches high, 3 feet long, and 19 inches wide (90cm x 45cm 50cm) for more than 22 years. The legacy of this cage, now

© KONINKLIJKE BRILL NV, LEIDEN, 2015 | DOI 10.1163/9789004293090_007

stacked with a pile of other rusting torture traps in the grounds of our Moon Bear Rescue Centre, stayed with Franzi throughout her life. The depleted shell of an animal that emerged from those cruel bars was just three and a half feet (100cm) tall and weighed just 105 pounds (48kg).

At first, Franzi wouldn't look at us. She stared at the bottom of her cage, her chest rising and falling as she breathed great gulps of fear, dreading what would befall her next at the hands of humanity. Then her nose quivered, and her head turned towards me—she had caught the smell of something new, and too tempting to ignore—a fruity shake with strawberries, apples, mangos, jam—and so much more—just in front of her nose. Even more astonishingly, it was all for her!

Gingerly extending her soft, pink tongue, Franzi sampled the delicious drink—and there was no going back. She closed her eyes and slurped, and slurped, and slurped. As she got to the bottom of the pot, I poured the rest onto my fingers—not the most sensible thing to do with a newly rescued bear; but I was rewarded for my carelessness with the softness of her velvety lips as she gently sucked the remainder of her first smoothie—her first taste of kindness.

From that point on, Franzi took charge of her diet. She would sometimes refuse to eat "proper" bear food, standing firm for two or three days while we patiently encouraged her to behave like a bear. Inevitably, she would win and we would wearily relent, offering her exactly what she was holding out for—her favourite sachets of dog food with gravy. She even trained us how to offer her grapes (peeled and deseeded) by contemptuously spitting out the skin and pips.

In January 2003, a month after her arrival, Franzi continued to worry us with bouts of ill health, and by occasionally refusing to eat. Our head veterinarian was particularly worried, calling attention to Franzi's laboured breathing and associated lung problems. Over those weeks, she felt it was her duty to prepare us for the worst, noting that it "didn't look good" for this elderly female with multiple health problems. But Franzi, in her normal style, now well-loved and well fed, ignored sound veterinary science and happily puttered around the garden for special-needs bears for seven years, demanding her favourite foods, and sleeping in the sun.

When we weren't fretting over her health, Franzi always made us laugh. Politely described as a "windy" bear, she burped and farted with abandon—most frequently when I was showing her off to a very large group of visitors. She timed the passing of gas for those special moments when visitors stood respectfully around her den, listening to the poignant story of her tragic past. How could any of us keep a straight face after Franzi let rip with all the smugness of an elderly Aunt?

Bears and Bile

Bears are the only mammals to produce significant amounts of ursodeoxycholic acid (UDCA) in their bile. This is the much-sought "magic" medical ingredient: Bear bile brings a tidy U.S. $585 per kg on the streets of Chengdu, and far more on the overseas black market. It is illegal to export bear products from China, but trade thrives nonetheless. Malaysia, Korea, and China have the highest demand for bear bile. Australia, Taiwan, Indonesia, Japan, Vietnam, Singapore, the U.S., and Canada also have a market for bear bile. Consumers are predominantly of Chinese, Vietnamese, Japanese, and Korean origin.

There are eight bear species in the world, and the Asiatic black bear (*Ursus selenarctos*, moon bear) has been most affected by the ongoing human demand for bile acid. Consequently, these bears are listed under Appendix I of the Convention on International Trade in Endangered Species (CITES), the most critical category of endangerment. Though their range extends from Iran to Japan and across Southeast Asia, today as few as 16,000 individuals are left in the wilds of China, and perhaps as few as 25,000 across their range in Asia.

Moon bears have been killed for their gall bladders for thousands of years, but only recently, in the past 20 years, have entrepreneurial farmers in Korea, China, and Vietnam discovered that enslaving bears in tiny cages and milking them regularly for bile is far more lucrative than hunting them down in the wild.

"Bile" bears are usually milked twice a day in China, a process that is excruciatingly painful. Since Franzi's rescue, the Chinese government has banned the use of catheters to drain bile. Instead, farmers must use the free-drip method of bile extraction—which is every bit as agonizing for the bears as the previous technique. Under the free-drip system, a permanent hole is cut into the abdomen, clear through to the gall bladder, from which bile drips. The wound is invariably infected and inflamed. To keep the hole open, the bears' abdomens are prodded and poked with metal rods or tubes. Sometimes, against regulations, Perspex catheters are concealed underneath the skin—cut flush with the wound—to keep the hole open.

Today, Animals Asia estimates that more than 14,000 moon bears are trapped on farms across China and Vietnam. (Animals Asia operates bear rescue projects in both countries.) The Vietnamese government, with the help of the World Society for the Protection of Animals, attempted to protect the country's few remaining wild bears by microchipping all 4,000 bears on farms, and banning the extraction of bile. Bears can now only be kept in cages as "tourist attractions," but allowing some endangered animals to be exploited for profit ultimately endangers the entire species. Too often, bears kept as "tourist attractions" are exploited for bile. In Vietnam, bile is collected illegally with the assistance of an ultrasound machine, catheter, and medicinal pump. The bears are drugged (usually with an illegal drug, ketamine) restrained with ropes, and jabbed with a four-inch needle until the gall bladder is located and robbed of bile. Busloads of visitors arrive at these farms from such destinations as Korea, where bile is a popular hangover "cure," and leave with viles of bile, fresh from the body of an anaesthetised bear.

Bears farmed for bile are fed just enough tasteless gruel to keep them alive—starving a bear produces more bile. They do not have free access to water, even in mid-summer. Some cages have sliding metal grilles inside, which farmers use to push the bears flat to the floor of the cage, making bile extraction easier. Sometimes these grilles rust so that they will not move, and bears are held immobile for weeks, or even months.

Bile farmers brutalise bears to destroy their natural defences. For example, their paw tips are hacked away to ensure that their claws will never grow back, and their teeth are smashed from their powerful jaws. Consequently, it is unlikely that any bears rescued from bile farms can ever be released back into the wild. They also lack basic survival skills (because they have spent their lives behind bars), and they are ill from neglect and abuse. Rescued bears from bile farms often suffer from an array of debilitating ailments, such as severe arthritis, peritonitis, and weeping ulcers. They die of liver cancer at a troublesome rate, though liver tumours are normally extremely rare among all but the oldest captive bears. Many farmed bears are missing limbs because they have been illegally caught from the wild with snares or leghold traps, and some are blind from malnutrition or trauma. The bile of bears who are milked for years in unhygienic conditions is often contaminated with blood, urine, faeces, pus, bacteria, and cancer cells—they are only alive because they are pumped full of antibiotics. Vets describe their bile as "black sludge" (a healthy bear's bile is a yellow-green liquid).

Bears exploited for their bile have a plethora of medical problems, many of which are not only incurable, but debilitating. Kiki, for example, a young male rescued in 2008 from a Chinese bile farm, arrived with necrotic flesh, with his right eye literally rotting away. Most of his teeth were shattered, and several had been pulled from his jaw, which was broken.

Animal Asia's veterinary team is collecting evidence, and working with independent pathologists, to convince authorities that the bear bile industry is not only cruel and unnecessary, but also a serious health risk for humans. Through posters, ads, the media, and public education campaigns, we are informing consumers in the hope that they will turn away from medicines or tonics that could harm rather than heal their bodies, and which definitely harms bears. Meanwhile, we continue to work with the governments of China and Vietnam to close down the worst bile farms, and to provide sanctuary for as many bears as possible. Every rescued bear becomes an ambassador for the cause—the eradication of bear farming. These bears, with their compromised physical or psychological health, give us tangible proof that bile farming is unconscionably cruel, unnecessary, and should be closed down.

All animals are remarkably similar in their capacity to experience pain and suffering, and we all have a complex range of emotions. The feelings a bear or pig experience are every bit as profound as our own. It is a shameful reflection of human nature that we are cruel to other sentient beings, treating them dismissively, as if they were "things" rather than individuals.

As the fullness of our responsibility for the health of the environment becomes clear, we must also recognise our responsibility for non-human individuals, and acknowledge that our treatment of cattle, chickens, tigers, and bears affects the fragile state of the earth. It is time for us to change. To care about bears means to care about the forests they inhabit, the water they drink, and the air that they breathe. Striving for a cruelty-free lifestyle is perhaps the greatest gift we can give this planet. Breeding animals for human food takes up huge amounts of land, water, grain, and fuel. The antibiotics and other drugs that are used in modern farming methods ultimately seep into the soil. Growing vegetables and grains takes up just a fraction of the land and requires far fewer resources. When we choose vegetables and grains over meat, we choose to save the natural habitat of bears and other endangered animals around the world.

As consumers, even the smallest change in our lives can have the most profound effect on the lives of animals everywhere. Along with choosing meals that do not include animal products, we can make many other cruelty-free choices as shoppers. We can buy cosmetics and soaps that have not been tested on animals, coats and accessories without fur trim, and "pleather" instead of leather, for example. These are simple of choices, but they mean the world to nonhuman animals.

Losing Franzi

There was no better ambassador for exploited animals than Franzi, who came to trust and enjoy the company of the very species that tortured her for decades. She showed us all what it means to forgive. Though she was wracked with constant pain for 22 long years, trapped in a pitiless existence, her zest for life was an inspiration. She survived for three decades (almost 100 years in human terms).

But Franzi grew old, and tired, and we knew it was time to let her go. On that sad and memorable day, we had only one last chance to spoil her. As I went to collect her favourite foods there were no words to describe my sadness. She was sitting up at the bars of her cage in her perfect "teddy bear pose," which we taught her so that we could easily listen to her heart and lungs with a stethoscope while she received her treats.

She began her small meal with a taster of rich dog food, followed by a piece of fruit mince tart. The latter because Franzi wasn't going to be seeing Christmas, and also in memory of her encounter with Australian conservationist Steve Irwin (rest in peace), who called her a "hot little tart" when he set eyes on her determined expression and luscious fur.

As it turned out, Steve was spot-on about Franzi. She was rather choosy about her company, and seemed to hate the presence of other bears in "her" space. Nonetheless, she finally grew attached to brain-damaged Rupert, with his slow, clumsy reactions and strangely lopsided face. A unique and loving friendship was born. Sweet and gentle Rupert had a "central brain lesion," most likely caused by the free-drip bile-extraction hole in his abdomen, through which bacteria had entered and infected his brain. (Although in no pain and deeply contented during his years at our sanctuary, Rupert's condition was a poignant reminder of why the free-drip method of bile extraction is every bit as cruel and damaging as the older method.) Franzi and Rupert adored each other. Even though Franzi was dwarfed by Rupert, who was three times her size, she dominated him from beginning to end. She flirted and flounced during spring mating season, then mischievously walked away—even though he appeared interested—leaving Rupert to cosy up to a bag full of straw. The only time Franzi honoured love-struck Rupert with anything resembling intimacy was on the coldest of winter days, when she cheekily snuggled up to him for warmth. Most of the time, she kept him on his toes, and showed him exactly who was boss.

I slowly and deliberately prepared Franzi's last meal; my heart was breaking for Rupert. But also for Peejou, a tortoiseshell cat who had taken up residence at our bear sanctuary. Peejou had always seemed to know instinctively that Franzi wouldn't mind if she explored her secret garden, and indeed Franzi never did—the two eyed each other with great interest while Peejou sniffed her way around, maintaining a respectful distance. Franzi was not aggressive, and was willing to share the delights of life at the sanctuary with a small cat. Peejou would miss Franzi, too.

Preparing Franzi's last meal brought back a flood of memories. She loved nuts but disliked cherry tomatoes. Most bears love cherry tomatoes, but Franzi preferred to play with them instead, and had a quirky and endearing habit of carefully clutching them in her clawless paws, then raising her arms to throw them over her shoulder. And pity poor Rupert if he came too close, hoping to hoover up her tomato rejects. Franzi never hesitated to place a well-aimed thwack on Rupert's tender nose. Always the gentleman, Rupert knew the rules, and would back off respectfully, returning only when Franzi walked away, leaving her leftovers.

Slowly peeling the last of Franzi's grapes, I remembered the cold, winter's day, when I looked out of my window onto the garden for special-care bears, which lay just outside my room, to see her carrying a huge pile of straw in her mouth, striding purposefully back to her den. Bears normally create dens for the winter, and Franzi could see that this straw would make a warm cosy bed for the cold weeks ahead—just how she liked it, thank you very much.

While Franzi sat in front of me one final time, gently taking and relishing each grape (seedless of course), her posture reminded me of how she stuck out her little disfigured chest, allowing the vet to place a stethoscope over her fading heart—her eyes glancing sideways, anticipating the treats she would receive if she could just hold still. She trusted us, yet now we would take her life. Her heart and lungs were failing. The vet team had removed six litres of fluid from her chest cavity, but it was refilling. The scales had tipped, and her quality of life was sliding. Even with regular medication and the best of veterinary care,

FIGURE 5.1 *Asiatic Black Bear*

Franzi's abdomen was unnaturally distended and no doubt uncomfortable. We knew what her trust required of us—it was time to let her go.

Franzi gently accepted the last of the peeled green grapes as we told her, for the very last time, how much we loved her. Then we made room for the veterinarian, who silently administered the anaesthetic. Franzi slipped into a deep sleep, blissfully unaware that her special care area was filled with adoring visitors. We, her family, had gathered to hold her tiny clawless paws and say a respectful, tearful, goodbye.

While we held vigil, the vet team injected sodium pentobarbital that gently ended her life. Franzi's body was shrunken—as small as a cub, yet larger than life—her spirit was bigger than China. Franzipants, our teacher, our friend, our hot little tart—sleep well, little bear.

CHAPTER 6

Little Bears, Big Trees, Tiny Insects: Protecting Sun Bears and Their Rainforest

Lisa Kemmerer, Siew Te Wong

Mary

Every day someone takes the orphans for a walk. There are many orphans—too many orphans. They have sleek black hair, and little bowed legs. They are only about a foot tall, and look up with dark eyes in front of little round ears. They have sharp canines, long claws, and stubby tails. These orphans are sun bears.

Last year in Ranau Township in central Sabah, the Bornean Sun Bear Conservation Centre (BSBCC) rescued a tiny bear named Mary from a villager who claimed that he had "found" the little bear while hunting for bearded pigs on a palm oil plantation. Like most baby mammals, bear cubs require intense maternal care in their first few months of life. As cubs grow and gain mobility, they romp and play, but they never stray far from their protective mothers, who keep them safe from predators and other mishaps. Mothers also teach cubs the secrets of survival—where to find food, and what to eat. When she arrived at BSBCC, Mary was probably only two months old, still very much in need of her mother.

"Walking" orphans permits young bears to learn what their mothers would normally teach them—how to forage for invertebrates and wild fruits, and which sights and sounds to avoid. BSBCC staff seek ways to reawaken and strengthen natural behaviors in the hope that rescues can be released back into their natural environment when they are adults.

As she walks through the forest, Mary often stops to forage for tiny termites at the base of massive dipterocarp trees. She busily digs with her strong sickle-shaped claws for a termite nest deep in the earth, which she is able to smell with her sensitive nose. As she digs, Mary breaks off small chunks of decaying wood, exposing termites. With a fast-flicking tongue, she feeds furiously on the terrified termites, catching them up as they swarm from their broken home. She seems as oblivious to the giant trees that stand over her like friendly giants as she is to the sound of cicadas and other forest insects roaring all around. The lush vegetation holds Mary in her dark safe-haven, a world that seems to have been created specifically for sun bears. The friendly people at

BSBCC who "walk" Mary hope that she will have a chance to reclaim her birthright in the wilds of Borneo—a little bear among big trees eating tiny termites.

Sun Bears

Sun bears (*Helarctos malayanus*) are one of the least studied bear species—it is likely that they are more neglected by scholars than *any* other bear. There are two sun bear subspecies: The Bornean sun bear (*H. m. euryspillus*) on the island of Borneo, and Malayan sun bear (*H. m.malayanus*) on the Asia mainland and Sumatra. The Bornean sun bear is smaller in size, with males weighing only about 45 kg (100 pounds); Malayan sun bears weigh as much as 90 kg (200 lb.).

Sun bears live in fragmented forests in Myanmar, Thailand, China's southern Yunnan Province, Laos, Cambodia, Vietnam, Peninsular Malaysia, Sumatra, Borneo, and on the eastern tip of India. Asiatic black bears share the northern portion of sun bear habitat, but the sun bear is the only bear living in the tropical forests of Southeast Asia south of Thailand. Sun bears have been driven from most of Southeast Asia by deforestation.

Female sun bears den in hollow tree trunks, or cavities in huge trees that have fallen onto the forest floor, where they give birth to one or two cubs. Tree cavities are the safest dens for sun bears because they are relatively dry (in a moist rainforest), relatively cool (in a hot tropical climate), and relatively warm even on cool nights. Newborns are only about 0.3 kg (0.66 lb). They are naked, blind, and helpless. Sun bear cubs stay with their mothers for at least two years in order to learn all that they need to know in order to survive.

Sun bears are unique among bears. Most noticeably, they are the smallest bears. They also have ample, loose skin, which some biologists believe allows them to turn and bite more quickly and easily when attacked, helping them to escape predators. Sun bear claws are unique not just among bears, but among species labeled as carnivores: A piece of bone inside each claw grows slowly throughout their lifetime. As a result, older sun bears have longer, more curved claws than younger bears. This clawbone is attached to a relatively large muscle at the tip of their paws, giving each claw the necessary strength to break through hard surfaces in order to open termite nests and logs, while also helping sun bears to climb trees. Finally, these bears have very long tongues. From the base, sun bear tongues can be up to 18 inches long—a perfect tool for collecting minuscule food items deep inside holes.

Like all bears, sun bears are opportunistic feeders. They are omnivorous, and the bulk of their diet consists of fruits and insects. In season, sun bears feed on more than 100 species of wild fruits. Most trees in sun bear habitat fruit only intermittently—once every two to eleven years! This intermittent fruiting cycle is known as "mast fruiting," or simply "masting." When masting, trees usually fruit for a few months, during which time sun bears spend a great deal of time high in the trees, gorging on pulpy fruits (with higher sugar content), storing up fat for lean periods ("intermast intervals"), which can last for several years. During these lean times, sun bears feed on non-masting fruits, such as figs (*Ficus spp.,* family *Moracea*), or on invertebrates—especially termites. Figs are a "keystone species" in sun bear habitat—fig trees each fruit on their own schedule throughout the year, and many local species depend on figs for survival. Because invertebrates are miniscule in comparison with sun bears, bears must constantly wander, smell, and dig if they are to eat their fill.

Selling Forests, Selling Out on Sun Bears

Habitat loss is by far the greatest threat to sun bears. As human populations grow exponentially, the demand for agriculture, logging, and mining also grow exponentially. Because bears require forests, and because logging brings roads, industries, settlements, and poachers into bear habitat, selling timber in Southeast Asia is synonymous with selling out on sun bears. Southeast Asia's forests are some of the oldest and most biologically diverse forests anywhere in the world—and they are home to a host of key species that are now critically endangered, including two species of Asian rhinoceroses, orangutans, Malayan and Sumatran tigers, Asiatic elephants, and sun bears. With few exceptions, all of Borneo's remaining forests are open to logging, including national parks, conservation areas, wildlife reserves, and sanctuaries. In 2008, sun bears were upgraded from "Data Deficient" to "Vulnerable" on the IUCN Redbook List of Threatened Species. Experts indicate that sun bear populations have declined by more than 30 percent in the last 30 years. If this process continues, sun bears are doomed to extinction.

Lowland rainforests in Malaysian Borneo have been selectively logged since the 1960's, targeting big trees and lucrative hardwoods, including dipterocarp trees. Some of these trees were more than 800 years old, offering a lush forest canopy 80 meters (262 feet) above the rich soils that fed their strong roots. Because of selective logging, thick forests across Southeast Asia have been thinned and reduced to stands of younger, smaller trees. It will take 700 years to replace these rainforest giants. Few studies examine the effects of losing old trees, or of reducing tree diversity. Changing forest structures certainly affects forest ecology. For example, smaller trees yield comparatively less fruit, and it is more difficult for wildlife (from hornbills to bears) to find suitable tree trunks for nesting and denning. Human populations continue to swell, simultaneously increasing logging, mining, and agriculture. With ongoing logging and limited forests, loggers claim smaller and smaller trees—and a larger variety of trees in more remote areas.

Logging not only robs endangered wildlife of essential habitat, but further threatens depleted species by running roads through previously remote landscapes. Roads offer easy access for poachers—or anyone with a gun who feels like shooting wildlife. Once roads are built, bears become almost impossible to protect. Poachers do not stop at the boundaries of protected forests—they know that protected forests are where bears are most likely to be found. From a poacher's perspective, every part of a bear's body has value as food, clothing, or medicine. Their gall bladders are particularly lucrative, selling for $150 in Malaysia, and up to $2000 in Hong Kong. Other body parts, including claws, paws, and canine teeth sell for a high price. Many local people continue to believe that bear canines and claws possess supernatural powers that repel bad luck and evil spirits.

Roads running through previously remote areas also increase the likelihood of conflicts between wildlife and human beings. Sun bears who only recently roamed vast forests where humans could not easily intrude, find their habitat flattened, and strange new forests growing—most often palm oil plantations. When bears wander into plantations, or into recently planted crops of fruit or coconut trees, men with guns protect their investments. Settlers emerge at night with spotlights and guns, eager to shoot bearded pigs, wild boars, and sun bears. When they shoot a mother bear, the helpless cubs are usually kept as pets.

Sun bear cubs are extremely cute, so there is a market for these little bears, and this market stands as just one more threat to declining sun bear populations: The only way to catch a cub is to kill the mother. Unscrupulous and/or ignorant people buy these adorable cubs as if they were kittens, stealing their lives and sealing their fates—cubs rarely have a chance to be rehabilitated and released once sold as "pets." But the "cute-cub phase" does not last long (typically less than a year). By the time they are ten months old, sun bear cubs are extremely strong—capable of destroying pretty much everything in a domestic household. (Sun bears have a stronger bite relative to body size than any other bear species—and *any* bite from a bear would be a threat to human beings.) Some stoop so low as to have a bear's canines filed and his or her claws surgically removed. Of course this does not solve the problem—the problem is that bears are wild animals who do not belong in human households. The most common next step is to lock these unfortunate young bears in small cages, where they usually remain for the rest of their lives. Others are soon backpedalling, desperately seeking somewhere to unload their "pet" bear. Mary was one such cub, though she was comparatively lucky—whenever possible, BSBCC staff rehabilitate cubs and return them to their forest home.

Southeast Asian Forest Ecosystems and Sun Bears

Dynamics between living organisms are continuous in the tropics. With a growing "season" of 365 days, plants thrive and animals remain active year-round. Sun bears are central to this ongoing tropical interchange in at least three critical ways.

First, by consuming millions of termites, sun bears act as "forest doctors," helping to maintain the health of forest ecosystems. Termites, who feed on dead plant material, are probably the most important invertebrate decomposer in Southeast Asia's tropical rainforest ecosystems. Termites also enhance soil structure and quality by loosening the earth, enriching mineral content, and assisting nitrogen/carbon cycles. But as with all species, they can be too much of a good thing. Some termite species (such as *Microcerotermes dubius*) also attack living plants—most notably, trees. These termites are indiscriminate, consuming trees of any species and size, and they are capable of gobbling up entire forest areas, leaving significant gaps in the trees. Sun bears help keep termite populations under control. When fruit is not available, sun bears feed extensively on invertebrates, and termites are by far the most important group of creepy-crawlies in the sun bear's non-fruit diet. In the course of a day's feeding, a single sun bear consumes thousands of termites, including larvae and eggs. In this way sun bears are "forest doctors," controlling the number of termite colonies in order to maintain the health of tropical forests.

Second, sun bears act as "forest engineers," reshaping trees to help create vital nesting sites for woodland animals. The local name for sun bears in the Malaysia and Indonesian language is *"beruang madu"*—honey bear. In the lowland rainforest of Borneo, stingless bees (*Trigona spp.*) build nests in tree trunk cavities, which they fill with honey. Some of these nests are 20 meters (65 feet) above ground, but sun bears are like Winnie the Pooh—honey is their favorite food and they will go to great lengths to taste this sweet nectar. When they reach bee nests, sun bears extract the honey and simultaneously "excavate" nests with their strong claws. When the bear climbs down from the tree, filled with honey and bee eggs and larvae, only a large cavity remains. These cavities later serve as homes for species that require large cavities for nesting, but are incapable of digging such hollows themselves (such as hornbills and flying squirrels).

Third, because they consume vast quantities of fruits—seeds and all—sun bears serve as "forest farmers," sowing seeds throughout local ecosystems. Ideally, seeds are dispersed far from mother-trees—young trees are unlikely to thrive in the shadow of their tall parents. Sun bears are critical for seed dispersal—especially for larger seeds, such as those of durian trees (*Durio spp.*). Sun bears carry seeds in their digestive tracts for up to eight hours, wandering as much as 5 km (3 miles) in a day, depositing seeds far and wide— "planting" seeds in the rich remains of whatever else they have eaten. As "forest farmers," sun bears assure a future crop of fruiting trees.

Little bears, big trees, and tiny termites have been central to the ecosystems of Southeast Asia's lowland tropical rainforests for thousands of years—each has evolved in the presence of the other, and they depend on one another. If we lose sun bears, the ecosystem to which they belong will be significantly altered, having far-reaching consequences.

The Bornean Sun Bear Conservation Centre

BSBCC stands on the northern edge of Sepilok Forest Reserve, in Sabah, Malaysian Borneo, witness to the many severe dangers facing these bantam bears. In order to protect sun bears and their habitat against the onslaught of human activities, which rob them of their homes and their lives, BSBCC has adopted a four-pronged program:

·   Provide sanctuary for bears in need,
·   rehabilitate and release captive sun bears when possible,
·   foster outreach and provide education, and
·   engage in research.

Sanctuary is important if bears are to have somewhere to go when they are orphaned and/or injured. BSBCC rehabilitates bears for release back into their tropical forest home, and provides safe haven for those who cannot be released. Education is critical because BSBCC cannot single-handedly assure the survival of sun bears. For example, BSBCC needs the support of the larger community to pressure law enforcement to crack down on poaching, the sale of bear cubs, and the sale of bear body parts, and to prevent unsustainable logging practices. Neither can BSBCC secure the support of the larger community if there is not a general understanding about the needs of sun bears, why they are disappearing, and why we must protect these bears. Raising awareness—both locally and internationally—is essential to the survival of sun bears.

And if BSBCC is to offer sanctuary, rehabilitate, and educate, personnel must first educate themselves. BSBCC must engage in research in order to understand sun bears—including basic facts that have long ago been collected on most other bear species, such as how far sun bears roam, how long they live, how mothers tend cubs, and how these pint-sized bears are affected by the loss of great big trees. In the well-stated words of Jane Goodall, "Only if we understand can we care. Only if we care will we help. Only if we help shall they be saved."

Saving sun bears requires an international effort, and BSBCC encourages people around the world to help in whatever ways they can. Please consider the following possibilities.

· Donate: The amount of work that BSBCC does for sun bears and their habitat is directly linked to the amount of funding received.
· Be Wise Consumers: Do not buy bear parts or products containing bear parts. Additionally, do not buy products containing palm oil or wood from Southeast Asia (unless they hold a sustainable seal that you can verify as legitimate).
· Network: Sun bears are perhaps the least known bear species. To gain public support, people must first know that sun bears exist, why they are endangered, and that they are not only a beautiful and fascinating species, but that they are also important ecologically. You can help spread the word by joining BSBCC's social network online (www.bsbcc.org.my; http://www.facebook.com/sunbear.bsbcc); by talking about sun bears with friends, family, and coworkers; and by mentioning them in the classroom or at environmentalist or animal activist gatherings. If you attend a meeting or conference for environmentalists or animal activists, set up a roundtable on palm oil plantations or Asian wood products—promote sustainable products (RSPO—www.rspo.org).
· Report Illegal Activity: If you hear of someone selling bear body parts or bear cubs, inform local authorities and NGOs working to protect wildlife, habitat, and/or animals.
· Volunteer: Volunteers help BSBCC to accomplish many tasks while supporting our work financially, allowing us to accomplish more for less. Volunteers bring home specialized training and unforgettable experiences, serving as overseas ambassadors for sun bears.

FIGURE 6.1 *Sun Bear*

Conclusion

Little bears, big trees, and tiny insects are part of an intricate, complicated web of life in Southeast Asia's tropical forests. Mary is part of this beautiful web of life.

Most people have never met Mary—or anyone even remotely like her. Most people have never watched a young sun bear dig vigorously for termites under an ancient dipterocarp tree. But knowing Mary—watching her sniff hopefully for grubs on this rich forest floor—it would be difficult to dismiss her needs, to leave her to the harsh fate of orphaned cubs.

BSBCC is doing all that they can for Mary and her forest home—and hopefully for Mary's cubs. But BSBCC cannot protect Mary or her forests without support. International effort is essential if we are to secure a future complete with ancient tropical rainforests where little bears dig tiny termites under giant dipterocarp trees.

CHAPTER 7

Libearty Sanctuary Zarnesti: Sharing Love and Sheltering Life in Eastern Europe

Cristina Lapis

First Friends: Lidia, Cristi, Viorel, and Maya

At a 1998 international conference addressing the concern of stray dogs, I met a few people who were working for the World Society for the Protection of Animals (WSPA, now World Animal Protection, or WAP). In the course of conversation, they asked about several Carpathian brown bears they had heard about, bears caged near Brasov. And so it was that, on return to Romania, I went to see about these bears. I did not anticipate how that visit would change the course of my life.

Lidia, Cristi, and Viorel were held near a restaurant at Poiana Brasov, a sport resort, while Maya was held near the Dracula Castle in the city of Bran. Lidia, Cristi, and Viorel were housed on wet concrete in a dirty hole, without a pool, grass, or a single shrub. Nothing around them resembled the forests in which they had once lived. All that they had in their dank pen were beer bottle shards.

All of these bears suffered severely from neglect, and were chronically hungry, but Maya suffered more than the others. Maya, alone and miserable, lay lifeless on the concrete floor of her dirty little cage, surrounded by metal bars and cement. When I first saw her, she was so weak that she could barely lift her head. She had been waiting for days for someone to bring food. Forgotten by all, she seemed to wait for life to leave her thin frame. Compassion and horror welled up inside me as I looked into her dull eyes, and I felt a boundless rage toward those who could condemn her to such a painful life and drawn-out death.

Looking into Maya's eyes I could see something of myself. Her eyes reminded me that we are all creatures of God, sisters and brothers on a planet that doesn't belong to us! Human beings are merely caretakers on behalf of the Creator, with the sacred duty of protecting God's beautiful earth, and glorious creatures, charged with handing this amazing creation on to future generations— all of it, not just what is left.

In Maya's eyes I was confronted with the wrongness of what we have done to God's creatures. She had been stolen from her rightful home in the forests, deprived of the company of her own kind. Her teeth and claws had been removed so she could not defend herself against a cruel humanity. She had been placed in this cage to attract the attention of tourists—and then forgotten. I knelt down next to her miserable little cage, and cried.

Though she could never be returned to the wild without claws and teeth, I promised that I would do everything that I could to help her find a measure of happiness and freedom in her life of captivity. I was determined to keep her alive long enough to offer her a better life. My commitment to Maya extended to Lidia, Cristi, and Viorel, and *every* day for the next ten years my husband and I (and a few other compassionate friends) travelled more than 100 miles to feed and tend these dependent bears. Living alone and unwell, Maya needed the most care and attention. We included vitamins with her food, and hung a tire from a chain so she might have something to play with in her barren pen. Over time, her health improved and her spirits lifted. She recognized the sound of our car, and when we arrived she would stand up to greet us enthusiastically. Maya reminded us of the value of every soul, the strength of each individual's will to live, and the depth of gratitude that can be felt in the heart of an innocent bear.

In 2001 Maya began to show new signs of depression. I renewed my promise to her that one day she would again have a measure of freedom to run through woods and play in a pool. I asked her to be patient, to hang on; I begged her to trust me, to wait. But Maya had long ago lost her faith in humanity, and she started to self-harm, chewing her right paw almost down to the bone. When I saw the blood on Maya's paw, I understood that she wanted a way out—an escape from the endless boredom of confinement, the lonely hours between metal bars with no companion, no peace, no independence, no small pleasures to mark off another passing day. Despite operations from two wonderful vets, Dr. Liviu Harbuz and Dr. Monika Koller, who helped Maya in those difficult times, Maya died in my arms on March 11, 2002. I will never forget her soft fur and the depth of her sad eyes.

Much to our horror, we arrived one day to find that Viorel had disappeared. I knew that Viorel had been sold and would end up at a "game farm." His skin and fur, complete with head and claws, would become a trophy on some heartless human being's floor, a man who thinks that he can show his toughness by killing a worn-out, tame bear who is trapped in an enclosure and cannot escape his relentless bullets.

I was heartbroken. Maya and Viorel were gone. I had failed to rescue them, and now I could not ever bring them to a place of peace on earth. With Maya and Viorel's passing I was yet more determined to keep my promise to the other three Carpathian bears—to create a sanctuary where they could retire from the misery of confinement and be permanently offered peaceful, spacious, safe surroundings.

Bears at Libearty Sanctuary Zărneşti

There were no bear sanctuaries in Romania, or anywhere in the area. We continued to feed the remaining Carpathian brown bears daily, and wait for some way to offer Lidia and Cristi a better life. Bears cannot be rescued from the horrors of human exploitation—street performances, bile farming, and business props—unless we establish sanctuaries where they can be relocated.

The World Society for the Protection of Animals, which had initially introduced me to the plight of captive bears in Romania, generously offered to finance a Romanian bear sanctuary. Libearty Sanctuary Zărneşti is located on 170 wooded acres (70 hectares), and is capable of housing 80 bears. We dedicated Libearty to Maya, and in 2005 our first residents arrived: Cristi and Lidia. They walked out of their dank hole onto the biggest Carpathian brown bear sanctuary in Europe—liberated. They immediately began to investigate their surroundings. They wandered among oaks and other leafy trees, waded in natural ponds, and dug in the soft earth—like bears were meant to do. Over time they began to climb the many trees, hide among the bushes, and of course they love to lie in the sun. I wanted them to forget their past—I didn't even want them to remain Cristi and Lidia—foolish human labels. And with the advent of Libearty, all seemed possible. They could again be bears, as God intended. My dream had come true, and I had fulfilled my promise to Lidia and Cristi.

In the seven years since Libearty was built, we have rescued 80 bears—we can house only 20 more in a world of need. Bears at Libearty generally live with one other companion on 17 acres (7 hectares), complete with stands of trees, ponds for wallowing, grass to roll in, and plenty of fresh earth for digging. We also have training areas for new bears and cubs, and smaller pens for special needs bears, where we currently have an Asiatic black bear (Ursula) and a blind Carpathian brown bear (Max).

Max was kept on a short chain for the pleasure of tourists outside of an old castle. Did tourists ever think to complain about his plight? He is blind because his "owner" stuck needles in his eyes so that Max would be helpless and dependent. Animal Planet filmed Libearty, and was moved to send a team of vets from the UK to operate on Max's eyes, but his retinas are damaged beyond repair. He continues to live in darkness, and because he is blind he lives alone. He cannot forage for food like the other bears, so we have to place his food right in front of him.

Until recently, Max enjoyed the companionship of an old bear named Ben. Ben, who we found starving in a zoo. These two companions could not play like other bears, but were always near one another while eating or swimming—

just nearby, without disturbing one another, like old people quietly sharing space around the fireplace. Last winter Ben disappeared into in his den, and for two weeks we did not see him. It was December, with snow, so we thought perhaps he was hibernating ... but we were concerned. We dug into Ben's den and found him not just asleep, but in eternal sleep. At 36 years old, he sailed away to join the bear constellations in heaven.

Max was sad for months after Ben died, but he came to accept the ways of nature—and so we all must. Though he must miss Ben greatly, he swims in his private pool, lies under the trees, and listens for the voices of those who lovingly bring him any care that he needs.

Ursula was our only Asiatic black bear. She was smaller than the big Carpathian brown bears of Europe, with gigantic fuzzy ears and a cream-colored collar around her neck, and a light muzzle. Ursula, who was probably about 30 years old when we took her in, would have been euthanized in a miserable zoo if we had not found a place for her at Libearty—zoos always prefer to buy cubs because these cute youngsters are more likely to attract the paying public. Because she was not a brown bear, like the other residents at Libearty, she lived with a fox whom we rescued from a circus. Ursula left us last year, and we are comforted to know that she died free, rather than in a zoo, and has now joined the big constellation of bears in the sky.

Libearty has also become home to a handful of cubs. One of the cubs, Diana, had been exploited as a "pet." A veterinarian, who also happens to be a hunter, "found" this cub in the forest, and of course the cub's mother had been shot. He thought that his family would enjoy having a cub around, so with no consideration to the needs and preferences of the little bear, he brought her home. They treated her like part of the family: She ate at the table, slept in a bed, and played around the feet of the adults in the house until she was four months old. But as she gained size and strength, she began to destroy the house: windows, doors, the fridge, furniture. An adult had to stay home at all times to keep an eye on Diana, and eventually they figured out that a bear cub did not belong in a human house. So the veterinarian put Diana in the car, as he always did when the two of them were going for a walk, then abandoned her at the edge of the woods. Diana had no idea how to be a wild bear—her autonomy and freedom had been stolen from her the day her mother was shot. Diana sat there, on the edge of the woods, and when the veterinarian returned to check on her, she climbed back into his car and went home. And so it was that he called Libearty. The family cried real tears of pain on separation from the bear cub they had stolen from the forest, and Diana screamed for months—she refused to eat bear food, was no doubt missing her soft bed, and also must have missed the only "mamma-bear" she had ever known.

Out of ignorance and selfishness, some people want to have a bear cub in their home despite the fact that these same people would not like their children to be raised by bears—though there are stories of children lost in the forest who survived only because they were nurtured and protected by bears. Fools who seek a pet bear rather than adopt a dog who desperately wants a home, create a market for cubs ... or go out and kill a mother bear themselves. Needless to say, this does not work out well—especially for the bear. With their whole lives ahead of them, these cubs become human dependent. Even at Libearty we can only provide them with the best possible captive life—not the full life of a wild bear. Diana now lives happily with other young bears. She climbs trees in search of acorns, roots around in search of tender leaves, and lives almost as God intended a bear to live. Almost. It is the best Libearty can do for bears whose lives have been disrupted by hunters. I tell Diana's story to children who dream of having a little bear in their house. I try to teach visitors to leave things as they ought to be, as God intended—animals free and autonomous, except when humans must step in to protect their lives and welfare.

Libearty Sanctuary has also rescued captive bears from restaurants, hotels, monasteries, fabric shops, and schools. We have adopted bears from zoos that were shut down (thankfully) because they could not meet European Union standards, and from businesses that no longer wanted to feed caged bears in the hope of attracting a few additional customers.

One of our more recent additions, Misha, came from Georgia on a DHL flight booked and paid for by the UK charity, Hauser Bear. Members of an EU Monitoring Mission (EUMM) in the war zone of South Ossetia, found this six month old cub chained in a village. They contacted Libearty, and we agreed to receive Misha. Hauser Bear put everything in place—notifying necessary officials, filling out paperwork, and making transport arrangements—then confiscated the cub and carried him to the waiting transport plane. We met Misha at the airport in Bucharest, and toted him the last 180 km to his new home at Libearty. Initially Misha was afraid of other bears—he was so afraid that he hid in his quarantine cage. Then one day he emerged to play with Zorro, a young bear we had confiscated from a private residence. Once they started playing, they just never stopped. It seemed that they had finally come into their own. Now a healthy one-year-old, Misha plays and roams with other young bears, free yet not free—safe in an enclosure with space to run and tumble and climb and wallow.

Some visitors are drawn to Max, others to Misha. I am especially touched by Mura. Mura was lifted from the side of her mother, dead but still warm, shot by a hunter. She was sold to the national circus in Bucharest, where she began a life of deprivation and suffering. She lived in a little cage, alongside many other caged and miserable animals. She was starved, beaten, and forced to ride a bicycle. After six years, she decided to die rather than go on—and she refused to go into the arena. No measure of cruelty could convince her to endure any more humiliation and abuse. The circus director eventually called me, and told me that he would not feed a bear who would not work, and that they were therefore going to kill Mura if I did not take her.

Of course I went to the circus to fetch Mura. I offered her a treat, looked into her sad eyes, and promised that she would never have to ride a bicycle again. We placed Mura in a holding pen where we could keep an eye on her and be sure that she was adjusting well to her new life. For 6 months she stood in one place and simply turned her back on us every time we approached the fence. She had 17 acres (7 hectares) to roam, but her mind remained locked in the tiny cage where she had spent her youth. Then one day, all on her own, she broke the bars of that imaginary cage, and joined the other bears in her pen for a swim in their pond. We were relieved—she was going to make it. Mura had readjusted to life in a safe haven, and time would allow her to slowly heal from the suffering and abuse in her past.

Mura now lives in a large enclosure with 20 other Carpathian bears. Her back legs are damaged from years of riding a bicycle, so she is easy to identify. Bicycles are designed for humans, not bears; it is not fun (or ethical) to watch animals who are forced to do unnatural "tricks" as a form of entertainment. Mura endured years of mindless "tricks" (torture) on behalf of thoughtless humans. How is it that some human beings believe that other animals have no soul, or feelings, when these other animals seem to have more decency than human beings, who exploit those who are weaker in cruel ways—not just in circuses and zoos, but for advertisements, for clothing, in research and education, and in our meat, egg, and dairy industries? When I tell children about Mura they sometimes cry—and they promise they will never again go to a circus. If these children keep their word, then Mura suffering is, in some measure, vindicated.

While bears are the focus of Libearty Sanctuary, they are not the only nonhuman animals we tend. Since 1997 we have worked with "Millions of Friends," providing shelter and care for more than 20,000 dogs—all of whom were spayed/neutered—8000 of whom found a big-hearted family to take them home. Though 20,000 dogs might seem like a whole lot of tails and legs, this number is a mere drop in the ocean of homelessness and hunger. We must commit to spaying and neutering all dogs and cats until every single cat and dog has a home. Dogs suffer in Romania not because people are poor, but because we let our companion animals breed indiscriminately, and because the human heart has forgotten how to love—because people of faith have forgotten their fundamental duties.

And of course we cannot turn away any needy individuals—why would only bears matter? We have rescued two horses and a donkey who gypsies long exploited as beasts of burden. (As I write, they enjoy the green grass of Libearty Sanctuary.) We also care-take five wolves and two foxes rescued from zoos and circuses. One of the foxes is missing half of her tail—the other half was burned off in a circus act that went awry. I hope that the humans who pay to see such nasty tricks have remorse when they see such unnecessary cruelty, and will never again visit the circus or zoo—except to protest. Zoos and circuses keep wild species only if they bring in money by drawing visitors. Their owners do not ponder what is best for nonhuman animals whom they buy and sell—they do not ask what is morally right.

Breaking the Cycle

We have been running Libearty Sanctuary Zărneşti for ten years. During this time I have seen too much horrific injustice. I have been amazed at the lack of compassion—the cold indifference that human beings commonly maintain with regard to other animals. I have come to see that sanctuaries are only part of the picture—we must teach the next generation not to abuse and exploit animals. We must break the cycle of indifference and cruelty. We must some-how instill a sense of compassion and respect for animals in children, so that they will never keep bears in a barren pit for human entertainment—or toler-ate such cruelty.

Toward this end, Libearty Sanctuary Zărneşti runs a program for school chil-dren. When I visit schools, I encourage children to listen to their hearts—to rediscover their innate compassion for bears and dogs and burrows—for all living beings. Our educational program includes videos that reveal the lives of sanctuary dogs and bears before and after rescue. I describe the sufferings of individual bears and talk to them about the importance of preserving habitat. I also speak out for farmed animals: I have created educational displays to explain how farmed animals are mistreated, and to teach children that they do not need to eat animal products to be healthy. I also explain why all dogs and cats must be spayed and neutered, and I invite children to visit Millions of Friends' shelter, in Braşov, to meet the 580 dogs who have found sanctuary with us, but who have little chance of ever finding a loving family. And of course I invite them to visit Libearty Bear Sanctuary.

Libearty receives groups of children, but not for their entertainment—we are not an exploitative nature park. We only receive visitors for educational purposes. Visitors must remain quiet and leave their cameras behind. They must respect the bear's place of peace. I explain how each bear was taken from their home for selfish human purposes, that some were stripped of their teeth and claws, that all were robbed of their freedom and independence. At Libearty, visitors learn the terrible truth of what happens to bears in the hands of unscrupulous human beings.

Libearty has grown considerably since we broke ground ten years ago, with seventeen employees, including personnel to maintain fences, video systems, and buildings, and of course specialists who feed and care for bears. Libearty's bears consume one ton of food every day, largely vegetables (including grasses and leaves from their forest home). Some people encourage us to open our sanctuary to the public, to allow visitors to come and see the bears for a fee, and to sell trinkets to bring in revenue. I do not want Libearty to become a commercial enterprise. Still, if we are to keep rescued bears, we must have funding. We hope that generous people will help Libearty Sanctuary remain an oasis of peace and safety. Love respects autonomy and does not exploit. Love does not possess. Bears at Libearty have been exploited by humanity, and now they deserve a chance to simply exist as bears—not for human entertainment, interest, or for monetary gain.

Libearty is about bears—it is for bears, not people. But on behalf of bears I educate human beings. I travel to many schools in the course of a year, but I cannot visit all the schools that would like to learn about our sanctuary—there are too many. I have asked the EU to support my educational program. If I am lucky—if the bears are lucky—I will have enough financial support to educate not only across my own country, but throughout the EU!

Changing Laws to Protect Europe's Bears

Romanian law forbids the capture or detention of protected wildlife. This law, which is critical to the protection of Romania's depleted bear populations, requires authorities to confiscate illegally held captive bears. But we need many more laws and much stronger enforcement—to protect bears throughout Europe.

If we are to protect bears and other endangered wildlife on the continent, the European Union must establish laws that prevent people from importing hunting "trophies." Because there are no longer any wild bears in France, Spain, Italy, Germany, or the UK, hunters from these nations, determined to kill a bear (usually in an attempt to prove their manhood), turn to Romania. In 2004, when King Juan Carlos of Spain came to Romania on an official visit, he killed five bears in just three days. Two of the bears were pregnant. If it were illegal to transport "trophies" from these kills across international borders, he would likely not bother with the hunt. A dead bear is of no use—it is "trophies" (such as claws and skin) that hunters are after.

Instead of sending royalty over to kill Romania's bears, other countries ought to help support Romanian efforts to protect Eastern Europe's tiny remaining bear populations. The European Parliament must also require Romania to respect the Convention of Berne (also known as the Convention on the Conservation of European Wildlifeand Natural Habitats, signed in 1979). This Convention was designed to conserve wild flora and fauna and their natural habitats, to promote co-operation between states, and to monitor and control endangered and vulnerable species such as *Ursus Arctos*, the brown bear. Many European countries signed the Convention of Berne, committing to work together to protect endangered wildlife and to protect necessary habitat, including all of the European Union, Burkina Faso, Morocco, Tunisia, and Senegal. But other nations have not yet signed the Convention of Berne, most notably Russia, as well as many less powerful nations, including Algeria, Belarus, Cape Verde, San Marino, and the Vatican. Despite the strength of the European Union, this Convention—like the bears I work with—has no "teeth": Current controls are inadequate to enforce the Convention of Berne. And of course bears (and other wildlife) have little or no protection in Russia, Georgia, and Ukraine—Eastern European nations that lie outside the European Union. At Libearty Sanctuary, we continue to work with governments in these nations, encouraging them to sign international treaties to protect endangered species, and to take a stand against the cruel treatment of wildlife in their nation—to establish sanctuaries and confiscate abused and exploited wildlife.

Tighter regulations are also required to protect nonhuman animals exploited by zoos and circuses. There are currently 400 bears in zoos around the world, all of whom are living in conditions that cannot simulate life in the wild, and many of whom live in unthinkably miserable conditions. Bears imprisoned by circuses and zoos almost always live in very small, barren enclosures— designed so that they cannot hide from the paying public. Bears in zoos and circuses are encouraged to reproduce, though their pens are not large enough for even one bear. Eventually, cute cubs, which initially bring in visitors, become adults who are no longer wanted. These bears often wind up in game parks— likely the horrific end to Viorel's life.

Finally, improved regulations must be designed to prevent countries who have wiped out their own bear populations from reintroducing bears. What right do we have to transport bears from their wild homes to distant forests just because human beings think this is a good idea? It is not a good idea. Officials may want bears, but citizens living near or in forests do not want bears in their neighborhoods. Farmers do not want to bears around their sheep and chickens, or around their homes and children. For instance, France imported Carpathian brown bears from Slovenia, but locals killed the bears in short order. Nations where people failed to protect bears must now live without bears. Instead of relocating bears to suit our whims, Europe must unite to protect remaining wildlife, including Romania's bears. If we do not, the outcome is as obvious as it is sad—there will be no bears left in Europe.

It Takes Only One

I am one of God's many servants—no more, no less. Only *through* God do I help others; only through *faith* can I continue to help nonhuman animals in this sea of suffering. For those who rest their case on science, please note that not only human beings have a central nervous system, but also all mammals, reptiles, fish, and birds. All beings who have a central nervous system can and do suffer. It is wrong to cause others to suffer. We do not need to permit bears in a pit, foxes under a circus tent, or dogs being bred. We do not need to eat other animals. We must choose what we will do—how much suffering we will cause. Our diet, entertainment, and decisions as to which organizations we will support decide which animals will suffer ... and which will be left in peace.

Libearty Sanctuary Zărneşti must always remain a holy place, a place of respite and peace—a place for God's will to be done on earth as it is in heaven. On their arrival, I promise bears that they will never have to perform, will never be hunted, and will be free to spend their days as they choose, in the safety of spacious pens that offer a natural environment. Lidia and Cristi come to the fence when they hear our voices, seeking treats and conversation, but bears at Libearty Sanctuary need not be gawked at by humans or beg for a piece of bread. They are free to hide in small forests. If they choose, they can remain out of sight and away from humanity all day every day—but they will always be fed.

When I sought sanctuary for Lidia, Cristi, Viorel, and Maya, I had no idea how many bears were suffering in captivity across Eastern Europe. Their stories are all unique, but they are united by human exploitation and pointless suffering, their tragic loss of family and forest home, and in long years of confinement and deprivation. We are all complicit in each bear's suffering. Hunters will only kill mother bears to snatch cubs if others are willing to buy cubs. Businesses will only buy cubs if customers are attracted by caged bears. Similarly, if no one pays to look at bears in zoos or circuses, we break the chain of cruelty and exploitation. And if we take the next step—if we contact businesses and tell them that we will not buy their products *because* they keep a bear—or any other captive animal—outside their store, we can make a difference. We can also let circuses know that we will not attend if animals are exploited under their tents. If we write letters of complaint to local papers, and protest outside businesses and circuses that exploit animals, we can help to end suffering. It takes only one human being—you—to bring change.

Sometimes children who visit the sanctuary ask where Maya is buried—they want to bring flowers to her grave. I remind them that neither the skin nor the bones matter. I point to the sky and remind them that Maya has joined the constellation of bears. Among stars that twinkle, Maya is happy to see that I kept my promises, that I created a little paradise on earth for needy bears. With Maya now joined by Ben and Ursula in the heavens, we have three stars to brighten even the darkest night.

CHAPTER 8

9,540,000 Square Miles, 800,000 American Black Bears, 3 Rescues

Charlotte Lorraine Cressey

In August of 2012, a scrawny, three-legged American black bear was lured to a suburban community by the lovely smells of human food. He had lost his leg to a trap, and finding food was not easy. Out of pity, construction workers began to share bits of lunch with the hungry fellow. Over time, he apparently grew more comfortable around humans and their dwellings and soon became "a fixture at an upscale housing community deep in the Blue Ridge Mountains of North Carolina, rummaging through trash cans and playfully ambling along the golf course" (Weiss). In storybook fashion, he went into a home and helped himself to two pies that were sitting on the counter. I can't blame him—if I were starving, I certainly would sniff out a pie!

In his quest for calories, the little bear caused minor property damage. The gated community's management team and local residents found a rescue center willing to take the bear. However, local wildlife officials were not receptive to the idea, and their assistance would be needed to transport the bear. Killing the bear was cheaper and quicker. The bear's rumbling tummy was finally silenced when "management" shot and killed him (Weiss). As is the case with most bears who become too comfortable with human beings, his story came to a sad end.

The hungry young bear in North Carolina exemplifies our attitude toward other species. We tend to think that it is okay to kill a bear (or raccoon or deer) just because we don't want her or him in *our* neighborhood. But given that human beings are comparatively recent immigrants to North America—especially Europeans—whose neighborhood is it?

American Black Bear

Perhaps as many as 800,000 black bears inhabit the North American Continent in 32 U.S. states, 11 Canadian provinces/territories, and 12 Mexican states (Macdonald 584, Pelton 547). These bears are nimble and strong—"no animal of equal size is as powerful" (Brown 87). Bears have incredible dexterity in their front paws, which allows them to open jars, doors, and pick pine nuts out of pine cones with their five toes. Also like humans, they are one of only a few

© KONINKLIJKE BRILL NV, LEIDEN, 2015 | DOI 10.1163/9789004293090_010

animals who stands on two hind legs. Unlike humans, a bear's nose "is its window into the world," and their sense of smell appears to be unparalleled (Brown 86).

Our relations with bears reveal much about our attitude toward other animals and the Earth. For instance, Teddy bears are named after Theodore Roosevelt, who was known as a "nature-lover," yet he was primarily a hunter. He killed many bears throughout his lifetime, and like many hunters, viewed nature as something to be conquered and controlled—including wild inhabitants. This sense of entitlement to "control" or "manage" wildlife is reflected in current hunting and trapping policies and laws. For example, though bears, like all sentient beings, desire to avoid hunger, and not be harmed, wildlife officials enforcing wildlife laws and policies—brought the death of the hungry little North Carolina bear—even though a sanctuary volunteered (and begged) to adopt the three-legged youth. Sadly, he is not the only victim of our lack of empathy, and our tendency to view other animals as expendable. In recent years numerous bears have been killed by wildlife officials because they are labeled "nuisance" or worse yet, "dangerous." If we are to have options beyond merely killing bears-in-need, our best bet is to establish and fund bear sanctuaries.

Bear Rescue, Rehabilitation, and Release

The need for wildlife rescue and rehabilitation increases as our human population expands: "An unprecedented number of [wild] animals are being brought to veterinarians suffering from human-inflicted injuries as the suburban population continues to boom and open space is gobbled up for development" (Hill). Human beings are the primary cause of black bear deaths, largely through hunting and trapping, but also due to human negligence and carelessness. Given our tendency to take over bear habitat, and to harm bears, rehabilitation facilities are essential if we are going to live peacefully and respectfully with other animals.

Until recently, we did not believe that bears could be rescued, rehabilitated, and released. We assumed that if bears were kept in captivity they would not assimilate back into the wild. Now we know that this is not the case, that young bears are prime candidates for rescue, rehabilitation, and release because once released, "they lead solitary lives and generally don't seek out people" ("Why").

In fact, the human fear of bears is unfounded. Human injury from bears is rare. A person is more likely to be killed by bees than a bear:

Only about three dozen human deaths from black bears have occurred across North American in this century, despite millions of encounters. To put this figure in perspective, for each person killed by a black bear in the United States and Canada ... 180 are killed by bees, 350 are killed by lightning, and 90,000 are murdered, according to data from the National Center for Health Statistics.

ROGERS 157

Even though human-bear conflicts are increasingly common, and even though we now know that bears can be rehabilitated and released, only three organizations rescue, rehabilitate, release and relocate bears across the vast expanse of North America: Appalachian Bear Rescue (ABR), Idaho Black Bear Rescue (IBBR), and Bear With Us (BWU). Most bears arriving at these sanctuaries are cubs who have been orphaned by hunters. They are often malnourished and sometimes injured. These rescue organizations provide veterinary care, allow cubs to grow and mature, then send them back to the wild—healthy and independent. Bears know what to do once released, provided they are mature and healthy.

Bear rescue and release organizations also offer educational programs that teach people how to avoid human-bear conflicts. Most importantly, bear sanctuaries remind people that those "who feed bears kill bears" ("Public"). Feeding bears, either intentionally or by leaving food in parked cars or garbage cans, creates human-bear conflicts. In fact, studies show that the lifespan of any bear fed by humans is likely to be cut in half ("Black"). This is largely because bears who are fed become habituated to humans, and are therefore not only more likely to be shot as "nuisance" bears but also become targets for hunters. Tennessee Wildlife Resources Agency (TWRA) explains:

Bears that habituate to human presence eventually become a threat to human safety. The end result is that such bears are often killed by intolerant and/or fearful landowners or have to be destroyed by the TWRA. The fact that "garbage kills bears" is irrefutable. The primary corrective action to this management dilemma is to simply restrict the access bears have to human foods. However, state and federal agencies have confronted significant challenges in bringing about even moderate changes to human behavior to achieve greater safety for humans and bears.

"BEARS"

Only when bear-proofing becomes a habit will bears be safe around human settlements. "We as humans can learn to coexist with less damage to our environment and the wildlife that inhabits the environment with us. Education, awareness and understanding bear behavior can reduce fear of the animal and increase appreciation and awe" ("Orphaned"). Public awareness is therefore crucial, and of course those who learn must be willing and able to modify their behaviors.

Bear rescues are important for bears and for science. North America's three bear rescues have collected a great deal of important information about American black bears—their growth and maturity, habits and tendencies, behaviors, and personalities. For example, they have learned that American black bears are rarely aggressive.

Perhaps most importantly, through much hard work, bear rescue organizations have changed, and continue to change, the way wildlife management and park rangers understand American black bears, and how they deal with orphaned cubs. Bear rescues emphasize human responsibility *and* compassion. Empathy guides those who work with and for bears. Caring about and helping individual animals is central to wildlife rehabilitation and relocation. Rescues model a kinder way of sharing the planet with wild animals.

When government wildlife officials are notified of an orphaned cub, their options are to: (a) do nothing (which will likely result in starvation or other form of death); (b) euthanize (shoot) the cub; (c) place the cub in a permanent facility such as a zoo (there are generally too many American black bear orphans, so zoos have no interest); or (d) transfer the cub to a rescue and release facility ("News"). Obviously, rescue and release is the best option, and increasingly, one supported by the public: "Although wildlife agencies deal with populations, management programs today need to recognize that the public cares about individuals" ("Why"). Who among us would not prefer to be helped in such a time of need, then released to a life of autonomy and freedom? Bears like space—miles of space—and though they can survive in captivity, it seems obvious that they would prefer to roam, to graze and breed, climb trees and raise young—to be free to make their own choices and live their own lives.

American black bear sanctuaries work with local government and non-profit wildlife organizations, and must be authorized by the government to rehabilitate bears. Rescue centers dream of a day when government wildlife agencies take responsibility for this important work: "As wildlife agencies become comfortable with the success of rehab and release, it is our hope they will consider starting their own rehab program. Our role then becomes one of consultation with both the wildlife agencies and the wildlife rehabilitators" ("IBBR"). Until such a day, rescue organizations—ABR, BWU, and IBBR—help bears in their respective areas, reaching across hundreds of miles to work in nearby states. For example, ABR assists local wildlife groups such as Tennessee Wildlife Resources Agency (TWRA) and Great Smoky Mountain National Park (GSMNP) when these organizations are contacted by the public about orphaned and/or injured cubs, or human-bear conflicts.

Until the day when our government takes responsibility for assisting wildlife-in-need, rescues and rehabilitation will be privately funded. American black bear rescue organizations must maintain facilities (bear-sized buildings and bear-proof pens), foot the bill for veterinary care, pay for necessary labor, maintain transport vehicles, and purchase vast quantities of food to nourish these large mammals. Across a rehab period of 9 to 15 months, "[c]osts associated with the rehabilitation of orphaned bear cubs are currently projected at $5600.00 for each cub" ("Bears First").

Appalachian Bear Rescue (ABR)

In 1989 there was a food shortage for bears in Tennessee, and hungry bears entered human communities, following their noses in search of food. People believed that these bears were dangerous, so they shot many of them, leaving a host of orphaned cubs. A group of locals empathized with these little furry orphans and organized to see what might be done for them. In 1991 this organization became Appalachian Bear Rescue (ABR) ("History").

Today, ABR is a large American black bear rescue facility, complete with a variety of enclosures and pens to suit the unique needs of each arrival. Pen placement depends on the level of care needed. Very young bears needing to be regularly bottle fed are kept in a small carrier. As they mature, these bears are placed in a large enclosure called "The Wild Side," which simulates life outside the sanctuary.

A unique feature of ABR, the Wild Side is rich with "trees, grasses, ponds, and foliage," where bears can "play and explore" ("Story"). "When cubs enter the Wild Side, their exposure to humans ceases" ("Story"). Food is thrown over a fence that works like a wall, preventing bears from seeing human beings so that the bears will not associate food with humans. Bears are largely solitary, but have complex social skills and methods of communication. Bears in "The Wild Side" may associate with other bears, or they may spend their time alone, depending on their unique personalities and momentary preferences. ABR staff has noticed that certain bears keep a watchful eye on sick bears. In The Wild Side, bears learn to forage and fend for themselves, living among other bears while still under the protective care of sanctuary volunteers and staff.

Ham and Sissy were two orphans who were rescued and rehabilitated at ABR. A hunter shot their mother. Concerned and responsible locals found the mother's body, and reported it to Tennessee Wildlife Resources Agency. A TWRA official came to check the body, heard crying, and found two tiny cubs in a nearby den. Under five pounds each, Ham and Sissy were much too young to fend for themselves, and would soon have starved, but TWRA contacted ABR.

Soon after arrival Ham and Sissy expressed their unique personalities. Ham loved to "ham it up." Sissy was shy, and didn't really come into her own until she entered "The Wild Side," where she especially loved to frolic in the water. Ham and Sissy thrived at ABR, growing into healthy, strong bears. They were released back into their home territory after nine months of care at ABR. Ham and Sissy are two of more than 200 bears who have been rescued, rehabilitated, and released by ABR.

Bear with us (BWU)

Bear With Us, founded by Mike McIntosh in Ontario, Canada, has rescued, rehabilitated, and released a whopping 311 orphaned and injured black bears ("About"). An avid nature photographer, McIntosh became acquainted with wildlife through photography. After visiting a local sanctuary, he established BWU to rescue and rehabilitate injured and orphaned cubs, and to educate people as to how we can avoid human-bear conflicts.

Bear With Us is the only American black bear rescue facility that serves as "a permanent home to a select few bears who cannot be returned to the wild" ("About"). The goal is always to help bears return to the wild, but some bears— most notably, bears who have been "owned" by people—cannot be released into the wild. Molly was one such bear. She had been exploited as a performing bear, and was forced to be a "dancing bear." Animal handlers working for circuses, or for TV and movie producers, use pain—whips, painful collars, and electric prods—as well as hunger and thirst, to establish dominance, and to force animals to engage in unnatural behaviors. For example, bear's front paws are placed on a very hot surface to "teach" them stand on their hind legs. A combination of abusive training techniques and confinement in small spaces often creates psychological problems for bears (as well as other captive animals). Molly exhibited many behaviors that stemmed from years of psychological suffering, and it took many years in a spacious (40,000 square foot), quiet pen at BWU for these psychological wounds to heal. She is now 27 years old, and has been at BWU for 19 years ("Bear Residents"). Her story serves as a reminder to all of us never to attend or—support in any way—any form of entertainment that exploits animals.

Idaho Black Bear Rescue (IBBR)

Founded by Sally Maughan, Idaho Black Bear Rescue has rehabilitated more than 200 cubs. IBBR is located in a region with comparatively large black bear populations, and accepts cubs from seven nearby states: California, Idaho, Nevada, Oregon, Utah, Washington, and Wyoming ("IBBR").

So it was that Kapalua, an orphaned cub, came to IBBR in May 2011 from Oregon. She was only six pounds (likely about 8 weeks old) when she arrived. A cub that young needs a lot of attention and tender, loving care, so Kapalua was bottle fed every 4 hours for the first few weeks. Around the same time, her IBBR "roommate" arrived from Utah, Hewech. The two orphans grew up together, and became best friends. One of their favorite games was hide and seek. Kapalua loved to hide inside a log until Hewech would notice that she was missing and go looking for her. Kapalua would wait patiently until Hewech had given up, then dart out and surprise her friend ("Hewech").

Eating, sleeping, and playing the two cubs grew healthy and strong, and it was soon time to release Kapalua and Hewech. Bears are always released with the assistance of local wildlife agencies in the state from which they were rescued. So it was that, after a year together at IBBR, Kapalua and Hewech were transported to their respective states, and released. Kapalua stepped tentatively out of her transport pen, scanned the area, headed toward the lush trees, then paused to munch on wild onions. Hewech also scanned the area and headed for the nearby trees, but before disappearing into the wilderness, she paused to play in a small pool of fresh water ("Hewech").

Conclusion

As humans overpopulate, extending across bear habitat, American black bear rescue, rehabilitation, release, and relocation are yet more essential. But government wildlife agencies in Canada and the U.S. do not rescue or rehabilitate wildlife, they merely "manage" populations. Consequently, publicly funded wildlife rescue and rehabilitation centers are essential not only for American black bears, but for all wildlife.

American black bears have long called this huge continent their home— they were here many centuries before human beings arrived. North America, a continent containing 9,540,000 mi^2 of land (29,709,000 km^2) is home to roughly 500,000 American black bears, and just three American black bear rescue facilities ("Map"). We need many more American black bear rescue facilities across North America, and we need to fund these facilities as a nation (rather than through private donations).

FIGURE 8.1 *American Black Bear*

Thanks to North America's three American black bear rescue and rehabilitation facilities, Molly, Ham, Sissy, Kapalua, and Hewech were given a
chance at life. These three facilities have made life possible for more than
700 American black bears, who would otherwise have been shot or left to
starve. If there had been a rescue facility serving the needs of American
black bears in the Blue Ridge Mountains of North Carolina, the hungry,
three-legged, little orphaned black bear, who came looking for food in
human communities, might have had a chance at life. As America matures,
citizens are coming to see the importance of every living being, and there
are few who would applaud the killing of a small, hungry bear, maimed by a
human trap. If we are to adequately address the problems that human beings
are causing for American black bears, we need to establish at least one rescue facility in every North American state and province that has a black bear
population.

References

"About Us." *Bear With Us*. Accessed March 30, 2013. <http://bearwithus.org/about-us>.
"Bears." *Tennessee Wildlife Resources Agency*. Accessed March 30, 2013.<http://www.
tn.gov/twra/bearmain.html>.
"Bears First." *Idaho Black Bear Rescue*. April, 2012. Accessed March 30, 2013. <http://
www.bearrehab.org/BFApr12.pdf>.

"Bear Residents." *Bear With Us.* Accessed March 30, 2013. <http://bearwithus.org/ bear-residents>.

"Black Bears." *National Park Service: Great Smoky Mountains.* Accessed March 30, 2013. <http://www.nps.gov/grsm/naturescience/black-bears.htm>.

Brown, Gary. *The Bear Almanac.* Guilford: The Lyons Press, 2009.

"Hewech and Kapalua Go Home." *Idaho Black Bear Rescue.* Bear Journal, 2011. Accessed May 14, 2013. <http://www.bearrehab.org/journal2011.shtml>.

Hill, James. "Some Wildlife Injuries Not Nature's Way." *Chicago Tribune.* Accessed March 30, 2013 <http://articles.chicagotribune.com/1992-08-14/news/9203130276_1_ animals-humans-and-wildlife-pellet-gun>.

"The History of Appalachian Bear Rescue in Townsend, Tennessee 37882." *Appalachian Bear Rescue.* Accessed March 16, 2013.<http://www.appalachianbearrescue.org/ history_abr.htm>.

"IBBR History." *Idaho Black Bear Rescue.* Accessed March 30, 2013. <http://www .bearrehab.org/history.shtml>.

"Map of North America." *Maps of World.* Accessed May 31, 2013.<http://www.mapsofworld .com/north-america/>.

Macdonald, David W., ed. *The Encyclopedia of Mammals.* Oxford U. Press, 2009. 574–588.

"News from Sally." *Idaho Black Bear Rescue.* Accessed March 30, 2013. <http://www. bearrehab.org/forthebears.shtml>.

"Orphaned & Injured." *Bear With Us.* Accessed March 30, 2013. <http://bearwithus.org/ orphaned-injured>.

Pelton, Michael R. "Black Bear: *Ursus americanus.*" *Wild Mammals of North America: Biology, Management, and Conservation,* 2nd edition. Ed. George A Feldhamer, Bruce C. Thompson, and Joseph A. Chapman. Baltimore: Johns Hopkins U.P., 2003. 547–555.

"Public Service." *Appalachian Bear Rescue.* Accessed March 30, 2013. <http://www. appalachianbearrescue.org/press_releases/public_service.htm>.

Rogers, L.L. "American Black Bear: *Ursus americanus.*" *The Smithsonian Book of North American Mammals.* Ed. Don E. Wilson and Sue Ruff. Washington: Smithsonian Institute Press, 1999. 157–160.

"The Story of Ham and Sissy." *Appalachian Bear Rescue.* Accessed March 30, 2013. <http://www.appalachianbearrescue.org/ham&sissy.htm>.

Weiss, Mitch. "Bear Killed In Mountain Air, North Carolina Angers Activists." *Huffington Post.* Accessed March 30, 2013. <http://www.huffingtonpost.com/2012/11/23/bear-killed- mountain-air-north-carolina_n_2176381.html>.

"Why Save Cubs." *Idaho Black Bear Rescue.* Accessed March 30, 2013. <http://www.bear- rehab.org/why.shtml>.

CHAPTER 9

Failing Giant Pandas: Captive Breeding and Conservation

Sarah M. Bexell

I was twenty-nine when I arrived in Chengdu (August 1, 1999), the capitol of Sichuan Province. I was warmly greeted by a young woman named Luo Lan, my translator and data-collection assistant. We were both working for long-term giant panda behavior studies sponsored by Zoo Atlanta, USA, headed by Dr. Rebecca Snyder. For the next five months Luo Lan and I acquainted ourselves with each other and with each individual panda, gleaning his or her personality and quirks, and personal story. While our love and understanding of these beautiful bears grew, so did our friendship and mutual respect. At the time, we had no idea that our working relationship would blossom into a long-term, close friendship sealed by a shared commitment to foster conservation and animal welfare in China.

Before Luo Lan came to assist Zoo Atlanta researchers, she had been working as an office assistant at the Panda Base. She had a degree in mechanical engineering—a field she had absolutely no interest in, which had been her ticket to a college education. Based on her English skills, she was asked to assist in behavioral research, an appointment that would bring her to the forefront of a new field of work in China—Conservation Education.

As Zoo Atlanta and the Panda Base contemplated launching conservation education departments in China, Luo Lan offered an insight that became central to our work. One day she said to me,

> Sarah, before I had the chance to watch giant pandas intensively, I had no idea that animals had feelings and personalities—that they were good mothers, that there was someone inside those bodies. In China we never really think like that. Now I watch pandas and try to understand what they are thinking, what they want, and how they are feeling. This is likely to seem very strange to other Chinese.

At that moment, walking together along a bamboo-lined path, we realized simultaneously that people must *see* animals as worthy of respect, as having interests of their own, and as worthy of care and protection, if conservation education was to be effective. Luo Lan's words ultimately formed the foundation of almost all of our work in conservation education.

© KONINKLIJKE BRILL NV, LEIDEN, 2015 | DOI 10.1163/9789004293090_011

Getting to Know Pandas

While I love all animals, including all giant pandas, my deepest attachment is with six individuals I came to know in those first five months of collecting data: Cheng Cheng and her son Shi Shi, Yang Yang (male) and Lun Lun (female) who now reside at Zoo Atlanta, and their twin playmates, Da Shuang (female) and Xiao Shuang (male). Each of these pandas was a critical part of Dr. Snyder's research in socio-behavioral development and mother-infant interactions—the latter four were all just two years old. These were my subjects and every day I collected data while Luo Lan ran the video camera.

Panda's like to play. Watching a mother with a cub, it is easy to see that cubs, just like other mammals, learn through play. Giant pandas usually appear pretty laid back, acting as if all is right with the world. Being solitary creatures from a remote and rare habitat, a quiet nap seems to be one of their most treasured pleasures, though this particular panda pleasure is becoming increasingly harder to achieve in our overcrowded world.

Pandas also love to eat bamboo. Foraging takes up an inordinate amount of time and energy each day for a panda, and they appear to eat with relish. They select bamboo stalks with care and precision, sniffing each stalk thoughtfully before taking a bite. If the stalk does not smell just right they toss it aside and choose another, and another, until they find just the right stalk. Then they begin the laborious process of eating the leaves (late summer and fall) or the culm (stem, in the spring and early summer). If shoots are available, they consume each shoot after removing the tough surrounding sheath. While they eat—whether leaves, pithy insides of the culm, or a shoot—they lie on their backs, looking as if they were in a wonderfully comfortable easy-chair. They often close their eyes when they eat, like a woman enjoying chocolate, as if those tough green grasses were ecstasy itself.

Cheng Cheng and Shi Shi

As noted, Cheng Cheng and Shi Shi are very dear to me. When I arrived in Chengdu, Shi Shi was about nine months old, living happily and securely with his mom, Cheng Cheng. In China's giant panda breeding facilities, cubs are typically taken from their mothers at about four to five months of age (a controversial practice that I don't agree with). This is done so that the mother will go into estrus the following spring. In many cases this means that she will become pregnant every year, boosting the captive population—the goal of those who control captive pandas. But this boost in population is gained at the expense of normal and natural family patterns, cycles, and behavioral development. In the wild, giant panda cubs separate from their mothers between eighteen months and two years of age, and an unnatural, early separation harms the behavioral development of cubs, threatening the well-being of both mothers and cubs, who form strong bonds. Luckily, as knowledge increases this practice is waning slowly, and some cubs are being kept with their mothers longer, or one experienced mother rears several cubs in small groups. Cubs need to be allowed to develop normal, species-specific behaviors if we are to conserve giant pandas.

Shi Shi was a lucky little cub for his time. As part of a research plan, he was allowed to stay with his mother until he was about one year old. My happiest memories of giant pandas stem from watching him and his mother in their huge outdoor yard amid a plethora of climbing structures, thick bamboo, tall trees, a flowing water pool, and a very deep, vegetated moat that provided endless fascination for Shi Shi. While officially collecting methodical data, I was unofficially observing two giant pandas in action, for the first time. I could see and feel their shared love and devotion. I could see and feel their joy at play, and Shi Shi's sense of security in snuggling with Cheng Cheng after nursing. I watched him study his mother as she ate delicious bamboo, and I watched him try bamboo for the first time, learning how to manipulate the difficult food source he would depend on for the duration of his life. I also watched as he learned how to climb a tree, and I think I was as proud as Cheng Cheng! I watched his confidence grow: He would leave Cheng Cheng's sight to explore, run through the vegetation, and roll down into the moat to explore. When Cheng Cheng felt he'd been away long enough, she would bleat to call her boy back. On hearing his mother, he would stop what he was doing and return joyfully. Each time I delighted in their reunion.

Sadly, all this joy in the mother-child relationship was nearing an end—and it was my duty to document the effects of separation, which proved to be most painful. Cheng Cheng was moved to another area of the Panda Base, and without her son, was devastated. She circled the enclosure, bleating for Shi Shi, only resting when she was exhausted. She was still lactating, and it was clear that this was causing her great discomfort; I am sure her physical pain added to her sadness, and stood as a constant reminder that Shi Shi was gone. She forced her nipples against the concrete to express some of the milk, leaving streaked pools behind her as she quickly kept moving in search of her precious son.

Shi Shi fared no better. At separation, she changed from a happy, secure individual to a fearful and despondent cub. He called for Cheng Cheng, but she could not come to him. He did not enter his beautiful yard, but remained curled up in his otherwise empty indoor enclosure, honking (a sad, distressed vocalization). He went into a fearful fit on hearing a goose honk—which of course was a natural noise, and one he had heard commonly at the Panda Base. In his terror at such common sounds as a goose, he scooted up the bars of the enclosure until his head was smashed into the ceiling, leaving a stream of diarrhea in his wake. Shi Shi was so unhappy that he would not eat. The keepers discovered that if they played with him for a little while, he cheered up enough to eat at least a little bit. I was asked to help with this duty, and while it was a joy to play with Shi Shi, it was heartbreaking—and I was angry that human beings had taken control of his life, and would not allow him to return to his mother during a time when he clearly needed and wanted her very much. Who would force panda cubs in such a state of terror, or leave a bereaved mother in physical and emotional agony, when they could easily be reunited for a little bit longer?

Though fearful that I would be seen as a meddler, and perhaps even be disciplined for violating cultural boundaries, I took my concerns to the curators. In Chinese culture, shedding tears is considered weak and shameful, but my empathy with Cheng Cheng and Shi Shi was unbearable, and I could not contain my grief. Maybe no one else could see that these bears were suffering, *but I could*. Though I knew they would not put Shi Shi back with his mother, I had to do something to ease their suffering. I asked that Shi Shi at least be placed with another young panda. The Panda Base had four cubs (Yang Yang, Lun Lun, Da Shuang, and Xiao Shuang) who were just one year older than Shi Shi. Unfortunately, they were close to double his size, and the curators were fearful that the older pandas would hurt Shi Shi. While I hadn't found young pandas to be particularly aggressive, I had only spent a little over eight weeks at the Panda Base, so I respected their fears.

Those in charge agreed that Shi Shi was not doing well, and that it would be possible to place him in a pen next to one of the more congenial young pandas, Xiao Shuang, also a male. They were very curious about each other, and only exhibited affiliative behaviors—sniffing and batting playfully at each other. It was evident that they were eager to rough and tumble. After a couple days of introductions, everyone agreed that the union looked safe, and we let Shi Shi and Xiao Shuang into the large yard that Xiao Shuang shared with his twin sister, Da Shuang (*shuang* means twin in Chinese; *xiao* means "small" and *da* means "large"—yes, his sister was bigger). Xiao Shuang was very excited to have someone to play with. His sister, being quite the princess—"too good" for play—was not willing to rough and tumble. As for Shi Shi, he seemed to let much of his fear and sadness go once he had a friend and playmate. Those of us watching smiled with satisfaction to see the two cubs play!

As a graduate student I observed many animals, but I had never so closely witnessed the security that a mother provides for her young as I did with Cheng Cheng and Shi Shi. I had learned about this bond, of course, and I knew how important the mother-infant bond is for animals—including human animals. But to see and feel the effects of premature, sudden loss of the mother-child bond between Cheng Cheng and Shi Shi was devastating, and reminded me of billions of animals forced into this situation by human beings—calves wrenched from their mothers for the production of dairy products, puppies torn from their mothers by breeders, and rabbits taken from their mothers by zookeepers and researchers either to feed other animals or for experimentation. Ultimately, the trauma of that experience—for Shi Shi, Cheng Cheng, and myself—further cemented my commitment to help giant pandas.

Conservation Education: Too Many Problems, Too Little Time

We are in the midst of Earth's sixth mass extinction, this one caused by just one species—*Homo sapiens*. Collectively, contemporary humans engage in the most widespread and severe animal exploitation and abuse in a long history of human atrocities. In the U.S., exploiters are quite skilled at hiding these crimes from the public eye, but in China human cruelty is painfully evident.

Most scholars believe that by the age of seven our ethics are well developed and defined. Consequently, we focus most of our efforts in conservation education on young children. Luo Lan's insight regarding how we view animals had started me thinking about the process through which people in my home country develop an understanding of animals as individuals. This led me to start a project where I interviewed preschoolers both in China and the U.S. in order to better understand how young children (our interviews being with four-year olds) in two very different countries think and feel about animals. I was amazed and pleased to discover that young children in both cultures seem to recognize animals as amazing in their own right, with feelings of their own, and that human beings ought to take responsibility to protect nonhuman animals. Children also expressed a strong desire to interact with other animals. These findings were so positive that I began to wonder, what happens to this compassionate tendency as we age? As we grow and are assimilated into our larger community, society robs us of this innate love for animals. How can we, as educators, empower youth to hold onto this initial empathy and compassion?

Most of our Conservation Education programs at the Panda Base include giant pandas, but we ask participants to think about all of their behaviors and how their daily choices are likely to impact nonhuman animals in general, and other humans. Our education programs emphasize the importance of ecosystems and biodiversity, including the importance of both for human survival: We greatly limit the chances of our own survival when we cannot control our numbers or our consumption. Though all of these topics are essential, I often ponder whether or not we have diluted our education efforts for giant pandas too much by including biodiversity and humane education in our core agenda. Hopefully, with pandas nearby, they are not forgotten in the midst of all of the new information that we offer.

While many of our conservation programs aim to instill compassion toward all living beings (including other humans), several programs focus specifically on certain species and/or on particular aspects of wildlife conservation, and/or on animal welfare issues. For example, we have run programs addressing the Asian turtle crisis and the fur trade, and we are currently developing a comprehensive wildlife trade exhibit and program. Almost all of our programs teach children, parents, and educators about the "exotic" pet trade and about humane care for domestic animals. We do this because we recognize that humane treatment of nonhuman animals in households and communities where children grow up is critical to how young people come to view and treat nonhuman animals as adults.

Our department strives to protect other bear species as well. We have partnered with the Chengdu Bear Rescue Center (run by Jill Robinson and her amazing team at Animals Asia) to teach youth about Asiatic black bears and the bear bile trade. The Panda Base also houses, breeds and cares for endangered red pandas, so our panda programs include information about and conservation behaviors for both giant and red pandas. These diverse programs are important because they help people connect personal choices, such as neglecting the needs of a pet or purchasing tiger body parts, with harms such as physical suffering and extinction.

With regard to giant and red pandas, threats are both domestic and international, and therefore require international cooperation. While it is true that red pandas continue to be taken from their wild homes for the pet trade or zoos, or killed for their fur or meat, the most pressing threats facing these two species are habitat fragmentation, degradation, and destruction. As the human population continues to surge out of control, our consumption choices threaten or overtly preclude the survival of just about every other species. Certain marginalized species, such as giant and red pandas, are losing ground at a staggering rate. While the Chinese government has made valiant efforts to support captive breeding (as a hedge against extinction), to establish nature reserves (to protect remaining wild individuals), and to curb human population growth,

China is running out of time to protect many endangered species and their essential habitat from the crush of humanity.

Giant pandas survive solely along the eastern edge of the Tibetan Plateau in six mountain ranges (Qinling, Min, Qionglai, Daxiangling, Xiaoxiangling, and Liang) in Sichuan, Shaanxi and Gansu provinces. Remaining habitat is highly fragmented due to human habitation and enterprises such as mining, forestry, infrastructure development, and agriculture. Consequently, giant pandas cling to a small vestige of their former range. As human beings push ever higher up mountain slopes—struggling locals seeking economic advantage while capitalistic businessmen greedily grab at profits from natural resources—bear habitat continues to disappear.

In China there are just over sixty nature reserves for giant pandas (red panda habitat overlaps with that of giant pandas), but almost every aspect of these nature reserves is up for grabs, upsetting ecological systems and damaging critical habitat. Locals continue to live a subsistence lifestyle, largely concerned with feeding themselves and their families, and occasionally squirrelling away a stash of cash as a financial cushion, or to buy a luxury item such as a mobile phone. This is not a phenomenon unique to China or giant pandas. As human populations grow, the unending human thirst for material wealth devastates the few remaining natural areas. As a result, both marginalized species and marginalized humans suffer.

Because giant pandas are one of the most critically endangered species on the planet, our education department has partnered with the giant panda nature reserve system since 2006, creating curriculum and training workshops for nature reserve staff and local teachers. We also partner with international and domestic NGOs to provide local communities living in panda habitat with sustainable livelihoods. However, the government and international community must make larger, deeper changes if China's endangered species are to survive. It is in this vein that our team, now employing 14 people, conducts conservation education programs and outreach.

Saving Giant Pandas

When people ask me what they can do to help protect pandas, I have no simple answer. Most importantly, we need to curtail our own breeding. No draconian measures are needed—simply empower women to make their own reproductive choices, and give them the means to make those choices. This has been proven to reduce human births significantly. Because the problem of human population underlies pretty much every other problem—especially the disappearance of both wild lands and nonhuman species—I no longer worry about offending people if I bring up family planning. If we don't speak the truth we become part of the problem, and we enable unsustainable and cruel human behaviors.

Our consumption—each one of us—adds exponentially to the problems that confront bears (and many other animals). We must stop consuming as if the planet has no limit. We must teach children and adults alike to ponder every purchase beforehand, and to carefully consider whether an item is necessary—and leave it on the shelf if it is not. We must constantly be reminded that everything we use takes something from the planet, and from others— both human and non-human. When we do make a purchase, we must consider the source of the materials and products that we buy, and we must think about who or what might have been harmed in the process of creating a given product or service. Every purchase ought to be a vote for a more humane world, and represent a sustainable lifestyle. No matter what country we live in, we are connected. What we do in the U.S. or England or Australia or New Zealand or Thailand or South Africa or Brazil affects giant pandas— and every other species, including our own. We must reduce both our consumption and our childbirth, and we must rethink global economic models and expectations.

Change Starts with You and Me

I visited a bear farm in China, where I saw the torture wrought on bears for the purposes of Traditional Chinese Medicine. When I see what we do to other animals, I do not wish to be associated with my own species. I have also visited Animals Asia's Bear Rescue Center in Chengdu, which provides a much-needed vision of hope for humanity. (If you want to help these suffering bears—if you want to undo just a little of the harm that we humans bring to bears and other creatures—I highly recommend supporting the efforts of Animals Asia (http:// www.animalsasia.org/).)

As a species, we humans are at a tipping point. We seem hell bent on destruction—even self-destruction. We have already grossly overstepped our boundaries. If we do not change, do we deserve to exist? It is time for us to collectively change, or perish because of our own cruelty and short-sighted vision. At the time of this writing, it is nearly impossible for me to have hope for the future of giant pandas. In truth, if we do not curb our numbers and our exploitative ways, I cannot see a future for any species—including humans.

FIGURE 9.1 *Panda Bear*

Greed, combined with ignorance of the interconnected nature of all things, is a deadly concoction. In the absence of an iron will for change, a deep compassion for others—including other animals—and a simple understanding of interdependency, we will not last much longer. Our big, misguided brains have gotten us into this mess, and now we must try to find empathy and a measure of generosity if we are to turn the tide toward harmony and respect for this beautiful, amazing Earth, and the many fascinating creatures that depend on this planet—including bears and turtles and butterflies and worms and cows and cats.

When I look into the eyes of a child, I see that he or she hopes for kindness, and some sign that we are on his or her side. I also see this when I look into the eyes of other animals. Giant pandas have been waiting for some sign of compassion for decades—for some sign that we are on their side—and that we care about their lives. I desperately hope that we do not continue to fail the world's few remaining giant pandas.

CHAPTER 10

Bear Baiting in Pakistan

Dr Fakhar -i- Abbas

Star

Last year, outside a remote village in Sindh province in Pakistan, a magnificent Asiatic black bear (Himalayan subspecies) was tied to a tree by a rope that ran through his brown-tinted muzzle. He had numerous wounds despite his coat of thick, black hair. Some wounds were older and had not healed well; others were more recent, and had become infected. He was malnourished, underweight and so weak that he couldn't stand on his hind legs.

I had seen this bear, whom we called Star, repeatedly pitted against dogs in bloody battles. I had noticed that he was too weak to put up much of a defense. He simply tried to protect his sensitive muzzle and vulnerable ears from the well-fed dogs' fangs. It was clear that Star had nearly reached end of the line.

Star, like most bears exploited for bear baiting, was poached from the wild—his mother was shot so that he could be captured. Local wildlife traders then "prepared" the young Star for a lifetime of misery in the bear baiting industry by removing his perfect little teeth—without any sedation—and blunting his growing claws. He was then sold to a nomad, called "a living bear owner," who traveled Pakistan's rural areas, offering Star for bear baiting events. Each month Star was forced into as many as 20 fights against dogs; in every event he was forced to fight more than once.

Star is typical of bears who are exploited for bear baiting in Pakistan. Though we have rescued many, there are still more than 60 bears like Star, cruelly exploited for bear baiting in Pakistan.

Dogs, Bears, Brits, and Warlords

Pakistan has three subspecies of Asiatic black bears, including two closely related subspecies—Baluchistan (*Ursus thibetanus gedrosianus*) and Himalayan/Tibetan (*Ursus thibetanus thibetanus*)—as well as one brown bear (Himalayan subspecies, *Ursus arctos isabellinus*). Each subspecies is endangered, with roughly 50 Baluchistan, 800 Himalayan black, and 120 Himalayan brown bears remaining in small isolated populations throughout their range.

"Bearbaiting," which began sometime in the 15th century in England, pits two dogs against one bear. The British constructed special buildings in London's Whitehall region to hold these fights, a gruesome form of entertainment for the elite. Bear baiting was introduced to the Indian subcontinent in the 18th century, in the hope of controlling Punjabi warlords, especially those in the area that has become Pakistan, who were fiercely resisting British rule. The British army officer in charge of gaining control and establishing order in the area had discovered that the warlords were fond of dog fights. In the hope of winning over these powerful rulers, he invited them to come in peace for a different type of fighting—bear baiting. This unique offer surprised and pleased the warlords, and successfully aroused their interest, and ultimately turned them into joint partners in the "game" of bear baiting. The British gained the loyalty of Punjabi warlords, opening the doors to British rule in the Punjab and Sindh, while throwing bears under the bus.

British rulers also introduced bull terriers to the Indian subcontinent, and they crossbred bull terriers with local breeds to develop the Gull Terr, often called the Pakistani bull terrier, a medium sized dog with short, smooth fur that resembles the Bull Dong (English Bulldog). Active, alert, and swift, the Gull Terr, though rare, is the preferred breed for bear baiting competitions. These dogs cannot be kept as pets because they are bred and trained to be savage, and are kept in separate quarters, maintained by rich landlords.

In Pakistan, bear baiting is a display of social status in which wealthy landlords display their wealth and virile power, while gypsies serve as their doormats. Pakistan's feudal elites arranged bear-dog fights as a mark of honour and as a form of entertainment at parties, feasts, and weddings. Hosting these violent but popular fights came to mark the strength and economic prosperity of a landlord.

Somewhere in the Balkan, at some point in our unrecorded history, gypsies started taming bears for entertainment and/or protection. The practice of keeping bears spread from the Balkan to neighboring regions and beyond. While places such as Bulgaria and Turkey have recently taken stringent measures to rescue such exploited bears, and close down such practices, other nations, such as Southeast Asia, have not. In these countries, bears can be purchased from a middleman or hunter, then forced to "dance" as a way of begging—people throw money, even though the beggars have done nothing to deserve pay, and are cruelly exploiting bears. Landlords maintain dogs, but not bears—though they sometimes own bears. For more than a century, wealthy landlords in Pakistan have purchased bears from gypsies, letting gypsies maintain and keep the bears, whom they exploit for small change. Gypsies, by their habit, move from place to place, but landlords and middlemen have sufficient influence to prevent them from absconding with their bears. Traditionally, as today, gypsies bring bears to matches. For gypsies, who bring bears to the fighting ring, bear baiting is a source of income.

For landlords, who own, breed, and train dogs, bear baiting is a way of showing their power and masculinity. Spectators, who live in the landlord's domain, are often in awe and terror of the landlord's power and dominance. Keeping this in mind, landlords raise their fighting dogs with great care, and at great expense. Even the food they feed these dogs is a symbol of their status, and they frequently boast that their dogs are fed on pure butter, kept in air conditioned rooms, and looked after by two caretakers. A pair of dogs is likely to fight for only three minutes, once in a season (whereas the unfortunate bear has to face several pairs of dogs a day, fight several times each season). Winning dogs receive excellent medical care, while bears receive very little veterinary care—if any—because gypsies are poor. For landlords, bear baiting is all about *their* power and masculinity, about padding *their* ego and reasserting control in their social arena. Consequently, when dogs lose a fight, the landlord kills them because his manhood has been publicly disgraced. (Like "fighting dogs" around the world, they are also nothing more than pawns and victims.) As a result, landlords take all possible precautionary measures to ensure that their dogs will prevail. All the rules of bear baiting are framed to favour the dogs, and bears are purposefully incapacitated: Their teeth and claws are blunted or removed, they are tethered during the fight, and one bear must face two dogs. If the bear gets the upper hand, attendants intervene with sticks and spears, to free the dog.

In Pakistan, bear baiting events are carried out in the countryside in front of crowds of up to 1,000 cheering people who have placed bets on the dogs or the bear. Only men are allowed to attend these fights, and the atmosphere is intense. Fights are usually staged in broad daylight in a dirt arena. One bear is tied to the ground in the middle of the arena, with a rope that prevents the unhappy bear from running away. The landlord's helpers position two dogs in a circle around the bear, and when given a signal from the jury, they turn the dogs loose on the bear. The dogs are well trained for these fights, and head straight for the bear's sensitive, vulnerable parts—the muzzle and the ears. Working together, they attack the bear's head, lunging at the bear from both sides. The bear, bereft of claws and teeth, tries to crush the dogs with his or her weight. After a time the jury stops the fight, and the dogs are pulled off the bear, though their teeth are still deep in the bear's tattered muscles.

Bear Baiting and Bear Populations

Bear cubs are captured young for bear baiting—before 3–4 months of age, in the hope that they can be sold to trainers before they are five months old, to "tame" and train them while they are still young. Those who capture bears for bear baiting kill the mother to take her cub. This means that for every bear sold into a gypsy camp, an adult female bear is eliminated from the wild population. Over time, this practice has seriously jeopardized the future reproductive potential of wild bear populations, and currently poses a major threat to the continued survival of Asiatic bears in Pakistan.

Brown bears, because they are more powerful than black bears, hold a special attraction for bear baiting events, though they are increasingly rare. Brown bears, normally living in cooler areas, are poorly suited to the hot conditions of the Punjab and Sindh—heat causes them to show yet more aggression, attracting even more spectators to bear baiting events. Landlords are wary of brown bears, however, because they are more likely to injure their precious dogs.

Wild populations of Himalayan black bears are currently the most seriously affected by bear baiting. (The Baluchistan black bear is already *very* rare—now too rare to be able to continue to supply bears for baiting). Himalayan black bears were once widely distributed in and around Pakistan. Bear-cub traders and middlemen were largely from Pakistan's Khyber Pushtunkhawa (Swat, Kohistan, Dir, Chitral), and cub-snatching was largely limited to this province. But as one might expect, bears in these areas declined considerably in late 1990s, forcing traders to search farther afield. In their search for a new supply of bears, they contacted grazers and Gujjars (nomadic grazers), who travel deep into bear habitat in search of grazing lands. Herders, who carry guns for protection, were more than willing to pad their income by killings sows, capturing cubs, and selling both. Grazers and poachers sell cubs to traders, who resell these little bears to gypsies. They sell the sow's fat and skin to merchants, and her gallbladder either to local merchants (Ayurvedic medicine) or into the international market for Asian medicines.

Needless to say, there is a very high mortality rate for kidnapped cubs, who are stressed by the loss of their mother, receive a minimum of care, are transported long distances, and change hands several times before they finally reach trainers or gypsies. Even this new supply of bears from remote areas of the region is running dry. There are now rumors of sloth bears (*Melursus ursinus*) being smuggled from South-east Asia to supply and maintain bear baiting in Pakistan. It appears that at least three sloth bears were smuggled from India for this purpose in the last twenty years. Luckily, sloth bears cannot be used for bear baiting because they are not strong enough to put up a worthy fight—and because gypsies in Pakistan do not know how to care for sloth bears well enough to keep them alive. Two of these imported sloth bears died, while the third was rescued and taken to Kund Bear Sanctuary in Pakistan.

Saving Pakistan's Bears

Efforts to curb the menace of bear baiting began in the late 1980s, when a forestry official working in Dera Ismail Khan (Khyber Pukhtonkhawa) shot home footage of a bear baiting event and gave the video tape to an international news channel. When the international community saw the brutality of bear baiting, a great roar of objection arose.

The World Society for Protection of Animals (WSPA), founded in 1981, decided to take on the challenge of putting an end to Pakistan's bear baiting. Unfortunately, in a nation with so many pressing problems, bear baiting is not a government priority, so WSPA has had to work with very little government support. In 1993, working only with local guides and collaborators, an 18-member WSPA team struck out in search of a bear baiting event. In the face of many lies and much fabricated information, they returned home empty handed. That same year (Benazir Bhutto's second tenure as Prime Minister of Pakistan), WSPA approached the authorities in Pakistan directly requesting a direct intervention on behalf of bears. Government authorities, in search of some excuse to ignore the issue, noted that there was no bear sanctuary in Pakistan. Why rescue bears when there is no place to house rescued bears?

In 1997 (Nawaz Sharif's second tenure as Prime Minister of Pakistan), WSPA returned to Pakistan to create a bear sanctuary. The government of Pakistan, for the first time, acknowledged the undesirability of bear baiting, and told wildlife authorities to put an end to this international embarrassment. Unfortunately, wildlife authorities were helpless: Pakistan's Wildlife Act contained no provision by which officials could raid bear baiting events, and no law against private bear ownership. There was only one antiquated act that might be used to protect Pakistan's imprisoned, exploited bears—the "Prevention of Cruelty Act 1890"—but the Wildlife Department was not authorized to enforce this law. Luckily, in time, Pakistan's bears were declared "protected" in the Wildlife Act, disallowing private ownership unless the owner held a permit issued by the Wildlife Department. No permits have been issued for bears captured since 1998, making any new bear acquisitions illegal.

WSPA had succeeded, but there was still much work to do if Pakistan's bear populations were to recover and survive. In 1998, WSPA began an awareness campaign, targeting schools. Simultaneously, a bear sanctuary was built at Kund (District Swabi, Pukhtonkhawa province), which was completed and opened in 2000. In 2001, WSPA also convinced President Parwaz Musharaff to issue a Presidential Order to provide a legal framework by which wildlife authorities could stop bear baiting whenever and wherever it was discovered. This Presidential Order was the most important achievement yet, and has been largely obeyed. Several bear baiting events have been raided under the guidance of this presidential order. Bears captured after 1998 are confiscated—rescued—and taken to the newly established Kund Bear Sanctuary. Bear baiting has declined markedly.

Pakistan's Bio Resource Research Centre (BRC) soon took charge of putting an end to bear baiting (with WSPA's generous financial support). BRC introduced alternative livelihoods for gypsies who surrender captive bears. They also extended WSPA's public awareness programme to village fairs, which had previously been a stage for bear baiting. Spectators were instead employed as entertainers, teaching conservation (infotainment!) by running a video of cartoons to educate children on bear welfare, including clips of real bears—happy, healthy, recovering bears at Kund Sanctuary. Afterwards, entertainers stage a bear baiting event where only humans participate, wearing bear masks and interacting boldly with the audience. These have been so successful that audiences prefer to watch infotainment—human mock bear baiting—than visit real bear-baiting arenas (which continue to pit dogs against bears who were unfortunate enough to be captured before 1998). This shift of interest cuts the landlord's audiences, and his pride, and makes bear baiting less attractive.

More recently, Pakistan's religious scholars have offered yet another breakthrough, noting that Islam, the major religion in Pakistan, strictly prohibits bear baiting. In fact, they note that Islam forbids any cruel or unjustified harm to animals. Local Islamic leaders began to offer teachings (Fatwahs) against bear baiting during Pakistan's most important religious gatherings, Friday sermons (Jumma Prayer), which draw the devout from a wide area. These talks have reached many Muslims with the message that Allah does not tolerate cruelty—including bear baiting.

Largely thanks to the efforts of WSPA and their many dedicated volunteers, laws against bear baiting are now strictly enforced, and bears continue to be confiscated from the miserable life of violence and suffering in bear baiting arenas. Field monitors keep an eye out for bear baiting in rural Pakistan, and are often able to prevent scheduled events and confiscate any bears acquired after 1998. Consequently, new bears continue to arrive at WSPA's Kund Sanctuary, and with 36 residents, the sanctuary is almost full to capacity. WSPA is planning another bear sanctuary at Balkasar (District Chakwal, Punjab Province), which will provide a safe refuge for every remaining battle-scarred bear in Pakistan. We are still working towards a complete end to bear baiting—a national recognition that this form of entertainment is both unconscionably cruel and irreligious. We have been very successful in closing down most bear baiting events, and we expect this barbaric practice to be completely eradicated in the next three or four years.

Kund Bear Sanctuary

Kund Bear Sanctuary was established by BRC and WSPA in 2001 to provide a suitable environment for bears rescued from the bondage and bloodshed of bear baiting. Most bears arrive with their muzzles half missing—chewed off by dozens of dogs—and their ears tattered and torn. We carry them in while they are sound asleep on stretchers. While they are under anesthesia, a vet cares for their infected wounds and provides restorative surgery, when possible. Bears at Kund sanctuary enjoy large enclosures designed to offer a natural environment and to minimize contact with humans. We make sure they have large water tanks to enjoy on hot days, and toys to enrich their environment. They are provided with a diet that is particular to and natural for each bear species. If one of our residents becomes ill, a vet is called. Kund is a safe haven for these wounded bears, the best that we can offer, given that they cannot be reintroduced to the wild.

Most Kund Sanctuary residents are Asiatic black bears (Himalayan subspecies), but we also care for one very beautiful female Himalayan brown bear, Neelum, with a distinctive, fluffy brown coat, and a bushy black sloth bear with long, curved claws, Karishma. Her name means "miracle," and it is a miracle that we were able to rescue her. She was owned by a powerful man—the provincial leader of a very strong political party. Rescuing bears from such powerful patriarchs requires diligence and diplomacy. Nonetheless, we were able to confiscate her and carry her away to safety. Karishma, never used for bear baiting (sloth bears are too small, unfit for the task), was exploited as a dancing bear. Now she dines on a special sloth diet of termites from Kund Sanctuary's termite farm, and spends her days high in the branches of trees, or playing with her soccer ball among the leaves and grasses of the soft earth.

Karishma, lives mostly with Kiran, a blind Baluchistan black bear. Their neighbor, Reshman, is a blind Himalayan black bear. Both of these bears were purposefully blinded to make them easier to handle. While we cannot undo the wrong that has been done these bears, they are at least free from torment, allowed to eat well and live peacefully, as is clearly their preference.

We also care for Star, whose coat is now shiny and full. He arrived with a tattered muzzle, hope gone from his dark eyes. His battles with dogs would have continued until his untimely death if we had not intervened. Luckily, we were able to rescue him last winter, and bring him to Kund Sanctuary. Our vet treated his infected wounds, and provided Star with an extra rich diet to help him regain strength. After a few weeks under close observation in our quarantine area, we were able to introduce him to some of the other older residents in the sanctuary. This past spring he was released into our semi-wild enclosure, where he wanders quietly through native brush, and lounges in a large water tank with other previously abused bears. It has been wonderful watching Star's spirit return, to see him begin to act like a bear once again after so many years of suppression, exploitation, and abuse. It is Star's recovery, and his bright future—in contrast with his very bleak past—that keeps me fighting to end bear baiting in Pakistan.

CHAPTER 11

Dirty Dancing: Caring for Sloth Bears in India

Lisa Kemmerer

An English literature lecturer at Delhi University, Geeta Seshamani, was cruis-
ing along the interstate between Agra and Delhi—a major tourist route—when
she noticed a large brown blob moving in a most unusual manner between the
two freeways. As she came closer, she could see that the brown blob was
fuzzy—some sort of a large mammal. Eventually she could see that the animal
was a bear—a sloth bear—pacing back and forth on her hind legs in response
to the tug of a rope that ran through her bloody, infected muzzle. She bobbed
while the man jerking the rope visited windows of cars that slowed or stopped,
seeking out tourists, inviting them to take a photograph with the bear, or ride
the bear, all the while begging for money. Some passersby were stricken with
pity for the bear, others empathized with the beggar, and so they pulled out a
few wrinkled Indian rupees; foreigners offered five or ten dollar bills—a small
fortune for a beggar in India.

Geeta was horrified—not because she had never seen a "dancing" bear ...
she had seen them all of her life. Not because tourists and passersby were foolish enough to pay someone to abuse an animal (again, she had seen this all of
her life). There was something about this particular bobbing, bleeding, beleaguered bear that stirred her compassion and sense of responsibility—perhaps
the despondent look in the bear's eyes.

Raised in a Hindu home—but not a traditional, vegetarian Hindu home—
Geeta had happened into the midst of a duck hunt in her childhood. It was then
that she first understood that she had been chosen to be a caretaker for animals.
The incident shifted her family to more traditional ways—to a diet free of flesh.
Geeta's natural compassion for all creatures continued to grow as she grew, and
so it was that, on seeing this bobbing bear, Geeta could not simply walk away
and forget. She decided to contact a distant cousin, Kartick Satyanarayan, who
also cared deeply about animals. As it turns out, he was working with the New
York Zoological Society on a Tiger Conservation Project in the jungles of India.
He readily agreed to help Geeta to do something on behalf of India's "dancing"
bears. The seeds for Wildlife SOS India had been planted.

---

* Many thanks to Arun Sha (Wildlife SOS veterinarian) and Kartick Satyanarayan and Geeta
Seshamani (founders of Wildlife SOS) for nuts and bolts information necessary to write
this essay.

Kalandar People and "Dancing" Bears

Marginalized geographically as well as by poverty and illiteracy, the Kalandar people live scattered throughout the nation of India (in the states of Karnataka, Andhra Pradesh, Madhya Pradesh, Bihar, Maharashtra, Haryana, Uttar Pradesh, West Bengal, Rajasthan, Delhi—the capital—and the newly formed states of Jharkhand and Chattisgarh). The Kalandars are traditionally a nomadic people living on the margins of Indian society in tents (bamboo and plastic) or mud huts, who often do not have access to potable water, toilets, or health care.

For centuries the Kalandars exploited sloth bears, forcing them to "dance" for money in the streets. They purchased cubs from a tribal poacher, who snatched them from the wilds of India, separating cubs from their mothers at a very young age, often killing the mothers in the process. Bears were important to the Kalandar people because they had so little. The income from a single "dancing" bear could support an extended Kalandar family of 10 to 12 members: During India's tourist season, which lasts about six months (October to March), dancing bears dependably brought in 150–200 rupees ($3 to $4) a day, considerably more if bolstered by the occasional $5 or $10 bill from a passing tourist. During the off season, Kalandars moved from village to village with these "dancing" bears, and in return for a village performance, received grain, wheat flour, vegetables, and so on. The annual income from one sloth bear would likely be something between 36,000 and 50,000 rupees ($600–$1000 U.S., and *per capita* income in India is just a little more than $1,500).

"Dancing bears" are one of India's most bizarre "livelihoods." For centuries marginalized tribal people poached sloth bears, trained them to "dance," and used them as street performers, soliciting spare change—often aggressively. Kalandars view sloth bears in the same way that people in animal agriculture view cattle and chickens and pigs—nothing more than means to an end, that end being money. Kalandars, like dairy and poultry farmers, do not recognize the animals in their care as individuals, capable of suffering, with hopes and fears all their own. Nor do they think of the suffering they cause when they exploit other animals for personal profit. Kalandars, like those working in animal agriculture, do not form emotional bonds with the animals they own. Dancing bears, like cattle and pigs and turkeys, are viewed as merely a source of income, and so they are disposed of and exchanged as deemed advantageous, and quickly dispatched if sick, old, or otherwise no longer profitable— just as dairy cattle are sent to slaughter when milk production drops. Parting with a bear is not an emotional issue for Kalandars; it is a financial calculation. When a bear cub is available at a reasonable price, they upgrade, selling their trained bear to another Kalandar family for $300 to $500.

Determined to help India's dancing bears, Geeta and Kartick headed straight to the headwaters of the river of suffering—Kalandar villages scattered across India. They traveled to a battery of these remote villages, intent on pinpointing forces supporting the ugly trade in dancing bears, especially socio-economic forces. They quickly realized that asking families to give up their most dependable source of income was not a viable long-term solution ... nor was such an approach compassionate. Instead, in 1995 Geeta and Kartick founded Wildlife SOS (WSOS) in 1995, and set plans in place to help the Kalandar people, to offer them alternative livelihoods—and much more—in exchange for their "dancing" bears.

Over the next decade, Geeta and Kartick spent a great deal of time in Kalandar villages, seeking ways to offer tribal people a brighter future *without* the dirty business of dancing bears. Wildlife SOS also helped Kalandars to improve life in their villages with grants to repair damaged roofs or to establish village wells. Thanks to Wildlife SOS, more than 3000 Kalandar families received micro-funding, job training, skill development, and other vital trainings and grants. To receive such assistance, the Kalandars were only required to surrender their bears peacefully and voluntarily, and sign an agreement stating that they would never exploit wild animals again. In return for bears and guarantees, Wildlife SOS provided each family with seed funds ($1000) to help them establish an alternative business. Once WSOS was well established, complete with bear sanctuaries, Kalandars were offered jobs at Wildlife SOS bear rescue centers. Wildlife SOS bear sanctuaries now employ more than 50 Kalandars, simultaneously promising a brighter future for Kalandars and captive bears.

Kalandar women and children were also offered opportunities to learn skills and work outside the home. More than 600 Kalandar women, once utterly dependent, are now earning an income. Additionally, Wildlife SOS sent Kalandar children to school, paying school fees and buying necessary books and uniforms. Over time, WSOS has enabled more than 800 Kalandar children (whose parents could not afford to send them to school) to attend school. Rather than simply become an additional set of hands for labor, these young Kalandars will have many more possible options for earning an income.

Wildlife SOS offered the Kalandar community a much brighter future than "dancing" bears could ever provide, and as a result, Kalandars surrendered bears and promised never to exploit wildlife again.

India's Bears and Wildlife SOS: Mowgli and Champa

India is home to four bear species—all endangered: Asiatic black bears (Himalayan/moon bears), sun bears (only in north-eastern India, along the border with Burma), Himalayan brown bears (only at higher altitudes), and sloth bears, which also live in Nepal and Sri Lanka. India's bears are threatened most decisively by human encroachment—by a rapidly expanding and sprawling human population. Human babies grow up to seek jobs, establish homes, and usually create their own babies, an ongoing cycle that has led our species to spread across landscapes, mowing down trees to build homes and plant crops in places where wildlife once lived. India's bears—and many other wild animals in India and around the world—are in grave danger because of ongoing, out-of-control human population growth and subsequent human sprawl.

Sloth bears are listed on Schedule 1—the most protected rank—of India's 1972 Wildlife Protection Act (WPA). Under WPA, it is illegal to "own" bears. (Frankly, "owning" another individual is perverse in any case.) Under WPA laws, forestry officials can arrest anyone caught with a bear. But the Government of India and India's state governments were unable to enforce this law because they had no facilities for rescued bears. Rescuing captive wildlife is not possible without sanctuaries and trained professionals to house and tend displaced individuals. With the help of India's Forest Department and organizations such as International Animal Rescue (IAR) and Free the Bears (FTB), Wildlife SOS provided such facilities. In December of 2002, Wildlife SOS established The Bear Rescue Facility in Agra, in the state of Uttar Pradesh. As a result, between 2002 and 2009—in just seven years—WSOS rescued more than 600 sloth bears. Needless to say, it was necessary to establish three more sanctuaries (in Bangalore, Karnataka; Bhopal, Madhya Pradesh; and Purulia, West Bengal). Wildlife SOS sanctuaries enabled government officials to confiscate any bears who were not voluntarily surrendered. Wildlife SOS success provides a working

FIGURE 11.1   *Sloth Bear*

model for activists in other nations seeking to enforce wildlife laws that are currently blocked by a lack of facilities and/or trained professionals.

Wildlife sos also models a host of happy bears, such as Mowgli and Champa. Wildlife sos staff found Mowgli shivering over a bowl of milk in a Kalandar village when he was yet too young to drink from a bowl. His tiny nose was bleeding profusely from the coarse rope that his "owners" had already inserted into his body. He had recently been castrated—likely with a rusty metal blade—and infection had set in. He was just four weeks old, and it is unlikely that Mowgli would have survived if wsos staff had not found and confiscated the wee bear—cub survival rates in Kalandar villages (at the time) was less than 50 percent.

A few days later, Champa, was discovered in the same village, about the same age and in about the same condition as Mowgli. When wsos staff introduced Champa and Mowgli, the two babies ran around each other, dashing here and there, leaping and bounding as they went, tumbling and rolling on the ground. Since that day, they have been inseparable ... and have stirred up their share of trouble. Champa and Mowlgli love to ambush other bears—especially if they can sneak up while neighboring bears are peacefully at rest. If they cannot find a napping neighbor to startle, they seek out wsos staff in the hope of waylaying caretakers who are busy burying or hanging food (part of enrichment feedings). Champa and Mowgli are always right in the middle of things, disturbing sleepy bears and derailing constructive staff efforts.

It is almost certain that Champa and Mowgli, rescued from the same village at roughly the same time, so visibly happy to see each another, are brothers. At wsos, despite having been robbed of their mother, despite the painful future they once faced, these two naughty youngsters are busy about the business of being bears. When they are on good behavior (not often), these two pals dig for hidden treats, clamber in the branches of trees, or splash vigorously in their pools. Rather than shifting their feet at the end of a biting rope, they are relaxing, playing, and causing trouble at wsos, where we hope they will live a long and peaceful life—despite the trouble they stir up for their good natured caretakers.

Ravena: The Beauty and Pain of Rescue and Rehabilitation

Raveena is another bear who found her way to The Bear Rescue Facility in Agra. Like most arriving bears, Raveena was timid and malnourished—almost 70 kilos (154 pounds) lighter than she should have been. On arrival, Dr. Arun Sha, a wsos Wildlife Veterinarian, assumed responsibility for her care. She was kept as quiet as possible during her first week in quarantine. In her second week, she was placed under anesthesia and the rope that had held her in slavery throughout her life, up to that point, was removed. After living at the end of a rope for many years—years in which any unwanted behavior was savagely punished—she was visibly distressed by the rope's removal, unsure what was expected, fearful of what would next befall her. She rocked back and forth in her cage, her eyes expressed resignation, confusion, and outright terror.

Each step in Raveena's recovery and rehabilitation was a struggle—as for most rescues. She had learned to fear human beings, and she had learned to live with a great deal of pain. Dr. Sha cleaned the pus and blood from Raveena's torn muzzle, sutured the flesh, then applied a topical antiseptic and antibiotic to help her wounds heal. Dr. Sha also removed what was left of her canine teeth, which had been shattered by the Kalandars, along with any other teeth that had been damaged and eroded by years of malnutrition. He ran blood tests on Raveena to check for lingering infection, and took a preliminary ultrasound of Raveena's abdominal cavity to check for respiratory diseases via thoracic radiography. As the weeks passed, Raveena slowly but surely gained weight on a special WSOS diet of fruits, honey, and porridge, which she received twice daily. Eventually she began to take an interest in her surroundings, and to demonstrate less fear and dread—she was on the road to recovery, even showing signs of trust.

Raveena had been confiscated from a Kalandar community in Uttar Pradesh, and it is safe to assume that her past was probably typical of many rescued bears. She was torn from her mother at a very young age, likely at about four weeks, when her eyes and ears were on the verge of opening to the wind-shifted leaves and bustling insects that enlivened her natural home. No doubt she had at least one other sibling to tumble and explore with—but her mother was the center of Raveena's world. Mother bears are fierce, protecting their cubs at any cost—even against hopeless odds. Doubtless, Raveena's mother bravely defended her little ones, but a mother bear is no match for a hunter's gun. So it was that Raveena lost her mother, her freedom, and her homeland in that fraction of a second in which a poacher pulled the trigger. The poacher scruffed her and her siblings and tossed them into the darkness of a course, rough sack woven from jute fiber. No doubt Raveena screamed and cried for her mother, but the poacher held fast to his loot—worth as much as 20,000 rupees ($400 U.S.), several month's worth of income for many Indian people.

Raveena was terrified, especially of her captors. Everything that would happen to her in the hands of the Kalandar villagers who bought her would reinforced this initial fear of human beings. First, without anesthesia, a crude red-hot iron rod was inserted through the flesh of her soft muzzle and tiny nostrils, searing holes through her flesh. Her new "owners" thrust a thick, coarse rope through these fresh wounds. Next, Raveena was pinned against the ground while they knocked out her canines with a metal rod. Her new masters were not done disfiguring her tiny body—she still had claws with which she might one day fight. Again without anesthesia, Kalandars extracted her claws, causing unbelievable pain, and removing her last means of defense.

With a dirty rope running across raw edges of fresh wounds, Raveena's nose and muzzle bled and swelled, and was soon infected. Her muzzle, likely the most sensitive part of her body, was in excruciating pain—a pain that she would have to learn to live with. She whimpered and cried when Kalandar's yanked on the rope and beat her feet with sticks, forcing her to lift her feet in agony and terror—forcing her to "dance." Nocturnal by nature, Reveena was expected to perform this bizarre dance-of-agony for many hours each day. If she was lucky, she would be fed one thick roti and a small bowl of milk in exchange. Oftentimes her "owners" only tossed scraps of junk-food in her direction—she was always hungry. At night, when she would normally have roamed the forests of India with her mother and siblings, she stood immobilized at the end of a short rope—trapped in a human world of exploitation and deprivation.

Raveena's ailments and wounds were very serious when she reached Dr. Sha, but no worse than many other rescued "dancing" bears he had treated, who now contentedly slobbered while they ate fresh fruit in WSOS pens just beyond Raveena's quarantine area. Her future was certainly more hopeful than her past, and when Dr. Sha had completed WSOS quarantine protocol, Raveena was released into a special pen with other rescued bears to be socialized, where she settled in gradually and with visible pleasure.

But Raveena's ugly past was not so easily shed. After only a year with WSOS, she fell ill, showing signs of neurological trauma. With special permission and help from the local forestry department, Dr. Sha transported Raveena to a human hospital in order to perform a multitude of tests, including an MRI, CT-scan, and radiography. Unfortunately, these tests revealed nothing. With no clue as to what was causing Raveena's decline, the veterinarian could only treat her symptoms, most importantly, her pain. Dr. Sha watched her slide back down the mountain he had helped her to so laboriously climb, feeling helpless. Her rapid demise was made yet more painful to witness because of her growing trust and innate patience—she had clearly come to understand that WSOS staff were on her side—that she could trust them. Much to the sadness of those who knew her, Raveena slipped beyond the borders of life after only four days after being placed in intensive treatment, leaving shattered caretakers behind.

A post mortem exam revealed the cause of Raveena's sudden, acute misery and premature death—rabies. Raveena was the first bear in which a veterinarian had witnessed the symptoms of rabies, and her symptoms were not typical of rabies in other species. While unable to save Raveena, a new WSOS medical protocol was established with her passing—all quarantined bears are now routinely vaccinated for rabies.

Raveena came to WSOS riddled with physical and mental damage, in perpetual pain, as she had remained during eight agonizing years as a "dancing" bear. Under human control she lost her mother, her freedom, her habitat, her means of self-defense, her health and vitality, and pretty much every activity that is natural for a sloth bear. She experienced long days of hunger and the effects of serious malnutrition. Her paws were damaged and infected from walking on hot pavement; the rope wounds in her muzzle were always raw and infected, and her emaciated body was riddled with parasites. Tied to a short rope, devoid of claws and canines, she could not even protect herself against marauding nonhuman animals—which left her with a disease (rabies) that, despite excellent veterinary care, ultimately robbed her of her life.

Veterinary Care at WSOS Sanctuaries

Almost every sloth bear arrives at WSOS with an encyclopedia list of disorders, ailments, and peculiarities. Poor nutrition, lack of veterinary care, and never-ending stress create a host of predictable medical problems such as external and internal parasites, maggot wounds on paws, severe gum disease, and rotting tooth stumps where canines have been purposefully broken. Their immune systems are usually compromised, and some suffer from the onset of tuberculosis, which they contract from the Kalandars. Diseases, especially tuberculosis, remain a major cause of death among rescued sloth bears.

Nonetheless, if rescued sloth bears can be nurtured through their first year in sanctuary, they usually live for many years to come. Wildlife SOS employs nine veterinarians (and even more veterinary assistants) to care for the many needs of rescued "dancing" bears. New WSOS arrivals are quarantined for three months for tests and observation, during which time they are assessed, given primary care, and treated for ailments and injuries. A veterinary clinical record is established for each arriving individual, and human contact is minimized during this first week, usually to just 3 or 4 caregivers, reducing stimulation and stress for these traumatized rescues.

In the first week, a long-term program is set in motion. While much change is needed, sudden change is stressful, and initial bear-care is designed to encourage new arrivals to settle in peacefully. Consequently, the Kalandar rope remains throughout each bear's first week at WSOS, and his or her diet is only gradually changed. Digestion is a serious problem in the early stages of rehabilitation because "dancing" bears often live on white flour—unhealthy even for human beings who create this "food"—since they were very young. As a consequence, their digestive systems are not properly developed and their colons cannot cope with natural bear food. New arrivals are therefore given 50–100 grams of glucose and 20 grams of electrolyte powder mixed with 2–3 liters water, as well as 2–3 liters of milk (that has been boiled and cooled to be sure no pathogens are introduced). Only very slowly can natural foods (such as seasonal fruits—watermelon, papaya, pineapple, jack fruit, graphs, and oranges) be introduced into their diets.

In the second week, the Kalandar rope is removed, usually leaving a rescued bear confused and nervous. Sometimes they shake their heads violently, as if still fighting a rope. Most often, they stand in one place, neurotically rocking back and forth. During this second week, veterinarians inject liver stimulants (belamyl, stronic, etc.) to help restore liver health, and routinely examine scat and urine to detect any abnormalities. Staff also observe the temperaments of new arrivals in order to assess how best to serve a particular bear's needs.

In the third week, rescued bears are dewormed, and vaccinated against infectious diseases (rabies, leptospirosis, tetanus). In the final week of their first month of quarantine, they are tranquilized for a complete clinical examination. While bears are "asleep" veterinarians inspect ears and eyes and perform a clinical analysis of various biological parameters, including full body measurements. Veterinarians also test for TB on a bear's eyelids and ears, and collect blood in order to test for hepatitis, rabies, TB, and leptospirosis. Finally, before the bear returns to consciousness, necessary X-rays are taken, an ultrasound performed, and visible injuries are treated.

In the second month of quarantine, veterinarians firmly establish normal parameters for a given bear through continued urine/scat analysis, blood samples, and observations. Bears are given booster vaccines, and ongoing treatment is offered for any medical problems detected in their first month of care. These treatments continue through the last month of quarantine, as necessary. WSOS staff watch each bear to be sure that he or she is healing and adjusting as expected. They also expose rescues to WSOS fencing, and assess each bear's compatibility with others in preparation for release into the best-suited sanctuary pen. During this last month of quarantine, rescued bears are introduced to their first enrichments—food puzzles and toys!

After three months of quarantine, assuming rescues prove to be healthy, they join other bears in a WSOS sanctuary pen, where they begin a much longer, slower process of recovery. They are provided with round-the-clock veterinary care and enrichments that allow sloth bears to "forage." In time, rescues discover their inner bear—they climb trees, dig shallow pits (for napping—a favorite sloth bear activity), play in water pools, roll in the dirt, and wrestle or mock fight with other bears. While wsos bear sanctuaries cannot provide sloth bears with anything like their normal range or natural habitat, or anything like a natural foraging experiences, compared with life at the end of a rope in a Kalandar village, they have entered paradise.

It is important that rescued bears find a slice of heaven at wsos sanctuaries because they can never be released into the wild. Most of them have been in captivity since they were very young cubs. Their mothers did not live long enough to teach them how and where to forage, or what dangers to avoid. Additionally, Kalandars mutilate "dancing" bears—breaking teeth, pulling claws, castrating males—rendering them defenseless. Rescued bears also tend to show signs of psychological damage, exhibiting stereotypic behaviors such as endlessly weaving their heads in a particular pattern, or pacing. Rescued "dancing" bears at wsos sanctuaries are almost always home to stay—and wsos provides a very fine home, indeed.

Caring for hundreds of sloth bears over the past two decades, wsos veterinarians have established basic standards of care, and collected vital medical information on this reclusive, endangered species, including statistics regarding blood-work, skeletal structures, and diseases such as tuberculosis, leptospirosis, rabies, infectious canine hepatitis, and canine adeno viral infection. wsos veterinarians have unexpectedly become a source of vital information internationally, helping others who rescue and tend captive sloth-bears.

Wildlife sos Projects and Possibilities

Wildlife sos currently cares for more than 400 rescued sloth bears—much more than any other organization in the world. Each bear will hopefully live a long, full life (20–25 years), with all the advantages of a nutritious diet and regular veterinary care, protected by well-maintained, secure enclosures. Rani, the very first bear rescued by wsos, still naps under the trees of her ample pen, and rolls in the grass, flashing her teeth or swatting at youngsters when they get out of line.

wsos continues to work with the Kalandar people, fostering sustainable livelihoods and ensuring that these distant communities are not tempted to exploit sloth bears for profit, thereby working to prevent any resurgence of the trade in bear cubs. By eliminating demand, wsos has seriously diminished poacher profits, protecting mother bears and their cubs even in India's most remote regions. With cooperation of India's government enforcement agencies, wsos has also been effective in uncovering and cracking poaching rackets and smuggling rings. As humans encroach more and more on less and less wilderness, poachers have gained increased access to once secluded habitats and wildlife, and the international trade in bear parts is lucrative: Body parts (gallbladder, penis, paws, bones, etc.) are now worth more than a live cub.

Geeta and Kartick continue to guide Wildlife sos on a course that they hope will bring lasting change to protect India's wildlife. Wildlife sos is collecting and saving funds in order to purchase private agricultural land adjoining bear habitat in the state of Karnataka. These lands will be reforested, providing both worthy jobs for interested Kalandars as well as a safe haven for bears and every other creature who lives in the area. wsos is also implementing programs designed to mitigate the causes and effects of climate change, and fostering research directed at a richer understanding of biodiversity and the specific needs of India's ecosystems and wildlife. wsos has even founded and now manages sanctuaries for leopards, reptiles, and Asiatic bears, and is currently establishing an elephant sanctuary.

Any one of us can help wsos to carry out these worthy programs. wsos maintains a strong volunteer and internship program through which volunteers from around the world are able to work at India's rescue centers, learn about caring for wildlife at sanctuaries, and at the same time, experience local culture and traditions. (Living in India is comparatively inexpensive for Westerners, and India is a fabulous place to visit.) Volunteers and interns pay a comparatively small fee (put towards boarding and lodging), and of course they pay for their journey to India. In exchange, volunteers gain precious hands-on experience working alongside experienced wsos staff with India's remarkable wildlife, including sloth bears. (For details, email info@wildlifesos.org or visit http://www.wildlifesos.org.)

But we need not go to India to help wsos—or to help bears or other endangered or harmed beings. If we come upon *any* abused animal—whether in India, Thailand, or Italy, whether exploited for entertainment, labor, or food— *we must never offer any incentive or encouragement.* Instead, take pictures and send photos of the animals (and their exploiters) to an organization working such as Wildlife sos (wsos), International Animal Rescue (IAR), World Society for the Protection of Animals (wspa), People for the Ethical Treatment of Animals (peta, which has affiliates around the world), or Human Society International (hsi). Use caution, but do not be intimidated by abusers. Without help from those of us who pass their way, these helpless victims are unlikely to ever escape the grip of abuse.

Seven years after Geeta noticed that bobbing, brown "dancing" bear along the Agra-Delhi highway, that very bear was rescued by Wildlife sos, and she is alive and well in the Agra Bear Rescue Facility. Now a senior bear, she naps peacefully in the sun in her ample, forested enclosure. Because Geeta did not pass by and conveniently forget what she had seen, because Geeta and Kartick took action, that very bear found a slice of heaven—and there are no longer *any* "dancing" bears in India. India's last "dancing" bear was rescued and carried to the safety of a wsos sanctuary in 2009. It just goes to show what can happen when those who witness animal abuse take responsibility and take action.

CHAPTER 12

Sliding Down Mountainsides on My Butt in Search of the Elusive Andean Bear

Dalma Zsalakó

The spectacled or Andean bear (*Tremarctos ornatus*) is easily distinguished from other bear species. Most Andean bears have spectacle-like markings around their eyes, and a light muzzle, creating a facial expression resembling utmost curiosity. Some even appear to have their eyebrows raised in surprise or doubt.

The Andean bear is the only bear species living in South America, and the only remaining species of short-nosed bears. While numerous publications and documentaries offer insights into the natural behavior and private lives of other bear species, little is known about Andean bears. This may be partly because the home of the Andean bear is difficult to access. Their natural habitat includes the *páramo* (high altitude grassland) on the windy peaks of the Andes, the cloud forest with moss and lichen covered trees, and impenetrable bamboo thickets. This environment can be rather inhospitable and thus poses a bit of a challenge for scientific research and long-term monitoring. Nonetheless, the field staff of the Andean Bear Project are working in this region to protect Andean bears and their habitat, and to study the behavior and ecology of this endangered species.

Tracking Bears with the Andean Bear Project

In 1995, The Andean Bear Project ("The Project") was founded by bear biologist Armando Castellanos, who still heads the organization (now revamped and renamed "Andean Bear Foundation"). With the help of staff and volunteers, he gathers data on the ecology and behavior of Andean bears, and his work has become central to the international research effort to better understand this elusive species. Castellanos' team also works with locals—a vital aspect of protecting Andean bears—educating them about bears and about the importance of protecting these magnificent animals and their habitat. Additionally, The Project helps to mitigate human-bear conflicts.

Going to Ecuador was just one of many "jump into the deep end" decisions that I have made in my life, along with studying in England and taking a job in China. I was attracted to Ecuador and the Andean Bear Project by the Spanish language, the exotic location, and the chance to radio-track bears while hiking in the Andean mountains. Although some seemed to think this was a rushed decision, it was definitely the right choice for me—working with The Project (including time spent with local Ecuadorians as well as foreign volunteers who chose to spend vacation time working for a cause) helped shape the course of my future, and left me with some of my dearest memories.

I spent 6 months working as a volunteer coordinator for the Andean Bear Project (2007–2008), during which time, among other things, I tracked five radio collared bears with the help of volunteers from around the world. While working with the Andean Bear Project, I lived at The Project's base camp in Pucará, 2081 meters (6827 feet) above sea level. This little hamlet is very rural—situated in the Andes, more than 2 hours by bus from the nearest town, which happens to be Otavalo, famous for its thriving indigenous market. Living in Pucará was a huge change of lifestyle—not just for me, but for other foreigners coming from around the world to help The Project. Life in such a small village offered a welcome break from deadlines, phones, junk mail, computers, and city traffic.

In Pucará, while lying in bed, we could hear the gentle buzzing of humming bird wings—a soothing remedy after the wake-up call provided by the smallest rooster I had ever seen, who compensated for his size with sheer volume in his morning regime of crowing. Through our bedroom windows, we enjoyed a stunning view of seemingly endless mountains and lush green forests. When we stepped out into the garden, we were surrounded by pineapples, orchids, and orange and avocado trees. The picturesque surroundings always lifted our spirits—even after a particularly exhausting day. The magic of the Andes was so profound that after months and months in Pucará I still found myself staring off at the untamed landscape with awe.

We arose early (not just on account of the rooster, but because work called), and after a hearty breakfast prepared by Celia, a local employee, we set off in search of bears. The Project could not afford a car, so we used any mode of transport that we could find—sometimes we took a local bus, but most often we hitchhiked (a common practice in Ecuador), flagging down anything with wheels and a motor. This turned out to be a great way to meet locals and practice our Spanish language skills. Often we were able to hitch a ride on the milk truck, which serves a large area that has no bus service, and is the only means of transport for many locals who live off the beaten track. It was always an interesting and educational experience because we stopped at farms along the way, picking up milk and other passengers—including dogs and a range of farmed animals such as chickens and pigs.

I have many vivid recollections from hitchhiking in Ecuador, but by far the most fun (and scariest) experience was when we flagged down a full bus, and the driver offered us a ride on the roof. We clumsily climbed up the ladder attached to the side of the bus, and crawled along the roof, as we had often seen locals do, praying that it would not collapse underneath us. The driver, most likely used to having roof passengers, did not consider what it might be like for us inexperienced *gringos* riding atop the bus, and continued at the same treacherous speed as before. We clung to the railing for dear life, ducking low-lying tree branches as the coach bounced over the rocky dirt road, laughing at each other's terrified faces, and occasionally screaming in a mixture of horror and exhilaration when we saw deep valleys below our dangling feet as the bus pulled to the edge of the road to overtake a slower vehicle on the narrow track. By the time we reached Pucará, our hands felt like they were frozen to the railing in such tight clenches that it was painful to let go. While we were truly grateful to be standing on the ground, alive and unhurt, the wild roof-ride was an unforgettable experience ... though I am not sure I would do it again.

We used several predefined routes to track collared bears, which were strategically chosen based on bear behavior and landscapes that maximized radio signal reception across a wide area. Some routes were easier (walking along a winding road), while others required us to hike above 3000 meters (9800 feet) through thick bamboo forests (suro, *Chusquea* species), scrambling up nearly vertical slopes despite rain and scorching sun (often 30 C/86 F). Our local guide, Alberto, led the way. He provided us with ample opportunities to improve our Spanish—when we weren't gasping for breath as we hiked rough terrain with food, water, and necessary equipment in our backpacks. Despite the inherently exhausting nature of tracking wild bears, we always had fun. For instance, we engaged in friendly contests to see who would fall the least number of times on the steep, slippery terrain. Alberto always won this competition, but I believe I set a record for distance covered sliding on my backside, while making "girly noises" that I am not proud of.

Each route had numerous "listening stations" (marked on a "master map" pinned on a wall at base camp). To us, the listening stations looked no different than any other place we passed along the way, but Alberto always knew exactly where they were—though sometimes we teased him, claiming that he was just making it up as we went along. We paused at each listening station to attempt to locate signals from radio collared bears. Each bear's collar emitted signals on a different frequency, so we always knew whose beep we were hearing. When we heard a signal, we noted which bear it belonged to, the time of day, and what direction it had come from (using a compass). On returning to base camp, I used this information to triangulate the location of that particular bear on our "master map." The results of this triangulation were then used to plan our route for the next day.

Though Ecuador's climate is by no means mild at all altitudes, bears need not hibernate in this region because they can find food year round. Consequently, the Andean Bear Project monitors bears all year long. Despite the simple technology used (a compass, headphones, and a radio with antenna), these data provide significant information on Andean bear home and core range sizes, as well as travel distances, use of habitat corridors, and activity patterns. This information enhances general knowledge of Andean bear behavior, aids rehabilitation and release efforts, highlights important areas for habitat conservation, and assists efforts to mitigate human-bear conflicts.

Even though I spent 6 months hiking in Andean bear territory, and listened to many radio signals, I never saw even one bear while I was in the field. Every now and then a radio signal's frantic beeping would indicate that a bear was within 500 meters (1600 feet) of where we stood, but we never spotted so much as a flash of this shy bear's black coat. Andean bears avoid humans when possible, and so it is rare to stumble onto a bear in the wild. Generally speaking, they are not aggressive and there are only a few isolated cases of Andean bears injuring humans; in such cases, as far as I know, the bears were either threatened or injured. For example, during his work in Peru, Bernard Peyton (a prominent bear biologist and Andean bear expert) reported that he had "heard of only one human death caused by a spectacled bear that fell on a hunter after he shot it" (Peyton 162). Thanks to their acute hearing, spectacled bears generally avoid human contact, but if people do surprise them in the wild, it would be quite unusual for Andean bears to attack—they usually seek the nearest escape route. Unfortunately, a startled bear may instinctively climb a tree in an attempt to escape, only to become trapped by humans below. Desperate to escape, they sometimes jump, falling long distances (even as much as 20 meters/65 feet), apparently without serious harm—impressive even among bears (Castellanos 20–21).

The Andean Bear Project invests considerable energy in raising public awareness, targeting especially children and local farming communities. Children are easy to win over, and are generally eager to support the protection of this fuzzy, huggable-looking bear. In contrast, gaining the support of local farmers is more difficult, particularly if they have had run-ins with bears, for instance, raiding their corn fields. In rural Ecuador, corn is an important crop, and bears who feed on corn are often killed by farmers. Unfortunately, in the process, many "innocent" bears might also be killed when they pass fields that have been raided by other bears. For ten years The Project compensated farmers for crop losses attributed to bears, which significantly reduced human-bear conflicts in the region. Farmers are also likely to hold a grudge against bears because Andean bears sometimes attack and kill cattle (Castellanos, Laguna, and Clifford 16–18). In their natural habitat, Andean bears are overwhelmingly vegetarian—fruits, bromeliads, *suro*, and palm hearts form the bulk of their diet, usually supplemented with insects, carrion, and occasionally small animals such as rodents. However, with ever increasing human encroachment into bear habitat, bears are more apt to seek alternative food sources, increasing human-bear conflicts.

Leo

The Andean Bear Project also rescues and rehabilitates bears for release in collaboration with partner organizations and private individuals. In the past sixteen years, The Project has released fourteen bears back into the wild. The majority of Andean Bear Project releases have been straightforward and without incident, but a bear named Leo managed to keep human beings busy everywhere he went. Leo was a bear that everyone seemed to have given up on—everyone except Armando Castellanos and his team at The Project. Leo was rescued as a cub in June of 2004 from a house in Oyacachi, where he was kept in a pen with hens. Allegedly, he had been saved by locals after his mother had abandoned him—a story Armando Castellanos and his team never believed, because it is inconsistent with most cases where cubs become captive. The Project did not have the necessary facilities to keep Leo, so he was transferred to a partner project, Santa Martha Rescue Center (another volunteer-assisted organization in Ecuador), which provided refuge for a large variety of rescued native wildlife. Due to financial constraints and other difficulties, Leo spent almost two years at Santa Martha. During this time, he became a cunning master of escape, keeping both management and volunteers busy recapturing him, while building safer and safer enclosures in order to contain this busy bear.

In June of 2006, rehabilitated and able to fend for himself, Leo was released in a remote part of Hacienda Yanahurco, a 26,000 hectare (64,250 acre) private ranch that prides itself in also serving as a Private Ecological Reserve. Unfortunately, a few months later Leo showed up around ranch buildings—and entered a house in search of food. Despite The Project's policy on returning "problem bears" to captivity, Leo was given another chance because it was possible that he had simply been released too close to human habitation. Project personnel captured Leo, took him farther into the wilderness, and then re-released him. This time it took four days for Leo to find his way back to the ranch, apparently famished.

Unfortunately now there was no alternative but to withdraw Leo's licence for freedom. However, no rescue or rehabilitation places were available, so he was temporarily housed in San Martin Zoo in Baños. Regrettably, Leo remained at the zoo for three years, during which time he caused untold headaches, even escaping twice by climbing an almost vertical rock wall around his enclosure—he was voting for freedom. Leo was clearly a liability, so the zoo's owner requested the bear's prompt transfer. With no other option available, Leo ended up back at Santa Martha Rescue Center, where volunteers nicknamed him "Houdini."

I met Leo at Santa Martha, and was amazed by the sheer size of this gorgeous bear. I knew other Andean bears at the Center, but none were anywhere near the size of Leo. At five years of age, he was enormous, with a powerful stride, jet black coat, light muzzle, and only a faint cream-coloured semi-circle around his eyes.

At Santa Martha, Leo's escape-proof cage was specifically built for bears, a design based on the Center owners' hard-won experience housing Andean bears. When Leo realised that he was held fast, he invested his excess energy in destroying the wooden structures we placed inside his enclosure. And so the contest began: We rebuilt interior structures for his entertainment and comfort, and Leo destroyed them, over and over again. Rebuilding Leo's cage became our primary "project" at Santa Martha. In the process, we carried out behavioral observations, applied a wide range of enrichments, and researched bear enclosure designs at other institutions. We even nominated a specific volunteer, who had a background in architecture, to design and rebuild the interior of Leo's cage.

Fortunately, Leo only spent two months at Santa Martha, or the rescue center might have gone bankrupt purchasing building materials for Leo's cage furnishings. This time the Andean Bear Project negotiated for the use of a helicopter from the Ecuadorian Army so they could carry Leo deep into the wilderness, far from human settlements. In June of 2009, when he was tranquilised for the journey and peacefully sleeping, we gave Leo (renamed Cenepa in honor of the Army's contribution) a farewell bear hug, and the army helicopter carried him to distant mountains for release. More than three years have passed without further incident, and for as long as his radio collar could be monitored (one and a half years) he remained active. Sightings since release have also confirmed that he is still alive and well (Castellanos, personal). Given not just a second chance, but many chances, Leo was finally given the freedom he struggled so hard to gain on his own.

Future Visions and Volunteering with the Andean Bear Foundation

Unfortunately, the Andean Bear Project closed its facilities in Pucará in June of 2011. The program continues, however, as the Andean Bear Foundation (ABF) at a new facility just outside of Antisana Ecological Reserve. This facility is designed to house up to 6 bears, with enclosures built specifically for cubs or adults. The new center has a restricted-access section for bears being rehabilitated for release, and an area where visitors can observe bears who cannot be released, and who will live with ABF for the duration of their lives. ABF continues monitoring and mapping bear movements and ranges, and is planning to use this information to help local communities plan agricultural expansion in areas with less bear activity. Interestingly, Castellanos plans to combine Andean bear research with studies on mountain tapirs (*Tapirus pinchaque*), and to investigate interactions between these two unique species.

The Andean Bear Foundation still has a volunteer program, providing enthusiasts with the opportunity to gain experience tracking wild bears and collecting field data, or working with captive Andean bears in the rescue center. Masters and PhD students in any wildlife or animal studies program are also encouraged to contact ABF for research opportunities. ABF is a dedicated and skilled conservation organization that needs our support if they are to continue their good work—if they are to succeed in protecting the unique habitats and wildlife of South America. Those who have volunteered will attest to the fact that the experience is worth every penny. Not only do adventuresome volunteers gain an unforgettable, life-changing experience, but they help to support an excellent program that cannot continue without funding.

FIGURE 12.1   *Andean Bear*

References

Castellanos, Armando. *"Andean Bears Jump from Treetops."* International Bear News, Quarterly Newsletter of the International Association for Bear Research and Management (IBA) and the IUCN/SSC Bear Specialist Group 15.4 (2006): 20–21. Accessed 18 Jan. 2012. http://www.bearbiology.com/fileadmin/tpl/Downloads/IBN_Newsletters/IBN_2006_November_for_web.pdf.

Castellanos, Armando, Andres Laguna, and Sarah Clifford. *"Suggestions for Mitigating Cattle Depredation and Resulting Human-Bear Conflicts in Ecuador."* International Bear News, Quarterly Newsletter of the International Association for Bear Research and Management (IBA) and the IUCN/SSC Bear Specialist Group 20.3 (2011): 16-18. Accessed 18 Jan. 2012. http://www.bearbiology.com/fileadmin/tpl/Downloads/IBN_Newsletters/IBN_Low_August_2011.pdf.

Castellanos, Armando. Personal interview. 19 Jan. 2012.

Peyton, Bernard. "Spectacled Bear Conservation Action Plan." *Bears: Status Survey and Conservation action Plan.* Eds. Christopher Servheen, Stephen Herrero, and Bernard Peyton. *Cambridge: IUCN Publications,* 1999. 157–164.

CHAPTER 13

Finding Enrico: Protecting Andean Bears and their Habitat

Lisa Kemmerer, Kerry Fugett, Simona Kobel

Packed with food for a week, tent, sleeping bags, and telemetry equipment, accompanied by a local guide named Alberto, two volunteers left the small village of Pucará in search of one of Ecuador's most elusive species, the Andean (or spectacled) bear. For more than five days, they had not received a radio signal from Enrico, one of six collared bears monitored by the Andean Bear Foundation (ABF). He could be anywhere within his estimated home range of 150 square kilometers (60 sq. m.) (Castellanos, "Andean Bear Project" 36). In search of Enrico's signal, the three weary walkers traipsed farther and farther into the cloud forest, a subtropical evergreen forest where fog usually sits down on the tops of trees and moss blankets the landscape. In this remote, high-altitude landscape, humans are limited to foot travel, aided only by machetes.

They were headed up to the *paramo* (high altitude grasslands). Camping at nearly 4,000 meters (13,000 ft.) would allow them to scan for radio signals in the finger-like valleys that spread out from every peak in the Andes, providing a better chance of catching Enrico's signal. The innumerable nooks, almost vertical mountainsides, and deep river basins of the cloud forest—all wrapped in a constant layer of mist—are an ideal home for Andean bears. Terrestrial radio telemetry is extremely challenging in this area, due to the complex topography, including very high altitudes and dense vegetation (Castellanos, "Andean Bear Home" 65). Signals often disappear into the forests and caverns, sometimes for weeks at a time, making research difficult, and demanding solid feet on the ground to manually collect data (Castellanos, "Andean Bear Home" 70).

As the two volunteers and their guide sweated and strained their way up the trail towards the open grasslands, they watched for claw marks on trees or scat along the trail, hoping for any sign of Enrico. They anxiously awaited the *paramo*, hopeful that they might hear the steady "Beep-Beep-Beep" of Enrico's collar.

Andean Bears and their Habitat

Andean bears are remarkably adaptable, at home in a damp cloud forest, dry desert lands, and high altitude grassland, they live throughout the Andes, which run from Venezuela through Colombia, Ecuador, Peru, and Bolivia to northern Argentina (Castellanos, *Guía* 1). Because this bear's habitat reaches across political boundaries, the Andean bear is dependent on coordination and teamwork for survival.

Andean bears are easily identified by their spectacle-like markings—cream or brown areas around the muzzle and eyes that sometimes run down onto the chest. These markings vary widely and are unique to each individual—some have no markings whatsoever. Evolutionarily distinct, they are the last of the world's short-nosed bears—no other living bear species shares the Andean bear's characteristically short muzzle. Their closest relative was the giant short nosed bear (*Arctodus simus*), who went extinct approximately 12,000 years ago. The Andean bear is the only bear native to South America (Castellanos, *Guía* 2).

Though classed as carnivores, these bears are omnivorous and opportunistic, and in reality are largely vegetarian. In the Intag region of Ecuador (20,000 hectares outside the 204,429 hectare Cotacachi-Cayapas Ecological Reserve) and on the western slopes of the volcano, Cotacachi, scat analysis reveals that one particular bamboo species (locally called *suro, Chusquea spp.*) serves as this bear's primary food source. Bromeliads and various forest fruits are important for bears living in the cloud forest, and bears throughout their habitat unearth beetles, worms, insects, and very occasionally, small mammals (Castellanos, "Andean Bear Research" 25). They also love carrion.

Ecuador's wild lands are one of the most biologically diverse areas of the world—home to a whopping 16,000 plant species, 15 percent of the world's bird species, 6,000 butterfly species, and 138 endemic amphibians, and are one of the last refuges for species such as the ocelot (*Leopardus tigrinus*), Quichuan porcupine (*Coendou quichua*), pacarana (*Dinomys branickii*), cock of the rock (*Rupicola peruvianus*), laminated toucan (*Andigena laminirostris*), toucan barbet (*Semnornis ramphastinus*), and Andean bears (*Tremarctos ornatus*) (Castellanos, "Andean Bear Home" 66). Habitats in Ecuador range from the rocky landscape of the Galapagos Islands through dry desert regions to the cloud covered, high-altitude mountains of the Andes. The high mountains, blanketed with forests and dotted with active volcanos, stretch eastward into some of the earth's most biologically diverse valleys, where massive rivers snake their way out toward the rich Amazon basin.

Ecuador, along with other South and Central American nations, is losing both forests and bears. Yet Andean bears are fundamental to healthy forest ecosystems. For example, Andean bears tear the bark from specific trees, eventually killing these trees, creating clearings throughout otherwise dense rainforests. This allows light to reach the forest floor, promotes seed germination, and encourages the growth of smaller trees (Castellanos, *Guía* 5). In addition, as avid fruit-eaters and long-distance travelers, Andean bears "plant" fruit seeds throughout their habitat.

Threats

Despite their ecological importance, the Andean bear is one of the least studied in the *Ursidae* family (Castellanos, "Preliminary Results" 60). Furthermore, Andean bears are listed as vulnerable to extinction on the International Union for Conservation of Nature (IUCN) Red List (*"Tremarctos"*). Fewer than 20,000 Andean bears grace their natural habitat. Their greatest threats include habitat loss and fragmentation (which heightens human-bear conflicts, leading to yet more bear deaths), and illegal trade in bear body parts.

Habitat Loss and Fragmentation

Since the 1960s, thousands of acres of native forests in the Western Andes have been logged, leaving less than 8 percent of original forests, greatly diminishing bear habitat (Castellanos, "Andean Bear Home" 66). The primary reason that rainforests are logged is to graze cattle, or to plant crops to feed cattle. For example, more than 70 percent of the Amazon's rainforests have been mowed down on behalf of animal agriculture (Oppenlander 22). New lands are plowed in Latin American countries largely for feed crops, "notably soybeans and maize" (*Livestock's* 12). Soy and corn, for example, is planted where rainforests recently grew, and 80 percent of all soy is fed to farmed animals (Oppenlander 23). Those who accuse vegetarians and vegans of destroying forests miss a vital point: Soybeans are raised largely as a feed crop for farmed animals, implicating those who eat cheese and chicken, not those who eat tofu.

Visiting the Andes, it is impossible to ignore the vast swaths of logged land, now riddled with new roads (Castellanos, "Andean Bear Research" 25). In the Andes, deforestation rates between 2000 and 2008 were 0.63 percent ("Estimación" 1). With ever-increasing human populations, and our endless array of livelihoods—agriculture, mining, and oil extraction—less and less land remains for bears. Making matters worse, lands in this region are developed with limited or no oversight, leading to yet more deforestation and fragmentation. If this continues—and there is no indication that we are planning any change—Ecuador will lose half of its forests in just 75 years.

Isolated pockets of intact forest cannot maintain a wide-ranging, thinly dispersed species such as the Andean bear—isolation leads to inbreeding and disease. Consequently, protected areas are essential. In 2008, 19 percent of Ecuador's land was protected, including 11 national parks, 10 wildlife refuges, and 9 ecological reserves, but these protected lands include only a fraction of remaining Andean bear habitat, and are still vulnerable to poaching (Ministerio del Ambiente). For this reason, research conducted by the Andean Bear Foundation focuses on bear distribution and habitat use, with the hope of focusing conservation efforts in areas where there are more Andean bears.

Poaching

Poaching "is a serious threat" to Andean bear populations ("*Tremarctos*"). Ecuador's adult bears are gunned down at an estimated rate of 70–120 bears annually, and this figure does not include cubs who are killed along with their mothers (or taken to be sold as pets, removing them from wild populations) (*Status* 180).

Local Farmers

When maize and pastures replace bamboo and bromeliads, human-bear conflicts are inevitable. Poaching is well documented across Andean bear range and "usually occurs when bears frequent either cornfields or grazing pastures" (*Status* 165). Across the Andean bear's range, "agricultural activities are reducing suitable habitats and forcing bears to predate crops, such as corn, to survive" (*Status* 180). Making matters worse, maize is "not tended on a daily basis," and is increasingly planted "in distant forest plots, away from the dwelling and protection of the gardener" (*Status* 177). It is therefore not surprising that "maize gardens are frequently and severely predated by bears," creating economic hardship for poor farmers eking out a living on the edges forested lands (*Status* 177). As a result, many farmers have come to see the spectacled bear "as a pest," and they are likely to shoot bears on sight (*Status* 180).

Bears are also "blamed for any cow killed or lost. Soon after a carcass is found, small hunting groups (2–3 people) are organized to go after any bears present. There are few accounts of people actually seeing a bear taking a cow" (*Status* 165). Despite this lack of concrete evidence, and despite this bear's natural diet of greens, fruits, and carrion, bears continue to be blamed for killing any cattle found dead—and are immediately targeted for execution. It is disconcerting that, in the Cosanga region (northeast Ecuador), fifty-five "bear attacks" on cattle were reported between 2000 and 2002. (Three blameless bears were killed before the targeted bear was shot.) Similarly, the Northeastern Chaco region of Ecuador reported 17 cattle deaths that they blamed on bears in 2007, and in Ecuador's northern Andes, 87 have been blamed since November 2009. (At least two innocent bears were killed in the northern Andes.) Although complaints usually revolve around cattle, bears have also been accused of killing sheep, horses, and donkeys (Castellanos, Laguna, and Clifford 17). It is likely that bears—opportunistic scavengers who love carrion—are attracted to and feed on carcasses, and are thereby accused of killing cattle who are long dead. Additionally, bears are likely to return to finish off a carcass, giving farmers the impression that they have returned to predate cattle.

Part of ABF's mission is to work with local communities in order to help provide long term solutions to human-bear conflicts—real or imagined—as well as to explain the ecological importance of the Andean bear, and the ineffectiveness of killing bears to protect investments. ABF also suggests alternative solutions, most notably a change in where herds are fed and where crops are planted, and a change in how both are managed (Castellanos, Laguna, and Clifford 17). For example, trained dogs can protect herds and crops, or ranchers might switch to Brahman cattle—a breed on which no attacks have been reported (Castellanos, Laguna, and Clifford 18). Identifying and protecting the Andean bear's primary sources of sustenance—local plants—is a critical long-term solution, but requires more data to know what these food are, as well as documentation demonstrating a correlation between scarcity of wild forage and reported crop raids (Castellanos, Laguna, and Clifford 17). Once this information is collected, reforestation plans can strive to enhance fruiting trees and plants favored by bears.

While these suggestions, if implemented, are likely to help minimize human-bear conflicts, underlying causes remain—ongoing human expansion into and destruction of bear habitat. For those of us living in Europe and North America, we can help Andean bears (and ourselves) by choosing a plant based diet, which leaves forests where they belong instead of bringing cattle and soy to the area, and protecting South and Central America's wildlife habitat.

Illegal Trade in Bears and Bear Parts

Logging and subsequent settlements bring roads into habitat that was previously virtually impenetrable, providing access for poachers. Poachers hunt bears for various reasons, including profit: They sell bear body parts and/or cubs. "Although hunting is prohibited, bear parts are openly sold in rural markets" at least in some areas of Ecuador (*Status* 180). Some locals buy bear parts because they believe that these body parts have healing properties: "Bear fat is used to heal bruises and broken bones. The meat and baculi are used to enhance health and vigor" (*Status* 180). Other bear parts, such as skulls, claws, and hides are sometimes also sold in local markets (*Status* 180).

Due to a growing international market for bear gallbladders (used for traditional Chinese medicines), Andean bear body parts are also sold abroad, posing a major threat to bears (*Status* 173). In Ecuador, "farmers living adjacent to Cotacachi–Cayapas and Cayambe–Coca reported that Asian merchants offered economic rewards for bear gallbladders. . . . In December 1992, a Korean offered farmers US $150 (five times the minimum monthly salary) for a bear gallbladder and US $10–15 for each paw" (*Status* 190). With so much money at stake, it is increasingly difficult to protect South American bears.

The Andean Bear Foundation

The Andean Bear Foundation (ABF), founded in 2005 by Ecuadorian biologist Armando Castellanos, has brought international attention to Andean bears. ABF's purpose is three-fold:

. research (with intent to learn more about this relatively unknown species),
. rehabilitate and release captive bears, and
. raise local and international awareness regarding the ecological importance and plight of Andean bears through education and outreach (Castellanos, *Andean*).

Research

ABF sends volunteers out in the field with guides to collect data. Research at ABF focuses on bear activity patterns and home ranges (via radio and satellite telemetry). Between 2001 and 2006, researchers and international volunteers captured, radio collared, and released twelve Andean bears (six females and six males) (Castellanos, "Andean Bear Project" 36). Like Alberto and the two volunteers traipsing through the Andes with backpacks and tracking equipment in search of Enrico, many volunteers help to record information from collared bears collected at specific sites at regular intervals.

Preliminary results suggest an average home range of 150 km^2 (58 sq.m.) for males and 34 km^2 (13 sq.m.) for females (Castellanos, "Andean Bear Project" 36). Females have well-defined, stable, but overlapping home ranges, often with multiple females in a particular valley, while males travel long distances to maximize mating potential. Tracking studies indicate that the highest levels of activity are early mornings and late evenings (Castellanos, "Andean Bear Project" 36). ABF keeps a close eye on any change in bear behavior that seems related to human encroachment, focusing research efforts on areas with high incidences of human-bear conflicts.

Rehabilitation and Release

Among volunteers, rehabilitation and release are likely the most popular ABF task. Those lucky enough to work in rehabilitation and release have the opportunity to work directly with Andean bears.

Bubu was the sixteenth bear to be rehabilitated and released by ABF. Orphaned as a cub, he was rescued and sent to a zoo in Ecuador until funds could be raised for rehabilitation and release. Once transferred to ABF, he was placed in a remote sanctuary in Cotopaxi National Park, 120 km (75 miles) outside Quito, where human contact would be minimal. Special permission was required to travel through the park gate and onward, where roads disappeared amid vast grasslands, and the snowy volcano, Cotopaxi, loomed above. White painted stones, the only road markers, led the way to Yanahurco, a 26,000 hectare (approx. 60,000 acre) private hacienda (estate), where Bubu would be rehabilitated for release.

Keepers offered enrichment activities to teach Bubu how to survive on bamboo (*Suro*), bromeliads, forest berries, and worms. To a trained eye, it was clear that Bubu would thrive in the wild. He responded readily, keeping the ABF team on their toes in search of new, creative ways to imitate foraging in the wild in order to challenge this smart bear. Keepers hung and buried food around his enclosure, and hauled in full-sized bromeliads in the hope of teaching Bubu the work necessary to extract the plant's soft center. They also fed Bubu extra—he needed to gain weight before release, providing a cushion against any rough aspects of the transition from captivity to wildlands. Finally, the ABF rehabilitation and release team began to locate some method by which to transport Bubu to the far reaches of Llanganates National Park for release. This final objective proved the hardest.

ABF worked for almost a year to secure transport for Bubu. Fueled by petitions from the international community, ABF ultimately engaged the Army of Ecuador to transport Bubu—a helicopter would be perfect. Due to unpredictable weather, the necessity of a remote release, and Bubu's size, only a few helicopters could handle the mission. When transport was finally secured, and weather was favorable, a helicopter carried Bubu to Llanganates National Park, one of only a few parks in Ecuador where he would have limited human contact. While heartbreaking to watch this vibrant bear disappear into the forests of Llanganates, every bear counts. Releasing Bubu back into his native habitat was the ultimate success for all who hope to save South America's Andean bears, for all who work with ABF—and for Bubu.

Education and Outreach

ABF recruits volunteer artists to paint murals in rural communities, and sends staff into the field to work with villagers, seeking to inform locals and mitigate human-bear conflicts. When a village in Northern Ecuador blamed bears for 25 cattle deaths in the course of a single year, ABF sprang into action.

Tensions were high when ABF staff arrived on the scene, but ABF ran a three part educational series for five communities in the area, including classes catering to the needs of youth and classes designed for adults. Classes high-lighted likely reasons for human-bear conflicts, and possible solutions. ABF suggested that villagers rethink pasture locations—especially new pastures. For example, vulnerability to bear attacks could be reduced by planning fewer (and/or eliminating) isolated, unmonitored fields, and by choosing not to place crops and farmed animals along forest borders. Proximity of forests and crops or grazing lands is a common denominator for most human-bear con-flicts—most incidences are reported in fragmented bear habitat close to diminished forests. Additionally, farmers were encouraged to synchronize calving season with fruiting season to ensure an abundance of natural food sources for bears during a time when calves are most vulnerable. ABF also stressed the importance of immediately eliminating cattle carcasses in order to avoid attracting these opportunistic, carrion-loving scavengers (Castellanos, Laguna, and Clifford 17). Finally, by comparing the bear's diminished habitat with drought, ABF helped locals to empathize with Andean bears.

While on the job, volunteers also trek throughout remote regions of Ecuador on a daily basis, looking for bear signs and signals, activating and monitoring bear traps (set to catch and collar bears for research). Villagers meet volun-teers on busses, or at the local market, and are amazed to learn that people travel from all over the world to work with and for Andean bears—a bear that lives around their villages but can be found on no other continent. Wherever they go, volunteers spread the message of ABF. Such encounters with foreign-ers tend to leave locals with a sense of national pride and heightened ecologi-cal interest. And of course ABF sends foreigners home with a much richer understanding of bears, and a strong commitment to their protection and preservation.

Tracking Enrico

Far from human civilization, three weary people climb from thick forests onto the windy *paramo*; one pauses to raise a telemetry antenna into the wind, slowly turning 360 degrees to scan for a signal. Each person tries to catch their breath while simultaneously struggling to hold silence, listening for a response from distant valleys. They gaze out over miles of rough grasses stretching down into forests—perfect bear habitat. Surely Enrico is out there somewhere?

Those working for ABF come to appreciate these shy, elusive forest residents, agile in the high forest canopy and able to find food even in desert regions. No price tag can be set on this fast diminishing species. Andean bears, ancient short-nosed bears—the last of their kind. Yet how can bears coexist with humans if we do not curb our population growth, and our tendency to sprawl into surrounding wilderness? How can bears compete with modern guns and rich profits, whether profits from bear body parts or agriculture? If we care about the Andean bear, we must reduce our environmental footprint. Whether we live in Zurich or Quito, our lifestyle (especially what we choose to eat) affects wilderness and wildlife.

Where has Enrico gone? The three weary humans disappear into the stillness and quiet of the *paramo* as they listen hopefully for a response from Enrico in the remote river canyons below, that run outward in all directions. They can feel that deep fear, quiet inside them—fear that Enrico is gone and will never send a signal again. Will never climb trees or wade in a cool pool on a hot summer day, will never eat sweet fruits or have offspring. In the next moment the silence is broken. The monitor returns to life: Beep-Beep-Beep! The three tired travelers continue to hold their breath and listen—the only motion is the broad smiles that inadvertently spread between their rosy-red cheeks. Beep-Beep-Beep!

Somewhere in the distance, on the rugged slopes of the Andes, Enrico is quietly foraging through what remains of his habitat. ABF intends to do all that they can (and hopes you will join them) to ensure that Enrico—and his offspring—can always forage and foster cubs in remote, forested canyons, far from human homes, cattle, and guns.

References

Castellanos, Armando. *Andean Bear Conservation Project.* 2007. Accessed Nov 25, 2012. <www.andeanbear.org>

———. "Andean Bear Home Ranges in the Intag Region, Ecuador." *Ursus* (March 23, 2011): 65–73.

———. "Andean Bear Projet, Ecuador." *Final Proceedings, Zoos and Aquariums Committing to Conservation* (Conference held January 26–31, 2007, in Houston): 36.

———. "Andean Bear Research Project In The Intag Region, Ecuador." *International Bear News, Quarterly Newsletter of the International Association for Bear Research and Management (IBA) and the IUCN/SSC Bear Specialist Group* (May, 2004): 25–26.

———. *Guía para la Rehabilitación, Liberación y Seguimiento de Osos Andinos (Guide to the Rehabilitation, Liberation and Tracking of Andean Bears).* Quito, Ecuador: Imprenta Anyma, 2010.

———. "Preliminary Results of the Three-Year Telemetry Study of Andean Bear in the Intag Region, Ecuador." *Abstracts Program Information, 16th International Conference on Bear Research and Management* (Conference held Sept 27-Oct 1, 2005, in Riva del Garda, Trentino, Italy): 60.

Castellanos, Armando, Andres Laguna, and Sarah Clifford. "Suggestions for Mitigating Cattle Depredation and Resulting Human-Bear Conflicts in Ecuador." *International Bear News, Quarterly Newsletter of the International Association for Bear Research and Management (IBA) and the IUCN/SSC Bear Specialist Group* (August, 2011): 16–18.

Christopher Servhee, Stephen Herrero, Bernard Peyton. *Status Survey and Conservation Action Plan: Bears.* Ed. Christopher Servheen, and Stephen Herrero, and Bernard Peyton. IUCN/SSC Bear Specialist Group. IUCN, 1994.

"Dirección Nacional Forestral. Estimación de la Tasa de Deforestación del Ecuador Continental." *Sistema de Información Marino Costera del Ecuador* (Feb 01, 2001): 1–10. Accessed Nov 25, 2012 <http://simce.ambiente.gob.ec/documentos/estimacion-tasa-deforestacion-ecuador-continental>.

Goldstein, I., Velez-Liendo, X., Paisley, S., and Garshelis, D.L. (IUCN SSC Bear Specialist Group) 2008. *Tremarctos ornatus.* The IUCN Red List of Threatened Species. Version 2015.2. <www.iucnredlist.org>. Accessed June 25. 2012. http://www.iucnredlist.org/details/22066/0.

Henning Steinfeld, Pierre Gerber, Tom Wassenaar, Vincent Castel, Mauricio Rosales, and Cees de Haan. *Livestock's Long Shadow: Environmental Issues and Options.* Food and Agriculture Organization of the United Nations. Rome: Food and Agriculture Organization, 2006. http://www.fao.org/docrep/010/a0701e/a0701e00.HTM.

Ministerio del Ambiente. "Àreas Protegidas." *República del Ecuador. Ministerio del Ambiente.* Accessed Nov. 25, 2012. <*http://web.ambiente.gob.ec/?q=node/59*>

Oppenlander, Richard A. *Comfortably Unaware: Global Depletion and Food Responsibility ... What You Choose to Eat is Killing our Planet.* Minneapolis: Langdon Street, 2011.

"*Tremarctos ornatus* Andean Bear." IUCN Red List of Threatened Species. Accessed Nov 22, 2012. http://liveassets.iucn.getunik.net/downloads/andean_bear.pdf.

PART III

Policy

∴

CHAPTER 14

Brown Bears, Salmon, People: Traveling Upstream to a Sustainable Future

Chris Darimont, Kyle Artelle, Heather Bryan, Chris Genovali,
Misty MacDuffee, Paul Paquet

On a crisp day in early May, a coastal brown bear and her tiny cub emerge from their den and slip-slide down a winter's worth of snow. Momma bear is focused on filling her belly with emerging vegetation. Calories from her last meal—a feast of spawning salmon consumed many months ago—have been spent keeping her and her precious daughter alive through the winter. Our team, a handful of conservationists, is at work just a few hundred feet below, inching up-slope, unaware of the furry pair above. Because it is early in the day, the wind rushes down the mountain, concealing our human smells and noisy grunts from the hungry and wary momma. Fortunately, we work hard for every foot of elevation on the steep gradient, allowing us time to scan the slope ahead and avoid a surprise encounter.

Beneath our feet, the earliest spring plants are already bursting from the ground: Cow parsnip, wild carrot, and other delicious bear foods push upwards from the avalanche shoot in search of every photon the sun has to offer. As we near the top of the morning's climb, we look forward to our own tasty snacks, stowed tightly in our backpacks. After snacks, the real work begins: We are here to install a non-invasive hair-snagging station, designed to snag hair from passing bears for analysis, which allows us to assess bear health. We have found an ideal spot for setting up our station: a bowl between two avalanche shoots that holds plenty of bear treats along a corridor linking the valley bottom to the high country.

Chewing on granola bars, we note incontrovertible evidence that this is indeed bear country. About fifty meters (150 feet) above us, momma puts on the brakes and raises her nose for a sniff. She is now aware of our presence. The cub, blissfully oblivious, skids into her rear end, almost knocking her down the steep grade towards our team. Fortunately, her powerful shoulders and robust claws prevent what would have surely been the mishap of the season. Oddly, having regained her balance, mamma bear sits with her cub to watch us work. Slower on the uptake, we are now also keenly aware of the two bears. We labor frantically to complete our task and get out of their way. They have much to accomplish, too.

© KONINKLIJKE BRILL NV, LEIDEN, 2015 | DOI 10.1163/9789004293090_016

Raincoast and the Great Bear Rainforest

Sometimes strokes of insight come from unexpected places. Canned salmon producers ran a lighthearted television advertisement extolling the lengths to which they go to provide the best possible product. Though unintentional, the commercial is a striking metaphor for human effects on fish populations, coastal ecosystems, and wildlife. The advertisement, filmed in Alaska, has become a YouTube©sensation.

The advertisement opens with a wide-angle shot of a pristine coastal river meandering through moss-laden old growth forests. While a narrator describes the ancient instincts that drive salmon on their relentless journey to natal spawning grounds, the camera shows bustling flashes of salmon jumping over fast-flowing rapids. Suddenly, a powerful brown bear claw enters the scene as the narrator describes how others, also driven by primal instincts, are awaiting the salmon's return. The camera zooms out and the mighty bear—iconic symbol of the northern Pacific coast—stands above the rapids eyeing the jumping salmon, mouth wide with hungry anticipation. In the next instant, a large salmon jumps straight towards the bear's open maw, while an angler in fluorescent hip waders dashes forward to intercept the fish as if it were a football. The bear looks shocked, and watches in dismay as the angler proudly holds his fine catch high above his head, hooting and hollering victoriously.

This commercial makes a memorable impression, as intended. But the unintended message is more poignant: The global human quest for fish snatches salmon from the mouths of bears. While some people seem to be slowly realizing that most contemporary fisheries management (or mismanagement) is morbidly unsustainable, there is still little thought as to how our fish intake affects other animals, who *must* depend on fish for survival and reproduction. Few seem to understand that the effects of declining fish extend beyond human interests—even beyond the interest of fish themselves.

We, the six authors of this chapter, are all affiliated with Raincoast Conservation Foundation ("Raincoast"), an NGO striving to protect Canada's Great Bear Rainforest. Ultimately, we work for bears. While numbers cannot do justice to the raw beauty and biological wonder of this region, it supports more than 3000 distinct spawning populations of salmon—5 species specifically returning to one of roughly 1000 streams that flow through vast and largely unspoiled watersheds in the Great Bear Rainforest. These watersheds also support the southern stronghold of North America's remaining coastal brown bears, a population that once stretched all the way from Alaska to northern Mexico. Hunters, ranchers, loggers, land developers, and the loss of healthy salmon populations—a lack of responsible management of fish and their spawning habitat—wiped out brown bears in more than half of their former North American range.

This chapter examines how British Columbia's management of wild Pacific salmon—managed solely for human benefit—is unsustainable. Current management jeopardizes fish populations, other wildlife populations, human livelihoods, and ecosystems in general that depend on spawning salmon for their sustenance for millennia.

Human Mis-management: Nets and Hooks versus Claws and Teeth

The annual return of spawning salmon to the coast of British Columbia (BC) is one of the true wonders of the natural world. From the moment they hatch until their final watery breath, salmon face a gauntlet of predators in frigid freshwater streams and the rough open-ocean. Salmon who escape predation hurl their exhausted bodies upstream against rocks and rapids in a final act of perseverance and endurance, en route to their natal spawning grounds, where they mate and promptly die.

The lifecycle of Pacific salmon defines the Northwest coast of North America. Ecologically, the migration of salmon (and the mass transport of their marine nutrients and energy into terrestrial ecosystems) parallels wildebeest migrations of the African Serengeti. Like their ungulate counterparts, spawning salmon provide wildlife with an exceptionally important seasonal food (*review in* Schindler *et al.* 31). Salmon are a crucial element in many ecosystems along the northwest coast of North America, as they are in many ecosystems throughout the world where they still run in strong numbers. They have nourished European settlers and their descendants—countless canneries and settlements were founded on fisheries that, until recently, seemed inexhaustible. Salmon nourished coastal First Nations nutritionally and culturally for millennia—and continue to do so. Bears, fishers, and killer whales are also dependent on Pacific salmon for sustenance. Even plant life is nurtured and sustained by salmon as fish nutrients pass through the bodies of bears and other wildlife (like wolves and birds) on their way to the forest floor.

Salmon consumption among bears correlates positively with bear size, reproductive rate, and population densities (Hilderbrand *et al.* 132). Although brown bears are omnivorous, with some populations persisting largely on vegetation-based diets, coastal bears (who are particularly large) have evolved in the presence of abundant salmon, and cannot easily replace this high quality, high calorie source of sustenance. In particular, it is difficult for larger males to meet metabolic demands when salmon are in short supply (Robbins *et al.* 161). Reduced salmon availability is likely to lead to poor physical condition, and subsequently, lower rates of reproduction. Poor survival rates are just as likely if hungry bears follow their noses to human food sources. A local study tracked brown bear numbers in the Rivers Inlet area of coastal BC for several years following a collapse in once world-famous local sockeye runs. This study appears to have detected significant bear population declines during the fisheries collapse (Boulanger 1267). Although unstudied, we predict that correlations between the decline of salmon and the decline of bears are widespread. Where bears remain, they likely exist only in relatively low densities in areas of precipitous declines in fish populations. For example only 10% of the sockeye salmon who once spawned in the southern portion of Western North America remain (Gresh *et al.* 15). Although coastal BC has fared better than other areas, many local salmon runs are chronically depressed. Less than 4% of salmon streams monitored in BC since 1950 have consistently met their target spawning numbers, with particularly precipitous declines in the last ten years (Price *et al.* 2712).

Declines in fish populations are often caused by shortsighted management strategies centered on human wants. Although salmon are an inherently hardy species, their resiliency has been undermined by decades of management focused on maximizing economic yields rather than focusing on ecological health. A major flaw in salmon fisheries management, for example, is that the "wealth" of fish has been increasingly usurped by humans. Fishing technology has made us exceptionally successful predators: Humans now kill an astonishing 50–80 percent of salmon before they spawn (Quinn 319). Predation rates of 50–80 percent are unheard of among non-human predators. Across the animal kingdom, and certainly among vertebrates, nonhuman predators rarely take more than 15 percent of any given population in any one year (Darimont & Reimchen *unpublished data*). A 50–80 percent extraction rate is unheard of in other species precisely because it is unsustainable. We are "super predators"— our predation has a stronger ecological influence than that of any other predator (Darimont *et al.*, "Human" 953). We are in fact taking more than the "lion's share." Recent declines in salmon populations (and prices—pink salmon was worth only 40 cents per pound in 2010) epitomize the folly of such a shortsighted approach to fisheries management. While fish die from diseases, natural predation, accidents, and when spawning habitat is destroyed, over-exploitation by industrial fisheries causes declines in fish population world-wide. Over-exploitation harms fisheries, and also harms wildlife.

Modern, technologically advanced commercial fishing fleets compete with wildlife who have relied on salmon for millennia. Even with salmon runs at record low levels, industrial fisheries engage in what ecologists call "exploitative competition," capturing salmon en route to freshwater streams, preventing spawning, and stealing fish from the mouths of waiting wildlife, bears included. In many cases, salmon population statistics predict that yet more declines are on the way, and that we therefore face a salmon shortage that will deepen if we fail to change our fish management policies quickly and decisively.

Individual, Personal Choice: What's for Lunch?

Dispassionate scientific statements about "salmon population declines" conceal the suffering of individuals who are dependent on healthy ecosystems for survival. Depriving wildlife of food can cause drawn-out suffering that is too often ignored by conservationists, wildlife scientists—even animal activists (Darimont et al., "Faecal" 73; Paquet and Darimont, 177).

When we contemplate salmon declines, we should consider not only salmon populations, but also salmon as individuals, and other wild individuals who depend on salmon for sustenance. Salmon suffer and die prematurely when we eat fish. This is an inescapable fact. As a result, a comprehensive examination of this issue requires that we examine our personal consumer choices. Furthermore, when caught industrially, fish are almost always left to suffocate on the decks of large fishing vessels, in great silvery heaps. Many birds and other animals—including endangered animals—are also drowned by fishing lures and nets. And bear are placed at risk when their richest source of food is eaten by ever-growing human populations. Hunger is not the only ill effect of our fish consumption: Malnourished sows are much more likely to lose off-spring. And when starving bears seek alternative foods in or near human communities, there is increased risk of human-bear conflicts that too often result in death—mostly for bears, but also occasionally for humans (e.g. Knight et al. 10; Gunther et al. 121). Following the failure of sockeye salmon runs in Oweekeno (Rivers Inlet, BC), at least ten apparently starving brown bears were killed by Conservation Officers and village residents in just one month in 1999.

A low salmon harvest for commercial fisheries is likely to cause financial hardship for a comparatively small group of human beings, but for wildlife who depend on salmon for their survival and reproduction, fish shortages could mean prolonged physical distress, pain, and even premature death for an entire population in a given area. We must quickly face the breadth and severity of this "fisheries" crisis. Science alone, however, is not enough to tackle this complex issue; such efforts must be coupled with policy intervention, outreach, and individual direct action—we must rethink our relationship with salmon.

Raincoast: Science, Policy, and Outreach

For 15 years, the Raincoast Conservation Foundation ("Raincoast") has been protecting wildlife (including bears and salmon) and their homes in the remarkably rich marine and terrestrial ecosystems of coastal British Columbia. We were instrumental in bestowing to this place its popular moniker—the Great Bear Rainforest, a name that speaks more eloquently of the nature of this ecological treasure than the previous designation—"Mid-coast timber supply area." "Great Bear Rainforest" conveys some of the beauty and magic of this unique, rare, and endangered temperate rainforest. Thanks in part to this fitting new title, the region is now receiving well-deserved global recognition, which is essential for this area's safekeeping. We are hopeful that new conservation-based plans will be implemented in the Great Bear Rainforest, guided by the increasing authority of First Nation stewards, who are in the process of reestablishing control over this region.

As conservationists, Raincoast's methods are somewhat unique. We employ rigorous, non-invasive, applied science, as well as ethics; we also engage with the public through education and outreach. Finally, we go out of our way to share the lessons we learn from working in one of the world's greatest ecological marvels, The Great Bear Rainforest, with both the public and the scientific community, and we make a point of describing how the lessons we have learned can help humanity to conserve ecosystems for countless beneficiaries—Pacific salmon, brown bears, cedar trees, avalanche lilies, as well as peoples and their economies—in perpetuity.

Raincoast blends the tenacity and acumen of seasoned campaigners with the rigor and authority of scholars, an approach we call "informed advocacy." Raincoast's applied conservation biology is also considerably enriched by local knowledge, including individuals from First Nation communities who have lived among bears and salmon in these ancient forests for millennia. Our approach couples the best available scientific evidence (including our own research, vetted by peers in academic journals) with informed, grassroots advocacy. Local team members bolster the knowledge and wisdom needed to guide science and advocacy, and also act as watchdogs and stewards for biological riches of this area. We strive for "pragmatic idealism": our actions are guided by absolute principles, but carried out through workable methods. We have learned that careful, deliberate steps towards well-defined goals bring the best results. In short, we advocate for bears, salmon, and ancient forests in academic journals, boardrooms, policy tables, and perhaps most importantly, in public discourse.

Science

Science is foundational to Raincoast, providing the "informed" part of our advocacy, complemented by the wisdom of local people. Research helps us to understand the unique ecological processes that connect BC's marine environment and coastal forests, and to monitor, predict, and prevent problems associated with declining salmon fisheries. We have developed a comprehensive research program that blends fieldwork with advanced laboratory techniques and computer-based mathematical modeling.

Fieldwork

How might we assess the effects of declining salmon on brown bears, who have a reputation for being naturally elusive and occasionally dangerous to humans? How can we study brown bears without further stressing these behemoths?

Amazingly, all the information we need to study brown bears is locked in a few tufts of hair. But how do we obtain hair samples from a bear? Should we lie in wait, scissors in hand, and then ambush a passing bruin to snatch and snip a tuft of fur? Or should we go with the more expensive, though decidedly safer method exemplified in TV documentaries: Capture bears in baited traps, tranquilize the great bruins with high-powered dart guns, *then* rush them with scissors?

True to our ethics, we chose a low-impact hair-snagging method. Working from dawn to dusk, we assemble and monitor about 75 hair-snagging stations each spring in our 5,000 km² (~1900 m²) study area. In a typical six-week season, Raincoast field crews set up and take down 2300 meters (~7500 ft) of barbed wire fencing, pound more than 600 fencing staples, pour more than 1100 liters (~240 gallons) of smelly bait, and are rewarded with ample but tiny milligrams of hair—totaling some 1000 samples.

Fine aromas are the key to success. Lured by the luscious fragrance, "eau de rotting fish" (a by-product of the fishing industry, typically used for fertilizer), bears travel to our baited stations from as far away as several kilometers (a couple of miles). The bait is encircled by a single strand of barbed wire that plucks—quickly, delicately, and bloodlessly—small tufts of hair from bears who step over or scoot under the wire for a whiff of fishy perfume. Despite the delicious scent, bears quickly realize that the anticipated food is nowhere to be found, and typically stay an average of just three minutes. The furry gold they leave behind provides a secret window into their lives.

We choose to employ this method because it is far less invasive than traditional approaches. Scientists generally capture, extract blood and muscle tissue samples, and attach radio transmission collars to bears before release. Recent analyses of information on captured and radio-collared bears has shown that collaring can seriously affect daily movements and body condition for months afterward (Cattet *et al.* 973). Based on this analysis, other similar studies, and our own gut feelings, we decided that the only ethical option was to create bear stations to snag hair. When multiple useful research methods exist, we have argued that the only ethical option is one that is non-invasive (Darimont *et al.*, "Faecal" 73). We place a high value on respecting the welfare of the individuals whom we study. Though these stations cause bears to wander in search of non-existent food, Raincoast's hair stations supply samples at a lower cost to bears than any other known method. Moreover, this non-invasive approach is more consistent with respectful relations between non-humans and humans that are foundational to Raincoast's First Nation partners.

Laboratory Work

At the end of each field season we use ecological sleuthing tools (likely to impress any fan of CSI) to translate our furry bounty into the stories of ursine lives. Extracted DNA reveals the species, sex, and identity of individual bears. This allows us to track bear population numbers over time, and to sound early warning bells if we detect population declines. Isotope analyses (a chemical tool that differentiates land-based and sea-based molecules) allows us to estimate how much salmon each bear has consumed. We are then able to examine the link between a salmon diet (or lack thereof) and overall population health. We also use hair samples to measure hormone levels. Hormones offer insight into stress levels and reproductive activity, which we suspect are also linked to salmon consumption.

Computer Models

Laboratory tests on miniscule hair samples tell us a great deal about the impact of salmon on the lives of these massive bears, but we can learn even more through data analysis and mathematical modeling. Some of this work is decidedly less sexy than traipsing through rainforests or high-tech lab work, but nonetheless offers critical insights into ecological problems.

With the help of modern computer technology, mathematical models allow us to calculate the influence of human fisheries on brown bear populations. Conceptually, we view the conflict between modern fisheries management and bear conservation as primarily a problem of allocation. Traditional single-species fisheries models, which manage each fish species separately, calculate an "optimum" number of salmon who "escape" human hooks and nets and return to spawn (termed "escapement"). Under this paradigm, managers achieve a "maximum sustainable yield" over the long run. In theory, this allows humans to control salmon breeding for the sole purpose of optimizing (*i.e.*

maximizing)—for humans and humans alone—annual fish catches. Despite being articulated through complex mathematical models, our goal is straightforward: Predict how bear population densities and fisheries (catch revenues) will likely respond to variations in salmon escapement. In other words, if human predators were to reduce (or increase) the amount of fish we catch each year, how would this affect bears?

Traditional mathematical models predict that when more salmon spawn ("over-escapement" in the jargon of fisheries management) fewer offspring are produced per spawning fish. Fisheries often cite this model in order to justify taking more than 50 percent of inbound salmon for human consumption. This sounds wonderful to fisheries managers, but how would it sound to bears? If they (and other fish predators) cast their vote, they would argue that there can *never* be "too many" spawning salmon.

Aware of this biased allocation of fish under the power of human fisheries management, Raincoast and our academic collaborators use computer models and data to evaluate how a range of increased "escapement" numbers (achieved through reduced human catch) would likely benefit bears. First we estimate the increase in salmon consumption among bear populations as escapement increases. Then we link this result to a known relationship between increased salmon consumption and increased bear density (Hilderbrand *et al.* 132). Thus, for each salmon system we can calculate expected bear densities over a range of salmon escapements. We are then able to estimate how reduced human fishing pressure could achieve a more equitable allocation of salmon between humans and bears (and by extension, other wildlife). Subsequently, we can calculate just how costly each scenario is likely to be for salmon fisheries.

In essence, this analysis permits us to assess tradeoffs between the needs of bears (and other wildlife) and human socio-economic interests. Practicing pragmatic idealism, we strive to maintain practical methods *and* ethics that take into account the needs and interests of nonhuman individuals. While aware of bear needs, we must also be mindful that our suggestions will be evaluated by managers of a multi-million dollar industry. As such, we must consider costs to fisheries. Ultimately, we hope to identify conservation targets for every salmon-run on BC's coast, targets that maximize benefits to wildlife and minimize costs to human fisheries.

Policy

Raincoast's Wild Salmon Program was founded on the premise that many coastal species—including bears—rely heavily on energy and nutrients from increasingly diminished salmon populations. To advance this policy perspective, Raincoast needed to secure a place in fisheries reform. We found an opportunity to climb onboard when Canada's Department of Fisheries and Oceans (DFO) put forward a landmark decision attempting to rectify decades of fisheries policies that focused only on economic interests. The DFO outlined a revolutionary *Wild Salmon Policy* requiring that ecosystems and wildlife, who are nourished by salmon (including bears), must be explicitly considered in salmon management policies. In short, salmon fisheries must allocate salmon *for ecosystems*. To ensure that these policy commitments were honored by on-the-ground salmon allocations, DFO created a multi-stakeholder "Integrated Harvest Planning Committee" (IHPC) as the chief advisory body to DFO with regard to the process of setting annual fishing plans. This body became a central forum for addressing salmon allocation issues.

We secured a place at the table, and as conservation representatives we soon discovered that the DFO and its IHPC committee lacked information as to *how much* escapement is necessary to support and maintain coastal ecosystems. Raincoast's computer modeling provides this information, indicating how policy and allocation can best be crafted to fit management objectives set forth in the *Wild Salmon Policy*.

Another Raincoast contribution to the *Wild Salmon Policy* has been to lobby for brown bears as ecosystem proxies in salmon-dependent ecosystems. In other words, bears are fitting indicators for the salmon needs of an entire ecosystem that supports salmon. As the last predators that salmon face on their multi-year migration route, brown bears live on salmon leftovers—salmon who have escaped every other predator earlier in their long migration route. Accordingly, sufficient salmon for bears—at the end of the salmon migration route— would likely indicate sufficient quantities for other salmon predators along the way. Brown bears are also appropriate indicators of ecosystem health where salmon are concerned because of their role as "coastal gardeners": Bears leave salmon remains scattered around the forest floor, providing nourishment to a web of life ranging from minute insects and grasses to scavenging mammals and large trees. Bears, with their sloppy eating, serve as one of the most important vectors in transferring salmon nutrients to marine-derived terrestrial ecosystems. Because of their "gardening" role, "sharing the wealth" of salmon with bears is a shortcut to sharing the wealth of salmon with an entire ecosystem.

Based in part on the notion of brown bears as ecosystem indicators, we recently made a bold proposal with regard to Canada's *Wild Salmon Policy*. Surprisingly, even in parks and other "protected" areas of coastal British Columbia, salmon themselves are not protected despite the fact that many of these areas were established specifically to protect salmon and salmon-dependent species (such as brown bears). As vital inhabitants of protected areas, we argue that salmon also deserve protection; moreover, without such protection the viability of these protected areas as a whole is jeopardized. From an ecological perspective, a protected area is not truly protected if key sources of nourishment (in this case salmon) are at risk—threatening the entire ecosystem.

To address this oversight, Raincoast proposed that some salmon runs in protected areas be managed *solely* for salmon and their recipients, like bears. In this model, bears (and other wildlife) would act as ecological proxies for the health of these particular forests and coastal ecosystems. Suspecting that this proposal would face strong opposition from fisheries, we carefully worked in the field, lab, and on the computer to outline how this management strategy would benefit bears, their habitat, and—as we outline below—humans (Darimont *et al.*, "Salmon," 379). Though we anticipated otherwise, responses to our proposal—even from government fisheries biologists—were surprisingly positive. This development provides great hope that fisheries management might embrace a policy paradigm that recognizes the non-consumptive value of salmon.

Raincoast is also working with the international Marine Stewardship Council (MSC) to "green certify" fisheries, offering salmon consumers more sustainable choices. Each salmon taken from an ecosystem for human consumption leaves one less salmon for wildlife. Green certification will provide more sustainable fishers with higher profit margins from a niche market. Toward this end, Raincoast (working with MSC, DFO, and the fisheries industry) has negotiated specific requirements for green certification of BC's commercial salmon fisheries. A "blue check mark" sustainability label is granted only to commercial fishers who meet 44 carefully outlined conditions (improvements). Increased fish allocation for wildlife, including bears, is central to green certification for fisheries.

Raincoast's Wild Salmon Program is a prime example of how our Raincoast research affects policy decisions in British Columbia, and has become essential to developing fisheries policies that protect bears (and ultimately, fisheries).

Outreach

Decades of collective experience have taught those who work for Raincoast that even the best science and fiercest policy interventions are not enough to ensure the protection of ecosystems. Public engagement and support is essential. From local British Columbian citizens to concerned individuals around the globe, we need many voices to join our cause if we are to succeed.

Raincoast works to reach as many people as possible, employing both tradi-tional and new forms of media. For example, Raincoast has been the focus of several television documentaries distributed internationally. We stood next to bears in National Geographic's *Last Stand of the Great Bear*, discovered wolf-salmon relationships for Discovery Channel's *Rainwolves*, and caught these elusive canines in the act of salmon fishing for Canadian Geographic's *Secrets of the Coast Wolf.* We have also received extensive international media cover-age, from the *Smithsonian Magazine, Canadian Geographic, New York Times,* the *Guardian*, the *Globe and Mail, Huffington Post,* as well as book productions and numerous other outreach publications.

We also share our knowledge with urban and rural communities through more localized outreach initiatives. For example, we dazzle viewers with com-pelling and informative slideshows that convey the mysteries of the Great Bear Rainforest. We expose the plight of coastal wildlife through advertisements on bus shelters and in magazines and newspapers. Finally, we reach the general public online through Raincoast Blog, Raincoast Facebook, Raincoast Twitter Pages, *Notes from the Field*, an e-mail journal devoted to sharing the progres-sion of Raincoast fieldwork, and short online videos highlighting the richness of our study area and the threats that face the Great Bear Rainforest.

Yet it is perhaps our programs for children that have the most impact. Our unique *Raincoast Kids* program develops scientific skills in young Canadians, offering the next generation the necessary tools to address the countless environmental challenges facing our coastal ecosystems. Key programs for children include *Discovery Week* at aboriginal community schools, and par-ticipation at a weeklong, locally-run camp for kids (in a remote valley in Heiltsuk Territory), where we offer programs on coastal rainforest and marine ecology. In the process, we also learn from children; in particular, we learn about their understanding of and relationship with salmon, bears, and the natural world in general.

Rethinking Relations: Brown Bears, Salmon, and Human Beings

This next generation could witness an exciting turning point in our relation-ship with the natural world along British Columbia's coast. Over-fishing damages not only fish species, but also (ironically) coastal fishing econo-mies worldwide. On the BC coast, conservation concerns have already prompted widespread commercial fishing closures. If salmon fisheries are to revive, we must develop radically new management policies. We must find other ways to earn revenue from salmon—we must shift to economies that value *living* salmon.

Several contemporary forces are conspiring to make this possible. For example, the Great Bear Rainforest has now received worldwide recognition for ecological diversity. Increasingly, First Nations are taking the lead in resource management, modeling far more cautious and respectful methods than the management methods that have dominated since Europeans arrived. Moreover, compared with the rest of the world, this vast area has a relatively unspoiled ecology, complete with large carnivores that have been driven from other areas of the world by humans. With the (albeit slow) implementation of DFO's *Wild Salmon Policy,* Canada's fisheries are shifting toward a recognition of the inherent value of fish—a value that lies well beyond profits from commercial exploitation. Canadian fisheries might even be on the brink of recognizing the importance of cross-boundary conservation, whereby decisions made at sea explicitly consider land ecosystems and fish-dependent wildlife, whereby the long-term sustainability of economies and cultures is ensured by protecting— rather than ravaging—local ecosystems. And doesn't this seem imminently sensible? The Great Bear Rainforest looks to be in a position to exemplify balance between the needs of humans and the needs of other living creatures and the environment.

While current threats to the Great Bear Rainforest, including those from climate change, trophy hunting, over-fishing, clear cut forestry, and oil exploration and transport may seem like a conservationist's nightmare, the opportunities presented by current shifts in policy and public opinion are in fact a conservationist's dream. Unlike many other conservation projects struggling to restore devastated ecosystems, in British Columbia we have the gift of intact species relationships that can still be preserved. If we act quickly (and thoughtfully), this region can remain a living library of functioning ecosystems, an inspiration to conservation efforts around the world.

As the sun sets on BC's excessive commercial salmon harvests, the rising popularity of ecotourism offers a promising and viable economic alternative. In the past 20 years, wildlife ecotourism in BC has more than quadrupled. This promising shift to a new coastal economy requires that we maintain healthy, functioning ecologies. Healthy salmon are inextricably linked to healthy bears— more salmon means more bears—and protecting both could protect economic opportunities in the form of eco-tourism (bear-viewing and other salmon-reliant activities) (*e.g.,* Clayton & Mendelsohn, 101).

Given the incredible potential of the burgeoning ecotourism industry (especially in light of decreased fisheries) Raincoast advocates for understanding that salmon are worth more alive than dead. Raincoast has shown that this shift of vision is beneficial not only in principle, but also in practice. In 2005, in an effort to save bears from the barrels of trophy hunters (sadly, BC laws still allow hunters to kill bears for sport), Raincoast bought the *exclusive* right to hunt "big game" in an area of coastal BC three times the size of Yellowstone National Park (~13,500 sq. m.). But instead of guiding hunters who shoot bears with guns, we guide tourists who shoot them with cameras. In one fell swoop, we replaced an economic venture that generated income by killing to one that generates income by protecting and preserving individuals and ecosystems. As a result, watersheds in this protected territory have again come alive with bears who delight ecotourists and support ecosystems.

Switching from a fisheries-dominated economy to an ecotourism economy makes sense, and the benefits are far more widespread and fundamental than mere economics: Commercial fisheries derive wealth by *extracting* and *depleting* the coast's natural wealth; ecotourism derives wealth by *protecting* and *preserving* the coast's natural wealth. This transition is possible without jeopardizing the sacred cultural association between local First Nations and salmon.

Conclusion

Perhaps brown bears can set an example for our own species. Brown bears receive their share of salmon only after all other predators have had their fill. They share and re-distribute the remaining wealth back into the ecosystem. Then they fulfill their roles as gardeners of coastal forests, leaving behind salmon remains that fertilize forests, which in a most elegant measure of reciprocity, fuels the food web in the streams on which juvenile salmon depend.

We need to learn to share the wealth of the earth with other living beings, thus protecting wildlife, forests, and peoples both ancient and new.

As we finish setting up our hair-snagging station, we look for the momma brown bear and her cub. They have wandered off to forage for delectable skunk cabbage shoots springing from snow-scrubbed subalpine meadows. Our minds and hearts follow the duo, but our feet carry us down the steep valley to our waiting boat. As we walk, we share our hopes—that these two beautiful bears will feast on salmon throughout their lives, and that their offspring will do the same. The thought of anything less makes our steps hasten; there is much work to be done if we are to secure their inheritance.

FIGURE 14.1   *Brown Bear*

References

Boulanger, John *et al.* "Monitoring of Grizzly Bear Population Trend and Demography Using DNA Mark-Recapture Methods in the Owikeno Lake area of British Columbia." *Canadian Journal of Zoology* 82 (2004): 1267–1277.

Cattet, Marc *et al.* "An Evaluation of Long-Term Capture Effects in Ursids: Implications for Wildlife Welfare and Research." *Journal of Mammalogy* 89 (2008): 973–990.

Clayton, Chris and Richard Mendelsohn. "The Value of Watchable Wildlife: a Case Study of McNeil River." *Journal of Environmental Management* 39 (1993): 101–106.

Darimont, Chris *et al.* "Human Predators Outpace Other Agents of Trait Change in the Wild." *Proceedings of the National Academy of SciencesUSA* 106 (2009): 952–954.

Darimont, Chris *et al.* "Salmon for Terrestrial Protected Areas." *Conservation Letters* 3 (2010): 379–389.

Darimont, Chris *et al.* "Faecal-Centric Approaches to Wildlife Ecology and Conservation; Methods, data and Ethics." *Wildlife Biology in Practice* 4 (2008): 73–87.

Gresh, Ted *et al.* "An Estimation of Historic and Current Levels of Salmon Production in the Northeast Pacific Ecosystem: Evidence of a Nutrient Deficit in the Freshwater Systems of the Pacific Northwest." *Fisheries* 25 (2000): 15–21.

Gunther, Kerry *et al.* "Grizzly Bear-Human Conflicts in the Greater Yellowstone Ecosystem, 1992–2000." *Ursus* 15 (2004): 10–22.

Hilderbrand, Grant *et al.* "The Importance of Meat, Particularly Salmon, to Body Size, Population Productivity, and Conservation of North American Brown Bears." *Canadian Journal of Zoology* 77 (1999): 132–138.

Knight, Richard *et al.* "Mortality Patterns and Population Sinks for Yellowstone Grizzly Bears, 1973–1985." *Wildlife Society Bulletin* 16 (1988): 121–125.

Paquet, Paul and Chris Darimont. "Wildlife Conservation and Animal Welfare: Two Sides of the Same Coin?" Animal Welfare 19 (2010): 177–190.

Price, Michael *et al.* "Ghost Runs: Management and Status Assessment of Pacific salmon (*Oncorhynchus* spp.) Returning to British Columbia's Central and North Coasts." *Canadian Journal of Fisheries and Aquatic Sciences* 65(2008): 2712–2718.

Quinn, Thomas. *The Behaviour and Ecology of Pacific Salmon and Trout.* Seattle: University of Washington Press, 2005.

Robbins, Charles *et al.* "Nutritional Ecology of Ursids: A Review of Newer Methods and Management Implications." *Ursus* 15 (2004): 161–171.

Schindler, Daniel *et al.* "Pacific Salmon and the Ecology of Coastal Ecosystems." Frontiers in Ecology and the Environment 1 (2003): 31–37.

CHAPTER 15

Cleaning up a Community for Black Bears

Mick Webb

Vancouver, in the province of British Columbia, Canada, is a beautiful city. Young and proud; she lies gracefully draped around the welcoming shores of English Bay. Caressed by balmy, Pacific breezes plucking at green, white-capped waters, her charm is further softened by the sprawling wooded acres of Stanley Park. A natural treasure which, like a verdant velvet purse, casually spills the diamonds of the downtown's crystal towers to lay sparkling in the sunlight.

Across the bustling harbour are Vancouver's northern guardians, the North Shore and the Coast Mountains, and for many, these are the real jewels in Vancouver's crown. Rugged, forested slopes provide a natural playground for hikers, mountain-bikers, skiers, and dog-walkers. Their cool, emerald depths, where even the shadows speak in whispers, provide escape from busy, stressful lives.

This mountainous paradise of peace, with an abundance of natural food, fresh, tumbling streams, and endless terrain to wander, is perfect American black bear country. And yet we seldom see this solitary, reclusive animal in these beautiful surroundings. Surprisingly, black bears are more commonly spotted on streets, and in gardens, where they venture in search of readily available calorie-rich food that humans have tossed in the garbage.

The Problem of Local Development

Old-timers of North Shore neighbourhoods accepted these visitors as part of the natural order of things, but over the years, as the human population grew— now approximately 170,000—a new breed of citizen arrived, and attitudes changed. The North Shore, with its natural bounty of unspoiled, scenic beauty, attracted middle-to-upper-income newcomers. Professional people in many cases, who related better to a world of finance, science, and power than they did to the natural forests that abutted their homes—homes that crept inexorably deeper and deeper into the bears' hinterland, as more and more subdivisions were built to house these new, affluent invaders.

Predictably, as is the way with human expansion, we caused problems as we sprawled across the land. The bears, constantly seeking food, continued to forage. However, with our rapidly increasing population, and subsequent expansion of garbage, bears overcame their innate wariness of humans, seeking readily available treasure troves in human communities. Locals noted more and more bears foraging along suburban streets, raiding fruit trees and bird-feeders. Police and the provincial Conservation Officers were constantly responding to fearful reports of bear sightings, and consistent with the new population's attitudes, offending bears were shot.

Inevitably, and fortunately (as it proved to be), the local media reported these deaths, often complete with photos of the dead bear. Hungering for a dramatic story, television news often covered entire pursuits, up to and including the actual shooting of the unfortunate scavenger. This wanton slaughter repulsed the public, and an angry flood of letters questioned these killings and demanded an explanation for such harsh measures. Public outrage reached a peak in 1999 when a total of 39 bears were shot on the North Shore. In some cases, entire neighbourhoods refused to inform relevant authorities of bear sightings, fearing bears would be pursued and slaughtered.

Community Conscience Awakened

About this time, a small group of environmentally-aware citizens banded together and formed what became the North Shore Black Bear Network (The Network). The Network was modelled after a similar organization in the popular resort community of Whistler, approximately two hours away, and a feeling of mutual cooperation quickly formed between our two groups. The basic intent of this fledgling organization was to stop the killing of local bears, and develop strategies by which bears and humans might successfully co-exist. At that time, I signed on as a volunteer, and the group flourished as more and more people joined. An invitation was extended to the Conservation Officers Service (COS)—those who had the onerous task of killing the bears—to participate in bringing about change. With their public image bruised and bloodied, they were ready to become part of some possible solution, rather than further angering the public.

The growing Network was soon able to implement a public education program. We created a Bear Line where residents could call to report bear sightings and concerns. Bear information pamphlets were included with property tax statements, and a small tax was levied against the garbage pick-up service to help finance the changes we hoped to bring about. Teams of volunteers canvassed neighbourhoods, distributing informational pamphlets that explained the lure of human garbage, and the need to securely contain such attractants against bears. Volunteers also answered questions, and whether or not they liked it, received responses ranging from genuine interest to total indifference, from verbal abuse to reports of problematic neighbours.

A surprising footnote was the many tales told—often quite proudly—of local bears and their antics. We heard how bears predicted garbage collection days, casually strolling the streets just before collection, tossing garbage bins aside in search of the choicest morsels. We heard about bears using swimming pools as impromptu lakes to cool off in the hot summer sun. And, of course, there were stories of bears—especially young bears—who enjoyed backyard play sets, probably as much as their human counterparts.

A Community Divided

We also heard tales of broken fences and damaged garden sheds. The community was now sharply divided on the issue of local bears. Some residents regarded the habitually visiting bears with affection, and often gave them names, referring to them in that exaggerated, tolerant tone generally reserved for a difficult family member. While many were supportive of our efforts, others opposed us, usually believing that bears posed a serious threat to children. Our door-to-door efforts were supplemented with public education presentations, culminating in a question-and-answer period. Many irate people vented their frustrations against bears at these talks, and against the Network, for trying to protect the bears. We had a long way to go.

Change was slow in coming, and if we were going to achieve successful co-existence between humans and bears, as the Network hoped, people needed to modify their perceptions about bears, and compromise, but many people simply weren't prepared to change. As one self-absorbed and indignant citizen argued, "I pay taxes, the bears don't, and therefore my rights come first!" As a result of this and similar attitudes, Conservation Officers were—unhappily—forced to continue to kill bears, although now they were often confronted by an openly hostile public.

The Network, seeking to project bears in a positive—and more accurate—light, capitalized on these situations with an official spokesperson, who was readily available to offer comment to the media. Devoid of the melodramatic, fear-provoking rhetoric favoured by newscasters, our Network spokesperson offered an informed explanation as to why bears and humans were clashing—poor garbage management. The spokesperson never missed a chance to remind residents of their personal responsibility to contain bear attractants, and how any failure to do so would inevitably attract bears.

Bear Response Officers

Untrained and unfamiliar in the handling of wild animals, and trained to protect human life rather than wildlife, police were often responsible for bear deaths. The COS eventually established a Bear Response Officer (BRO) Program in conjunction with local Park Rangers, which reduced police responses to bear sightings. Two officers worked the North Shore exclusively, in contrast with a single Conservation Officer who previously had to travel a considerable distance to respond to bear sightings, usually arriving long after the fact. Now BROs could be on-site in short order, to haze the bear back into the forest and find out what had attracted the bear. Ultimately, the Network arranged for condensed training sessions to teach police officers how to respond to bears, but bears fall outside their normal job requirements, and are a low priority for busy officers.

The Network's Sphere of Influence Grows

Membership around the Network's monthly discussion table continued to grow, and soon included representatives from all three North Shore municipalities, and even from further afield, as neighbouring communities sought answers to their own human-bear conflicts. We were joined by park rangers, police (briefly), biologists, and even manufacturers of bear-resistant garbage cans. Anyone who was willing to help find ways to co-exist with our neighbours of the forest, black bears, was welcome. People were finally facing and discussing the issue, and slowly accepting that their affluent suburb was undeniably linked to bear country, and that nothing was going to change unless our attitudes changed first. We needed to adapt.

Sadly, bears continued to be shot, though in greatly reduced numbers, and every new death brought public dissent and a smattering of angry letters to the editors of local newspapers. The COS recognised the public's wish for a more humane way of dealing with bears who had learned to scavenge for human foods, and implemented a program to trap and transport such bears to carefully selected, distant wilderness areas. While stressful for bears, this option seemed preferable to being shot. Unfortunately, in most cases, relocated bears returned, so this method is now only used for bears who Conservation Officers believe can successfully adapt to life away from human food sources.

The North Shore Black Bear Society

Around this time, a sister organization, the North Shore Black Bear Society (NSBBS—or "The Society") was formed to handle exclusively North Shore bear-related matters. NSBBS maintained an active role with the Network, and both groups work together, yet independently, to achieve common objectives.

Almost from the outset, we recognized that the basic challenge with "problem bears" was problem humans. The Society lobbied for by-laws that would help control careless garbage storage, the primary reason for bear activity in human neighbourhoods. However, our main focus was education. The Society placed information booths at all major North Shore community events, complete with volunteers and a wide variety of bear informational literature, prompting visitors to ask questions on a wide range of bear-related topics.

The Society's Education Coordinator, assisted by volunteers, also offered enormously popular and successful school presentations to children of all ages. Children, in turn, took these messages—with the righteous, unassailable conviction of the young—home to their parents. By reaching families—through children at school—we encouraged responsible garbage management at home.

North Shore Bear Festival

To further augment public education and understanding, a group of volunteers organized a local North Shore Bear Festival, financed entirely by grants from local councils and businesses. High-profile bear experts flew in to speak in a packed, local theatre. With PowerPoint presentations they introduced us to the interesting world of American black and brown bears. The festival included a family day at a public park adjacent to the white, sandy shores of English Bay, where gentle sea breezes cooled the warm sun while children played in Bouncy Castles, clambered over the COS vehicles, and explored many other bear-related activities. The focus of this grand event was bear education, including stands and displays explaining the needs of bears and the benefits of successful co-existence.

Christmas Fundraising

The Christmas fundraiser is an annual highlight for many, held in a local shopping mall amid the festive gaiety of the season. The Society's information booth is always swamped with teddy bears to help finance our ongoing efforts. After years of work, it seems that the North Shore's appetite for teddy bears is inexhaustible. The Society's booth is usually a social centre for bear talk, with countless residents stopping by to chat about their personal experiences with local bears. The old attitudes of fear and anger have largely been replaced by those of responsibility and even protectiveness. International visitors are often astonished at the level of co-existence that North Shore residents have achieved with local black bears. When visitors are fortunate enough to see a local bear, they are delighted at this unforgettable experience, one they will tell, and retell, in faraway places.

The Network and the Society have both grown, and continue to flourish in pursuit of their mutual goals. Since those tragic 39 deaths in 1999, the number of deaths has declined considerably, resulting in an average of 7 bears per year from 2000 to 2012. We lament the loss of even one bear, but these numbers testify to a community's changed attitudes.

A Personal Experience of Co-existence

Just last year I was walking my dog, Reggie, along a local woodland trail, when I came upon a large black bear. (By the breadth of the skull, I presumed the bear to be a male.) He was straddling an impressive berry bush, which he had uprooted and pulled across the narrow trail so that he could enjoy the fruits of his labours. I stopped dead in my tracks. We stared silently at each other for a moment. His coarse, coal-black coat shone with a clean, healthy gloss in the dappled sunlight. Following bear-encounter protocol, I spoke in a low, calm voice as I slowly reached down to snap the leash on Reggie (who was, fortunately, disinterested). The bear, unmoving, continued to gaze steadily at us.

Volunteering with the Network and Society had provided me with guidelines on how to behave in such circumstances. Most importantly, I knew that I should not

· panic and run (which could encourage a chase),
· allow my dog to chase the bear (which could bring both the dog and the bear right back at me), or
· threaten the bear by shouting or approaching.

Instead, I knew to speak gently to the bear to lower his or her stress level; and move slowly backwards, away from the area.

The intensity of the moment heightened my senses. Aside from my gentling words, the only sound was the sleepy, undulating drone of a bee. The air was spiced with a warm, loamy scent from the forest. There seemed to be a mutual acceptance between us. The bear calmly tolerated my presence in his natural environment—just as humans have been learning to respect and tolerate bears in our North Shore communities.

Soon the bear moved back from the berry bush, briefly stared at me, then ambled up the trail. He moved off in a rolling, shuffling plod, with an occasional glance over one shoulder to check where we were, then he took a trail to the left. Reggie and I, in turn, continued calmly along the original path, with me chattering so the bear could hear where I was—avoiding any element of surprise if the bear was anywhere in front of us.

In truth, the Pacific Northwest was and remains the bear's terrain. Consequently, we continue to see these woodland residents on our streets, and enjoy photos of bears in local papers, looking faintly ridiculous as they wallow in a backyard pool or explore a child's play set. In response, we will continue to place "Bear Sighting" signs in areas of bear activity, hoping to protect both the bears and the public. We have learned the secret to cohabitation: Eliminate bear attractants and offer no reason for bears to stay, thereby ensuring our safety, and theirs.

CHAPTER 16

U.S. Wildlife Agencies: Outdated, Misguided and Destructive

Lisa Kemmerer

In a functioning democracy, citizens have a very special power—they can affect policy. Unfortunately, this process is ineffective when citizens are uninformed. Wildlife policies are a case in point—outdated policies conflict with citizen's interests and harm wildlife, yet remain in place because so few of us are aware of these policies or the damage they do. Currently, wildlife policies in the U.S. benefit hunters and trappers, harm wildlife (including bears), and are contrary to the interests of the vast majority of U.S. citizens.

Historic Roots of the Problem

Theodore Roosevelt claimed that hunting had a civilizing effect on men, and advocated hunting as an outlet for a man's "virile impulses" (Kheel, *Nature* 70). For Roosevelt, the gentleman-hunter was the perfect model of manhood, wielding deadly power within the confines of prescribed rules—good sportsmanship rooted in the incongruity of "fair chase" ("History of the Boone").

In the late 19th century, Roosevelt, complained that commercial hunters had decimated wildlife—that a comparatively small population of "market" hunters profited while the nation was stripped of his favorite target species. To solve the problem, he founded the Boone and Crockett Club (BCC) in 1897, with the following mission: "to promote the conservation and management of wildlife, especially big game, and its habitat, to preserve and encourage hunting and to maintain the highest ethical standards of fair chase and sportsmanship in North America" ("About"). The BCC promoted laws to protect "every citizen's freedom to hunt and fish," and established wildlife as "owned by the people and managed in trust for the people by government agencies" ("About"). With this, the BCC put the government agencies in charge of managing wildlife *on behalf of hunters*: Early government wildlife conservation in the U.S. was thereby established *by* hunters *for* hunters in response to decimated "game" species (S. Fox 123).

Further sealing the fate of U.S. wildlife, Roosevelt placed his friend, Gifford Pinchot, in charge of the nation's freshly established National Forest Commission. Pinchot's family had earned their fortune logging; Pinchot was a member of BCC and an avid hunter. He believed that natural "resources" should be "managed" to offer the greatest good to the greatest number. Though not explicitly stated, he was only concerned about the greatest good *for human beings*—he viewed forests and wildlife as means to human ends, and therefore advocated that government managed forests remain open for capitalistic enterprises. In contrast, other members of this early National Forest Commission hoped to establish government lands as "locked reserves," where forests and wildlife would not be exploited for personal gains ("Gifford"). But President Roosevelt chose Pinchot as the first head of a newly established Forest Service in 1905, sealing the fate of U.S. National Forests as reserves for "resources" to be "conserved" for human ends.

Roosevelt also established the National Wildlife Refuge System (NWRS) with a network of 55 "game" reserves. These "refuges" have never been places where "game" animals can find refuge—they are lands where hunter-target populations are fostered on behalf of hunters ("History of Pelican"). The NWRS website provides "Your Guide to Hunting on National Wildlife Refuges," complete with a search engine that helps users "Find the Perfect Hunt" ("Your").

U.S. wildlife (and wilderness reserve) management was established by humans, for humans—more specifically, by and for hunters and trappers. Consequently, individual animals—especially non-target animals—are unimportant. Wildlife is maintained for the pleasure of the hunt. Few contemporary citizens are aware that wildlife agencies and their policies are designed to aid hunters and trappers—at the expense of wildlife *and* against the interests of the vast majority of non-hunting citizens. Federal and state wildlife agencies have preserved this special interest focus, and have therefore shown little interest in caring for injured or orphaned wildlife.

Power and Control Without Expertise or Responsibility

Given the history and established purpose of wildlife agencies, it is not surprising that relations between citizens engaged in wildlife rehabilitation and employees working for government wildlife agencies have often been less than ideal. Wildlife agencies in the U.S. are not concerned with maintaining balanced ecosystems or with assisting individual animals in need—they favor the interests of hunters and trappers: Thanks to Roosevelt, our wildlife policies are specifically designed to protect and enhance hunter-target species. For example, Alaska's wildlife management targets wolves in order to protect and bolster elk, caribou, and moose. Surveys now suggest that American black bears are killing young herbivores in Alaska, and state government agencies are looking to implement a trapping program to reduce black bear numbers on behalf of "big game" species.

Government officials are rarely educated or informed about (let alone trained or skilled in) wildlife rehabilitation—few have ever been directly involved with wildlife rehabilitation. Despite this lack of knowledge and experience, wildlife rehabilitation policies and procedures are controlled by government wildlife agencies. For example, rehabilitation facilities must be licensed by the government—it is illegal for citizens to keep wildlife without proper permits. Adding insult to injury, the government provides no financial support for rehabilitation, yet after months—or even years—of rehabilitation, government employees step in to control wildlife release. Needless to say, this is a frustrating situation for those working full-time in wildlife rescue, rehabilitation, and release.

Furthermore, because wildlife rescue, rehabilitation, and release are government controlled, relations between rescue organizations and government agencies are plagued by the hierarchical, red-tape-ridden, detatched-from-reality nature of government agencies. Wildlife policies are riddled with an unnerving array of procedures that must be followed in order to accomplish any given task. When dealing with wildlife issues, various state and federal government agencies also have to work with one another, and inter-agency interactions often come across as competition rather than cooperation, further foiling smooth interactions between government agencies and wildlife rescue organizations.

In contrast to government wildlife policies, rehabilitators devote tremendous time and effort to every injured or orphaned animal who comes into their care. Among government wildlife agency employees, many of whom are hunters, this is often viewed as sentimental, frivolous, and contrary to nature itself. Making relations yet more complicated, wildlife rescue and rehabilitation is often taken on by women of strength and courage, while government wildlife agencies tend to be conservative and conventional—and male-dominated.

Problematic Hunting Laws[1]

Bear hunting laws in the U.S. need to be revisited and revised. Current laws allow many questionable forms of sport hunting, forms that conflict with the hunter's own ethic of 'fair chase', and which are highly likely to result in orphaned cubs. In many states it is still legal to shoot American black bears in spring hunts, or with the help of either bait or hounds, and they may also be trapped.

---

1   Thanks to Adam Roberts of Born Free USA for necessary information on spring hunts, bear baiting, and hounding.

Spring Hunts

Bears emerge groggy and hungry from hibernation—a winter without food—and are therefore extremely vulnerable in the spring. Additionally many females emerge with new cubs who are completely dependent on their mothers. The hunter's ethic of "fair chase" ought to prevent hunting bears under these conditions, but in the absence of hunter commitment to "fair chase," most states have banned spring hunts. Other states have banned shooting mother bears in the spring, but given that it is impossible to visually distinguish a male bear from a female bear, this law is meaningless except when a cub accompanies the mother *and* the hunter notices this nearby cub. Not surprisingly, many mother bears are accidently shot in the course of spring hunts, leaving dependent orphans behind. Even though spring hunts are problematic on many levels, conflicting with the hunter's ethic of "fair chase," other states (for example, Maine, Idaho, and Montana) allow sport hunting for bears in the spring—both males and females.

Bear Baiting

Bear baiting is a practice whereby hunters repeatedly put out bait, such as a pile of fruit, both luring and habituating bears to a particular food site. Once the bears become frequent visitors to the food station, hunters hide with guns in hand in "blinds" (protected, hidden areas) to shoot bears who show up for a bite to eat. Bear baiting, like spring hunts, conflicts with the hunter's ethic of "fair chase," and is just as likely to result in orphaned cubs. Furthermore, bear baiting trains bears to seek out unnatural food sources—human food sources—drawing bears to human communities and campsites, increasing the likelihood of human-bear conflicts. Thankfully, bear baiting is illegal in most states, but again, this questionable sport is legal in some states (for example, Alaska, Wisconsin, and Minnesota).

Hounding

Some people train hounds to chase bears into trees, where bears are an easy target for hunters. This practice, called "hounding," is obviously stressful for bears. Even in rare cases where bears escape, the stress from such a chase can and does kill. In the spring bears are vulnerable because they have not eaten all winter. Bears chased in hot weather, or just before hibernation (when they carry a good deal of extra weight), can easily overheat. Additionally, hounding frequently separates mothers from cubs, leaving orphans to be consumed by predators, to starve, or to be torn to pieces by pursuing hounds. Does this not conflict with the hunter's ethic of "fair chase"? Either way, hounding remains legal in many states, only some of which have limited the number of hounds that may be turned onto an unsuspecting bear.

Trapping

Many U.S. states permit bear trapping (including Alaska and Maine). In some states it is legal for trappers to lure bears into snares and traps with bait, leaving food in a particular area for some time before setting traps, training bears to frequent areas where trappers intend to set traps.

Trappers use both cage traps and snares. Cages are more humane (and less common) provided they are checked daily. Obviously, it is inhumane to hold a wild animal in a cage, day after day, where they have no access to food, water, or shelter. Foothold traps are designed to clamp onto an animal's leg when their foot lands on a steel plate in the center of the trap, triggering two spring-loaded metal jaws. Foothold traps cause hematomas and deep lacerations, and can dislocate joints, cause fractures, and damage teeth and gums when wild animals turn on offending traps with their powerful jaws. Like those left in cages, animals caught in steel-jawed traps do not have access to food, water, or shelter, and they are also in severe pain. A snare is a wire noose designed to catch a passing animal and tighten when the animal struggles to escape, thereby, cutting off circulation, and often cutting through flesh to bone. Snares tighten on a bear's leg, foot, or neck—whichever body part becomes caught.

While state regulations sometimes require trappers to check cages, traps, and snares at regular intervals, usually every couple of days, such legislation is impossible to enforce. No one but the trapper knows where these devises are set. The reality is that trapped animals often wait, filled with pain and terror, without access to food, water, or shelter, for very long periods of time.

Rescue, Rehabilitation, and Release—Outdated, Unfounded Fears

Wildlife agencies in the U.S. remain under the shadow of Roosevelt's late 19th-century approach to "management," and by the tendency of these archaic institutions to attract employees who hunt and trap. These employees are therefore among a very small minority of U.S. citizens who tend to care a great deal about hunter and trapper target populations, but very little about any single wild animal. Government agencies are, by nature, slow moving. In any event, few government wildlife agency employees are interested in changing policies that have long favored hunters. And few government wildlife agency employees are interested in taking even a small measure of responsibility for the expense and labor of wildlife rehabilitation—though they certainly intend to continue controlling those who engage in wildlife rescue, rehabilitation, and release.

This outdated government wildlife management mentality hinders rescue and rehabilitation in the U.S., and harms wildlife in a handful of important ways—especially with regard to bears.[2] For example, Government officials continue to believe that it is best to kill a cub who was under the care of a mother bear killed for frequenting campgrounds. While it is true that cubs learn pretty much everything they need to know from their mothers, rehabilitated cubs are definitely not destined to become campground foragers just because their mothers were. Data demonstrates that rescued, rehabilitated cubs are no more likely to become "problem bears" than wild-reared bears.

Even more problematic, government wildlife "experts" have long asserted that orphaned cubs cannot be reared by humans and then successfully released back into the wild, because such bears will starve and/or become "problem bears." While it is true that mothers teach cubs how and where to forage, it has been demonstrated that human-reared bears do not starve without this natural and preferred education. Furthermore, human-reared bears do not automatically seek out human beings in the event of a food shortage. While bears are easily food conditioned—especially American black bears—the idea that hand-reared bears are destined to become "problem bears" has been thoroughly disproven by decades of rehabilitators. Nonetheless, this fear lingers in government agencies, and is sealed into policies and procedures, hindering—and even blocking—rehabilitation efforts.

Most disturbing, many government wildlife agency employees cling to the outdated notion that bears in rehabilitation—because they can be dangerous to human beings—ought to be kept in constant fear of caretakers. These stalwarts argue that cubs who do not fear humans will become "problem bears"— perhaps dangerous—once released. Accordingly, "old-school" wildlife "experts" suggest harming and terrifying cubs during rehabilitation—using cattle prods or clubs to establish an intense fear of humans. While this would definitely instill a lasting fear, this fear would just as surely erode a dependent orphan's physical and mental health. In any event, release data demonstrates (beyond a shadow of a doubt) that such old-school fears are unfounded—that such cruelty is entirely unnecessary.

Rescue, Rehabilitation, and Release—Legitimate Concerns

Fragmented, diminished habitat is the biggest threat to bears around the world (as for wildlife more generally). Humans have spread across the planet, mowing down forests, plowing prairies, and building settlements wherever we go.

---

2 Thanks to Sally Maughan and Valerie Stephan-LeBoeuf (from Idaho Black Bear Rehab, Inc.) for information on bear rescue, rehabilitation, and release.

Given that bears *already* lack sufficient habitat, and that bear habitat continues to shrink, one legitimate concern with regard to rehabilitation is where to release rehabilitated bears.

Any decrease in habitat is accompanied by an increase in the likelihood of human-bear conflicts. While American black bears aren't normally aggressive, they are quite capable of injuring or killing a human being. Many people don't want bears around their homes or neighborhoods. While this reluctance may be understandable, a lack of habitat (due to human breeding) is actually the problem—not bears. If we are to protect dwindling wild spaces, we must curb our population growth. For example, we will need to eliminate tax incentives that encourage larger families, and remind one another that no single person is entitled to more than one child—no two people are entitled to more than two children, no matter how many times they remarry, no matter how much they love children, and no matter how proud they are of their genetic inheritance. We must also revisit our unequivocal devotion to individual freedoms—especially with regard to reproduction—in light of the needs of other animals, and in light of our utter dependence on a limited planet.

Another common reason for killing (rather than rescuing) bears is a lack of rehabilitation facilities. Preferably, every state where bears live in the wild would have a bear rehabilitation facility—a place for bears-in-need to recover. But bear rehabilitation is land intensive, time consuming, expensive, and requires specialized knowledge and skills. Most states have a fair number of wildlife facilities, but there are precious few bear specialists anywhere in the world, likely because each rescued bear consumes large quantities of specialized foods, and requires a very secure enclosure and knowledgeable caretakers. While most extended communities are able and willing to sustain one wildlife rehabilitation facility (usually one that rehabilitates a variety of species) this same demographic is much less likely to be able and willing to support an additional wildlife facility designed for bear rescue and rehabilitation. Bear rehabilitators are often dependent on larger wildlife organizations, such as the World Society for the Protection of Animals, to make ends meet. Bear rehabilitation is also labor intensive—young cubs must be bottle-fed at regular intervals, day and night. All told, about $5600 will carry a bear (without special needs) through the rehabilitation process—it costs far more to see an injured bear through the same process. Initially, many wildlife rehabilitators work fulltime jobs to support their work. Given the plethora of expenses, and the initial investment required, bears often fall between the cracks. A more dependable source of funding is needed for wildlife rehabilitation.

Why Rehabilitate Bears?

Most citizens erroneously believe that government wildlife agencies help injured and orphaned wildlife. As may now be obvious, this is not the case (unless shooting such animals is viewed as "help"—and sometimes a quick end may truly be the kindest option). Wildlife agencies neither engage in nor fund wildlife rescue, rehabilitation, or release, though they control all three. It is time for relevant government agencies to shift focus and take responsibility for these essential wildlife activities. There are several compelling reasons supporting this shift in policy, procedures, and purse strings.

First, it makes no sense for government agencies to control policies and procedures for a specialized area of work about which they know little and in which they have little investment. It also makes no sense for wildlife rescue and rehabilitation to be left to citizens who, out of concern and compassion, take on this difficult responsibility at their own expense, with whatever funds they can muster. *The health and welfare of wild animals is a public concern, and a public responsibility*. Therefore, wildlife rescue, rehabilitation, and release ought to be tax-funded.

Second, rather than wildlife management on behalf of 5 percent of the population (hunters), as initiated by Roosevelt, government wildlife agencies ought to engage in rescue, rehabilitation, and release on behalf of the majority of today's tax-paying citizens. While hunters and hunting have declined steadily in the last fifty years, wildlife watchers have grown by one million *each year* between 1996 and 2001 (Robertson 153). Hunters declined 100,000 each year between 2001 and 2006—despite an overall population increase of 15 million—while wildlife watching enjoyed an 8 percent increase just since 2001 ("News"; Robertson 153). "The ratio of non-hunting outdoor enthusiasts to hunters grew more than 26 percent in the last ten years"—there are now six times as many nonhunting wildlife enthusiasts as there are hunters (Robertson 153). "Comparatively speaking, the body of hunters in America is withered and shrunken, only a wee fraction of its former self" (Robertson 152). Despite expensive hunter recruitment programs (many of which targeted women and children), even FWS was compelled to admit in 2008 that "the participation rates and economic impact of hunting and fishing now trail those of wildlife watching" (*2006* 5; Reed).

Funds for rehabilitation can be gathered by taxing outdoor recreation supplies. Today, "kinder, gentler outdoorspeople are far outspending hunters" with U.S. wildlife watchers contributing $46 billion to local, regional, and national economies (Robertson 153). For example, in 2006 hunters spent only $138.5

million in Wyoming, while wildlife watchers spent a whopping $392.4 million. Though hunting is considerably more popular in Wyoming than in most states, twice as many people watched Wyoming wildlife as hunted Wyoming wildlife ("Helping" 1; 2006 96, 102). Unlike citizens in Roosevelt's time, hunters now spend less than "nature lovers," who buy everything from "bird food to binoculars, from special footwear to camera equipment," spending large sums simply "to enjoy wildlife" ("Federal"). It would now be more effective to fund wildlife rescue and rehabilitation programs via an excise tax on outdoor recreation supplies such as tents, hiking boots, climbing gear, sleeping bags, binoculars, backpacks, life preservers, skis, canoes—perhaps even photography sales.

Many citizens, myself included, are deeply thankful to be able to turn to experts when faced with an injured fawn or raven in need of veterinary care. Similarly, those confronted with a orphaned cub eating garbage from local dumpsters likely prefer to call wildlife rescue rather than wildlife extermination, which is the dominant response of government wildlife agencies when faced with orphaned cubs.

Third, rescue, rehabilitation, and release yields valuable information that cannot be attained in any other way. Bear rehabilitators are able to gather information regarding diet and medical care, physiology and cub development, behavior, tendencies, and personalities. Even after rehabilitation, bears are released with collars that provide yet more information on bear behavior, ranges, and a variety of factors that affect bear survival. Information collected through rehabilitation and release has proven vital to individuals and organizations working to save endangered bears around the world—a worthy investment for government wildlife agencies in the U.S.—certainly more worthy in the eyes of the vast majority of citizens than manipulating wildlife populations on behalf of hunters.

Finally—and most importantly—wildlife agencies ought to rescue, rehabilitate, and release wildlife (including bears) because wildlife is a public responsibility, and because we owe them this basic decency as partial compensation for the many harms and injustices we bring upon them. Humans often cause suffering and misery for wildlife—we mow them down with vehicles, take over their essential habitat, and shoot nursing mothers, leaving orphaned young. Animals—all of us—suffer when we are injured, or lose our homes or are orphaned. We enjoy whatever pleasures life offers, and we strive to avoid misery and premature death. The best outcome for any orphaned or injured bear is, as it would be for any human being, to be rescued, rehabilitated, and released. To make this financially feasible and so that we might take responsibility for that which is rightfully our collective responsibility, government wildlife agencies ought to engage in wildlife rescue, rehabilitation, and release.

Change is Possible—Even for Government Agencies

Roosevelt and his BCC cohorts created a wildlife management program whereby "those who use the resource ... pay for its care and maintenance" ("About"). Today, surveys indicate that the vast majority of U.S. citizens invest in outdoor recreation that is not deadly, while less than 5 percent of the U.S. population hunts. Consequently, rather than manipulate wildlife on behalf of a tiny special interest group, it is well past time for government wildlife agencies to invest tax dollars to assist displaced and injured wildlife.

This shift in focus and purpose will place government wildlife agencies that already control policies and procedures for wildlife rehabilitation, in charge of what ought to be the most important aspect of wildlife "management"—the actual labor of rescue, rehabilitation, and release. As this change in duties is implemented, it makes sense to employ those who have long been working in rescue, rehabilitation, and release, and who already have strong skills and years of experience in this line of work. To fund this shift in responsibilities, taxes need to be redirected, starting with the $115 million now spent each year to eliminate predators (in order to bolster hunter-target species and on behalf of ranchers) and funds directed toward hunter recruitment programs. Additionally, outdoor equipment can be taxed—kayaks and camp stoves and climbing helmets. Taxing those who use wilderness, and who prefer wildlife on the hoof, can provide financial support for wildlife rescue, rehabilitation, and release.

While change does not come easily, placing government wildlife agencies in charge of rescue, rehabilitation, and release will bring many benefits. Government wildlife agencies have much to gain from realigning with the majority of citizens, and much to lose by continuing to cater to a dwindling minority of hunters. Moreover, they will be doing the work that they ought to be doing—"managing" wildlife on behalf of the American people. Those currently engaged in rescue, rehabilitation, and release also have much to gain—most notably, they will gain a say in policies, a dependable paycheck in exchange for their labor, and adequate funds to tend needy wildlife placed in their care. America's beleaguered wildlife also have much to gain. Instead of manipulating their populations to grow hunter target species, we can take responsibility for wildlife that we displace and injure. And where wildlife benefit, so do citizens: our lands will foster a natural mix of species (rather than a proliferation of hunter-target species and a dearth of natural predators), and we will have somewhere to turn if we come upon injured or orphaned wildlife.

Conclusion

We live in a democracy—each of us is responsible to help bring desired and necessary change. If we would like government wildlife agencies to cater to the needs of the majority in the U.S. (and the needs of wildlife), we must write to senators and representatives and ask that government wildlife agencies stop catering to minority hunters at the expense of wildlife and the majority of citizens. We must tell those in congress that we prefer tax dollars invested in compassionate wildlife programs designed to protect and preserve wildlife—and that we do not want to pay government employees to run a bullet through an orphaned bear on the assumption that an individual bear does not matter.

Until rescue, rehabilitation, and release are government funded—as they should be—we must support private rescue, rehabilitation, and release through donations—including donations of money, time, requested goods, and/or skills. When we help nonhuman animals—when we help those who are least able to help themselves—we foster a community of sharing, a community where no one is left out in the cold, a community in which we can be proud to live. Selfish gains end with us, but gains for the greater good have a ripple effect that continue long after we are gone.

References

"About the B & C Club: Boone and Crocket Club since 1987." Accessed May 25, 2012. <http://www.boone-crockett.org/about/about_overview.asp?area=about>

"Federal Aid Division—The Pittman-Robertson Federal Aid in Wildlife Restoration Act." *Conserving the Nature of America*. U.S. Fish and Wildlife: Southeast Region. Accessed May 24, 2012. <http://www.fws.gov/southeast/federalaid/pittmanrobertson.html>

Fox, Stephen. *The American Conservation Movement*. Madison, WI: University of Wisconsin Press, 1981.

"Gifford Pinchot." *The Environment: A Global Challenge*. Oracle ThinkQuest Education Foundation. Accessed June 10, 2012. <http://library.thinkquest.org/26026/People/gifford_pinchot.html>

"Helping them All: A Status Report on Wyoming's State Wildlife Action Plan." Wyoming Game and Fish Department. 2010.

"History of Pelican Island." Pelican Island National Wildlife Refuge. U.S. Fish and Wildlife Service: Southeast Region. Accessed May 25, 2012. <http://www.fws.gov/pelicanisland/history.html#immigrant>

"History of the Boone and Crockett Club: The Legacy." Boone and Crocket Club since 1887. Accessed Dec. 28, 2012. *<http://www.boone-crockett.org/about/about_history. asp?area=about>*

Kheel, Marti. *Nature Ethics: An Ecofeminist Perspective*. Lanham: Rowman and Littlefield Publishing Group, Inc., 2008.

"News Releases about Hunting and Fishing Licenses." U.S. Fish and Wildlife Service. Accessed May 24, 2012. <http://www.fws.gov/news/huntfish/>

Reed, Len, "Wildlife Watching Surpasses Hunting and Fishing." *Oregonion*. Sunday, Nov. 16, 2008. Online. Internet. 12 March, 2011. <http://www.oregonlive.com/news/index.ssf/2008/11/wildlife_watching_surpasses_hu.html>

Robertson, Jim. *Exposing the Big Game: Living Targets of a Dying Sport*. Jim Robertson. Winchester, UK: Earth Books, 2012.

"Your Guide to Hunting on National Wildlife Refuges." *National Wildlife Refuge System*. Accessed 27 Feb, 2012. <http://www.fws.gov/refuges/hunting/>

2006 *National Survey of Fishing, Hunting, and Wildlife-Associated Recreation*. U.S. Fish and Wildlife Service. **Accessed** May 24, 2012. <http://library.fws.gov/pubs/nat_survey2006_final.pdf>

CHAPTER 17

The Assignment: Breaking Laws to Build Laws on Behalf of Lake Tahoe's Black Bears

Ann Bryant

Meeting Natalie and Her Family

A few dirty piles of snow still lay in patches here and there on the West Shore of Lake Tahoe, an immense alpine lake on the border between the U.S. states of California and Nevada. My yard, shaded by large trees, had more snow than the rest of the area. It was spring of 1998, and as a wildlife specialist, I spent my days caring for orphaned birds and mammals. I was extremely reclusive and shy, and rarely ventured from the safety of my own yard. I had found my fellow humans to be scary, selfish, and mostly not from Planet Earth. Not so the wild animals whom I tended (instead of dealing with humans). At the time, I was taking care of several squirrels with various disabilities, and an opossum who had been run over by a truck—but had survived, for the most part—even though his right arm, left ear, and tail had not. This was my family. The world went on around us, but we were not really involved.

Living here with these unusual dependants, I had seen American black bears pass through the yard, making their way from the mountain slope behind my cabin to the lakeshore across the road. I even shouldered a bear off my porch once when 'Possum was out getting some fresh air, because I was concerned the bear might mistake him for a snack. The huge bear ran off so fast that 'Possum didn't even realize we'd had a visitor. I could see that the bear never intended to eat my friend, he or she was simply curious—there are no native marsupials (opossums) in Tahoe.

I did not know it at the time, but my life was about to change.

One day I looked out of my dining-room window and discovered a gorgeous, well groomed, dark chocolate-colored mama black bear accompanied by two tiny milk-chocolate teddy bear babies. They were playing in the safety and privacy of the natural shrubbery just a few feet from where I stood, watching from my window. The mother knew I was there but seemed confident that I posed no threat, perhaps because I was inside. I was awe-struck and deeply moved. I felt as though she knew exactly what I was thinking, and a few months later, I realized that she did.

© KONINKLIJKE BRILL NV, LEIDEN, 2015 | DOI 10.1163/9789004293090_019

Summer tourists hadn't arrived yet, and ski season fizzled out as the snow melted away, so my big woodsy yard was a comfortable, quiet place for this precious bear family. They came by just about every day, from that day onward, much to my delight. Within a week, I knew Mama Bear well enough to call her Natalie (after Natalie Wood because she was a beautiful brunette). She invited me to come outside and sit on the porch so we could watch the cubs together, while they romped and wrestled, which I happily did. I never fed them, never tried to approach, or touch them. I simply enjoyed their company, and their trusting friendship. These three bears became a part of my strange little family, and in a nation where animals are usually considered to be disposable, I felt extremely protective of my non-human family.

The cubs grew, summer came, vacationers arrived, and I told Natalie that she had to be more discreet, that she should only come to visit late at night. She agreed.

Summer continued, and in August a couple from the city rented the vacation cabin just behind my home. They foolishly kept their garbage in an unsecured crawl space under the living room. Consequently, a big, local, male bear lightly scratched the siding of the house one night in a lame attempt to score an easy meal. The people assumed he was trying to break in and eat them. First thing in the morning, they called the Department of Fish and Game (DFG), crying for help. Rather than tell them that bears naturally seek out anything that smells like food, and that they are especially attracted to garbage—instead of mentioning that the bears are not interested in eating people, as they should have—DFG brought in a bear trap, baited with mackerel and marshmallows. Two nights later, Natalie entered the trap and was captured. The big, male bear had a larger range, and had already moved down the shoreline, safely out of reach. The trapper also caught one of the 40 pound cubs. DFG took her and her mother away, and shot them both.

Soon I heard the other cub crying in a tree, and ran out to investigate. The trapper tried to come after the remaining cub, but I chased him away. I had seen the blood inside his trap, and when he said he had taken the mother bear and cub a few miles away and released them, I knew he was not telling the truth. I also knew that California did not have a relocation policy, and had not had such a policy for well over 20 years. The trapper cursed me, and reluctantly left, while the terrified cub cried for his mama. I was destroyed—as was the bear family.

Many hours later, darkness fell, and the hungry, scared cub, too terrified to come out of the tree and let me help him, finally climbed down and raced away into the woods, alone for the first time in his short life. I searched and searched for him until most of that miserable night had passed. Completely defeated, I returned home and tried to sleep at about three in the morning. Closing my eyes only amplified the horror, and sleep didn't come until the first hint of light.

When I finally dozed off, I dreamed that Natalie and one of her cubs came to my bedroom window. In my sleep I did not accept that Natalie and her cub were gone, I was thrilled to see her alive and well … even though they were floating above the ground and Natalie was speaking English. The dream was extremely vivid and I remember every word she said to me. In a nutshell, Natalie represented the spirit of all bears—she was the Bear Spirit, or perhaps the Great Spirit behind all that exists—and she told me to care for her orphaned cub, to speak out on behalf of bears, and to gratefully accept help that would come from countless individuals along the way.

BEAR League

When I called the trapper's supervisor, he admitted that the two bears were dead, and justified their deceit; he said that it was easier for the public if they believed the bears would be relocated. While I mourned the loss of these dearest of friends, my human neighbors, who also had grown to love the bears, wrote letters to the editor and contacted the media.

Meanwhile, I was secretly caring for the orphaned, nursing cub, who had returned, as his mother said he would. He was named Oliver, after Oliver Twist, because he was an orphan. The Department of Fish and Game threatened to arrest me (daily), unless I told them where the remaining cub was hiding. I knew that they intended to kill him, because all motherless cubs were shot—since there was no rehabilitation policy in California. I wasn't budging. I had become a fierce mother bear.

The tragic story of Natalie and her cubs had all the necessary elements for a media frenzy: Tourists causing the deaths of California's treasured wildlife, mother bear and cub killed, orphaned nursing cub, threats of arrest, angry exchanges in the local media: DFG vs. people who respect wildlife. I felt that I had no choice but to come out of my protective shell and deal with the growing storm. In any case, I was quoted daily in the news, and people started calling to offer help, including funding for Oliver's upbringing. As a result of this hubbub, a small group of concerned locals met at a coffee shop, talked it over, and formed a group to advocate for Tahoe's American black bears. We called ourselves the Bear Preservation League.

We set up a meeting with the Department of Fish and Game in order to extend the proverbial olive branch, and to discuss how we could work together to educate the public about bears and garbage. They seemed to like the idea, so a Memorandum of Understanding (MOU) was drawn up between us—the first (and last) of its kind. A press conference was called, and we signed the agreement with cameras flashing and reporters scribbling. A year later, we realized that the MOU was nothing more than a way to tie our hands. The DFG never honored any part of the document, but used this agreement to keep us busy and preoccupied while they killed bears. In any event, we had grown past the point of needing the DFG. The public was calling us directly for bear-related matters, so we legally terminated the MOU, changed our name to BEAR League, and began to answer only to our conscience, and the bears.

We immediately set up a 24-hour Bear Hot Line, inducted a board of directors, obtained 501c.3 tax exempt status, and printed educational bear literature of every imaginable type, including brochures, bumper stickers, posters, flyers and garbage can stickers. We were well received, and people called to offer help from all over the Tahoe Basin. We trained volunteers extensively in non-lethal bear/human conflict management. Within one year we had a trained BEAR League volunteer in every neighborhood all the way around the Lake, and beyond. We had more than 100 trained volunteer response team members responding to bear emergencies or telephone calls from the public, helping people understand American black bears, and mitigating bear complaints. Incoming calls increased as we proved our professionalism and demonstrated our expertise; soon we were receiving calls from all six of Tahoe's county law enforcement agencies—Police, Sheriff, Animal Control, etc. We formed respectful friendships with many of the officers, and as donation funds came in from a supporting public, and our membership grew, we purchased non-lethal bear aversion equipment for most squad cars, so that officers would have an alternative to killing bears. Instead, they could shoot the bear in the rear with rubber buckshot, and teach the intruder a lesson he or she wouldn't soon forget.

The most difficult and important part of our job—by far—was (and is) educating humans. We live right smack in the middle of bear territory. We don't need to kill the bears; we need to educate people—and bears. And we do. Bears are all around us, and being opportunistic, they will take advantage of our carelessness. Anytime they smell a tasty tidbit, they are drawn toward the smell. We are invited to speak at public forums of every possible kind, all year long. Working with bears has blessed us with amazing photos, so we bring a PowerPoint presentation to help pry open human minds, and allow respect to replace fear. Fear makes people do incomprehensible things—like kill. Recently we counted well over 15,000 attendees at our lectures for just one summer.

At the beginning of each presentation I show a photo of Natalie and the tiny cubs, and credit her with founding the BEAR League. Communities all over California now call us to provide non-lethal bear/human conflict resolutions. Citizens have learned that calling the DFG usually leads to a dead bear (and angry citizens), while calling the BEAR League means problem solved—with no one harmed. We are happy to help, and I find myself spending more and more time outside my prior comfort zone, far away from my home and yard. I continue to tune in to the Bear Spirit and the Great Spirit, asking them to give me courage. And they do.

The Deadly DFG

The Department of Fish and Game (DFG) is comprised mainly of men who hunt. They are therefore ignorant of the spiritual nature of wildlife, and feel threatened by this knowledge. And they should.

DFG employees also feel threatened by those of us who value individual animals because this point of view speaks against hunting. In their attempt to permanently silence and be rid of me and my organization, I have been arrested and booked on unbelievable charges. Consequently, they have pestered and harassed me beyond my wildest imaginings.

Just after BEAR League had gone to the State Capital to obtain a legal cub rehabilitation policy for the great state of California, I answered a call for help from a local ski area to rescue an emaciated, motherless American black bear cub. The presence of the cub forced the ski operators to close down one of their lifts each day around noon, when she smelled the outdoor BBQ. As an orphaned cub, she was starving, and couldn't resist the delicious smells. DFG told them, "Just leave it alone, it will go away and die." But she didn't, and the ski patrol asked for our help. After calling several BEAR League volunteers, we created a plan to rescue the starving cub, who was noticeably weak, and was hiding under a nearby restaurant. The task seemed relatively straight forward, but we needed to move quickly if we were going to save the cub's life. We called the DFG, brought them up to speed on details, and asked for their cooperation. Instead, the Captain told us to "beat her with a stick and run her off."

Instead, we did what we knew was right—what you should do whenever a baby is motherless and starving—we rescued her. We coaxed her into a dog kennel, carried her down the lift (with assistance from the ski area staff), and loaded her into my truck. I again called the Captain at DFG to inform him that we had the bear and would take her to our local wildlife rehab facility. I could not have anticipated what happened next.

As a state agency, the DFG has authority over county officials, and they ordered local law enforcement to chase me down, arrest me, and confiscate the hungry bear cub. The Sheriff's Deputies and local Forest Service personnel reluctantly took pursuit, and soon stopped me. But when they looked at the frostbitten, terrified cub huddled in the dog kennel in the back of my vehicle, they said I did the right thing. Instead of arresting me, they escorted us to our destination, where the cub received immediate veterinary care.

The little bear recovered well, and was soon adopted by a wonderful 80 acre wildlife sanctuary (which passed our rigid inspections), where she lives happily to this day. Nonetheless, the DFG filed charges against me. The court-house docket read, "Bear Poaching." There is no law against rescuing wildlife, so this was all that the DFG could come up with. We all laughed—hundreds of us. People who heard about the case of the starving cub came by the busload to support bear rescue. The judge listened to the truth from my pro-bono attorney, then pounded his gavel as he announced: "Case dismissed, in the name of justice!" The crowd cheered and applauded, and I got to go home instead of to jail.

This made the DFG even angrier, and a couple of years later they confiscated and threatened to kill my dear friend Marvin, a much loved, non-releasable porcupine, who had been run over by a car and was disabled. I called the Director and Deputy Directors at the DFG, and begged for Marvin's life and safe return. Unbelievably, these men listened to their hearts, and issued a permit for Marvin to live with me. Ultimately Marvin became a well known animal ambassador, accompanying the BEAR League to every public educational event for 10 years. It would have been difficult to bring a bear, and Marv volunteered for the job—simply by being who he was, he helped to open people's minds, allowing them to understand that even a prickly, waddling, rodent has a unique personality, enjoys life, appreciates love and kindness, and really isn't very different from what we are—except in looks. And we all know that looks don't matter.

When Marvin died of liver cancer, years later, his obituary was published in all of the local newspapers. Marvin was one of many individuals that Natalie sent to help me with the tasks with which I was entrusted.

There have been and continue to be good people in the DFG, but the DFG has fired many good employees who worked well with the BEAR League— perhaps *because* they worked well with the Bear League. One wildlife chief, who worked very closely with me, gave me permission to rescue many bears— he was fired. Other wardens have become very good friends of mine, and working together we accomplished much good for bears *and* local residents who live among bears. Unfortunately they were also fired, or left the department because they were sickened by the pervasive and perverse killing mentality.

Looking Back

It has been 18 years since the beautiful dark chocolate-colored bear was shot, and since that bleak day, the BEAR League has rescued many bears. Threats of arrest have gotten somewhat out of hand, backed by the DFG. I was arrested a second time for helping yet another bear, and have been threatened with arrest a handful of times since. When we rescued an orphan cub whose mother was killed by a hunter, we were threatened with arrest, but the District Attorney refused to charge me, and indicated that the DFG should leave me alone so that the BEAR League can do what it does best—help bears.

The BEAR League has implemented bear/garbage ordinances all around Lake Tahoe. We helped write the California State Parks Non-lethal Bear Policy. We trained the South Lake Tahoe Police Department on non-lethal bear response. Tahoe recently suffered two forest fires and a serious drought, so we implemented a successful supplemental/diversionary feeding program to stop bear incursions. We were featured on PBS's "Nature," on National Geographic's "Wild Chronicles," in an Animal Planet mini-series called "Blonde vs Bear," and on numerous other TV broadcasts and international publications. We pulled off the now famous Bear Rescue from the 100 foot high Rainbow Bridge by Donner Lake. (For which I was threatened with yet another arrest.) Sometimes bears die, but we continue to rescue bears and cubs; our organization continues to grow.

Much has changed in my life, too. I have suffered but recovered from a heart attack, and both of my parents have died. I still miss Marvin terribly, yet am comforted by two more disabled porcupines have found their way into my home, and have become part of my life. I've grown older, and I've learned with the years. Amazing friendships have been forged in the process of working with people and bears. I like most human beings now, and no longer consider them to be scary. In fact, I stand before audiences of hundreds to tell them what I know about bears, and Natalie is with me always. I've been told I am doing God's work. I'm honored and truly blessed.

I never dreamt that helping bears would require breaking laws. But I have learned that laws are by and for human beings; they do not protect the many other nonhuman animals. This needs to change. The BEAR League has been very successful in bringing new laws to California. It is no longer legal for residents or visitors to leave garbage accessible to bears in the Tahoe region. If they do, they are fined. Bears are no longer killed for getting into unsecured trash. Orphaned bear cubs are now rescued and cared for, and much more restrictive policies dictate when a "problem" bear can be killed. There is still much change needed, but things are looking a lot better for the bears in our area.

   As the years pass, I look back in amazement at the many lessons I have been gifted through Natalie. Her death required me to jump out of my comfort zone in more ways than one. Meeting Natalie pushed me to make the world better for nonhuman animals, and to let it be known that *all* of the myriad creatures deserve our respect, and our care—whether a porcupine, a bear cub, or any other sentient being.

   ### Epilogue

As our anthology finds its way to the printer, I am pleased to share a few important updates There has recently been a veritable 'changing of the guard' within the California Department of Fish and Game, and the bears have benefited. The name of this state agency was legally changed to 'Department of Fish and Wildlife,' and the BEAR League has since met often with department supervisors, as partners, to pave a pathway to a future where wildlife issues no longer focus exclusively on hunters and the "consumption" of wildlife. It appears that a more informed and balanced relationship between this state department and the Wildlife that this department is commissioned to protect is, at long last, becoming a reality. Wherever she is, there can be no doubt that Natalie is smiling.

CHAPTER 18

A Grizzly Battle: Government Agencies, Endangered Species, and the U.S. Legal System

Tara Zuardo

I first encountered grizzly bears in a court room—though not in the flesh. I was a student working for the Pacific Environmental Advocacy Center (PEAC)[1] a nationally-recognized, domestic environmental legal clinic of Lewis & Clark Law School in Portland, Oregon. As an independent organization, the Center's lawyers collaborate with students to protect natural resources through *pro bono* representation and litigation, training, and education.[2] Law students gain experience, while the natural world is defended by a host of eager young lawyers.

I had attended law school with the hope of effectuating some sort of change for the better for nonhuman animals—change beyond what activism could accomplish. I felt somewhat desperate about dwindling species and cruelty to animals. At the time, I was just beginning to understand the possibilities of the legal system for protecting animals, and this was my first chance in the court room. I had been assigned a lawsuit against the Forest Service and the Fish and Wildlife Service (FWS) for the Flathead National Forest. Though we were mere students working with supervising attorneys and professors, our job was to convince these government agencies to comply with their own forest plan standards for protecting brown bear (grizzly subspecies) habitat (Swan, "Lawsuits" 3). Government agencies—officially responsible for protecting wildlife—are too often the deciding factor between wildlife populations flourishing or going extinct. Yet convincing the Forest Service and FWS to comply with federal laws—and with their own regulations—can be nearly impossible.

With only two years of law school behind me, I could barely keep up with my supervising attorney while he explained the complicated legal system surrounding endangered wildlife, including brown bears, and the agencies charged with protecting these diminishing populations. At that time I still believed that Congress passed laws like the Endangered Species Act and the National Forest Management Act to legally provide animals and public lands with protection because this was sensible and necessary. I did not see that

---

1 Now Earthrise Law Center: http://law.lclark.edu/centers/earthrise/.
2 Special thanks to Professor Daniel J. Rohlf for his inspiration as a teacher and tremendous guidance.

agencies like the Forest Service and FWS perpetually created loopholes to get around these legal mandates, or that organizations had to bring these government agencies into court to combat violations, uphold laws, and protect species. I had no understanding of the ensuing "battle of the briefs," whereby each side would throw creative, complicated arguments at a judge in the hope that he or she would "take their side." I had no conception of the hours and hours that these courtroom battles consumed, or the cost of such battles to small environmental organizations, pitted against more expansive pockets of government agencies. At that time, I was a naïve student who believed that justice for animals would be served in U.S. courts because the Forest Service and the Fish and Wildlife Service were breaking their own laws. It seemed to me that all we needed to do was to point this out. In my mind, it was as simple as that. Indeed, I was naïve.

Grizzlies in Trouble—Gaps in the Endangered Species Act

Historically there were about 50,000 brown bears in North America. Their numbers have been reduced to somewhere between 1,000—1,200, largely as a result of human expansion and hunting. Brown bears in the U.S. now exist only in fragmented populations in Alaska, Wyoming, Montana, Idaho, and Washington (McLellan *et al*).

Bear habitat is harmed and diminished by our ever-expanding human numbers. Humans build homes and roads connecting homes. We log forests and mine deep in wilderness areas, forcing bears to move to less desirable habitat, including rugged mountains and remote forests. Bears wander into communities that have been built in their habitat, and are shot and killed because humans have claimed new land and have no intention of sharing "their" area with wildlife—especially grizzlies.

Grizzlies are listed as "threatened" under the U.S. Endangered Species Act (ESA), and remaining populations are therefore entitled to certain protections guaranteed by law (16 U.S.C. § 1531 et seq.). Most people would assume that this includes some bulletproof government protection, but this is not the reality. While laws such as the ESA establish general goals (like conserving threatened and endangered species), most of the details as to *how* this will be accomplished are left to government agencies. Still, the ESA does provide some important protections. For example, Section 7 of the ESA includes critical habitat designations and substantive consultation requirements for threatened species. Consultation requirements are designed to prevent federal agencies from jeopardizing the continued existence of listed species and from destroying designated critical habitat. Consultation requirements obligate federal agencies

whose plans are likely to affect listed species or their designated habitat to con-
sult with the Fish and Wildlife Service (50 CFR §402). If the consultation reveals
that the project is likely to jeopardize the species, the project is not permitted
to move forward.

This "jeopardy standard"—established for all species at risk—is crucial to
the ESA's ability to protect endangered species. However, lawmakers have
declined to define what constitutes "jeopardy," leaving interpretation to FWS.
Ironically, the evolution of the meaning of this word has affected the outcome
of species survival (Rohlf 114). Additionally, the jeopardy standard is problematic because it is a high standard to meet, yet serves as virtually the sole mea-
suring stick for determining the legality of federal actions that affect listed
species. Unless a federal agency (like FWS) finds that a certain activity is likely
to jeopardize the continued existence of a listed species, the ESA cannot pro-
hibit that activity (Rohlf 114). Consequently, many activities that affect endangered or threatened species, activities that the public would consider to be
harmful, are nonetheless allowed to move forward.

For example, the jeopardy standard has done little to protect brown bears in
Flathead National Forest. Despite the grizzly's threatened status under the
Endangered Species Act, the U.S. government continues to build public access
roads for loggers, hunters, and snowmobilers. These roads further jeopardize
threatened and dwindling brown bears. Statistics have clearly demonstrated
that areas of high human use—areas with roads that allow ready human
access—are mortality sinks for bears, who are killed inadvertently by drivers in
fast-moving vehicles, or purposefully shot, harming already diminished populations (McLellan *et al*).

The ESA prohibits "taking" (harassing, harming, hunting, shooting, wound-
ing, killing, trapping, capturing, or collecting) listed species. Although Fish and
Wildlife reserves the right to set a legal "take" limit on threatened species,
hunting brown bears is no longer legal. Increasing public access is clearly damaging to this "threatened" species, especially given that local agencies rarely
have adequate resources for monitoring access areas. Roads jeopardize grizzly
survival: More roads make survival yet more tenuous, and loosing individuals—even a few grizzlies—harms already diminished populations (McLellan
et al). Increasing public access roads is clearly damaging to this threatened species, especially given that local agencies rarely have anything like adequate
resources for monitoring access areas.

Both legal hunter kills and inadvertent deaths in front of rushing autos seem
comparatively benign in light of poacher activity. Poachers single-mindedly
hunt bears in exchange for a bundle of hard cash, and do not care whether
bears they kill are young or old, male or female—or pregnant. Poachers make a

gash in their victims with a knife, reach in to take out the gall bladder, leaving the body to grow cold. Park rangers have too often found yearling cubs dumped along public access roads in parks, bellies sliced open, gall bladders missing. Bears are no match for poachers, who use high-technology such as dogs fitted with radio collars, to track and kill grizzlies while they lie still in winter dens. New forest service access roads provide poachers with convenient access to previously inaccessible brown bear territory (McLellan *et al*).

Corrupt Agencies, Ineffective Courts

I was excited to take direct action on behalf of the great grizzlies in Montana's Flathead National Forest. In order to protect these bears, it was essential for forty-nine of Flathead's fifty-four non-wilderness Grizzly Bear Management Subunits to meet strict limits on roads and trails. These limits were designed to protect grizzly habitat from hunters, poachers, and the dangers of speeding vehicles (Swan, "Standards" 2). Without these limits, access roads would allow invasive human activities—legal and illegal, snowmobiling and poaching—in the habitat of threatened bears.

Nonetheless, the U.S. Forest Service began a management plan in 2004 that offered excessive concessions to snowmobilers. As any informed person might predict, this quickly devastated Flathead's brown bear populations. Thanks to plummeting grizzly numbers and the diligence of private citizen watch-groups (like Swan View Coalition), this important issue was brought to the attention of the courts. When a federal judge was presented with the Forest Service's extended snowmobile plan and its effects, he ruled that these excessive concessions were illegal under the Endangered Species Act. As a result, a lawsuit was filed, a settlement was reached, and a new Flathead management plan was established to protect half of the Flathead's forests (52,000 acres) from snowmobile use.

Unfortunately, this new management plan was manipulated by and for FWS. (While the Forest Service was the "action agency" for purposes of the ESA, FWS was the consulting agency charged with ensuring that the project would not jeopardize grizzlies.) With this new protective plan in place, FWS turned down additional brown bear habitat protection arguing that additional protections were no longer needed. As part of their scheme, the agency created and put forward a Biological Opinion (BiOp) stating that new roads would not have a significant impact on brown bears in Flathead National Forest.

A BiOp is created after a formal consultation between a federal agency (in this case the Forest Service) and the consulting agency (FWS). A BiOp is a scientific report indicating whether or not the project in question is likely to jeopardize the continued existence of a species listed under the ESA, or whether or not the project in question is likely to result in the destruction, or adverse modification, of critical habitat.

In this case, the FWS BiOp unfairly supported their interest in opening an area to snowmobiles that was legally closed in the previous settlement. Most fundamentally, the FWS BiOp started from an illegal reference point: It started with the base assumption that the entirety of Flathead might be open all year long for snowmobiles—a provision that was deemed illegal in the original forest plan. Furthermore, the BiOp manipulated the fact that the recent settlement had closed off certain areas of the forest to snowmobiles, and had required complete closure during certain months, to assert that there were plenty of grizzly protections already in place. By exploiting these previous protections, the FWS BiOp effectively defended the Forest Service plan to allow late-season snowmobiling in protected brown bear territory.

Fortunately, in May of 2008, U.S. District Judge Donald Molloy (Missoula, Montana) ruled that FWS' BiOp defending the Flathead National Forest's late-season snowmobiling plan violated the Endangered Species Act (i.e. *clearly* threatening grizzlies in the region). Judge Molloy promptly banned late-season snowmobiling until a legal BiOp could be issued (*Swan*). But the Forest Service, determined to placate snowmobilers by permitting access to brown bear habitat through the end of May, quickly issued a new BiOp, declaring Judge Molloy's injunction dissolved. To add insult to injury, rather than promptly submit the new BiOp to the court, FWS submitted this underhanded document only days before the late snowmobiling season began in April, effectively delaying the case in backlogged courts. As a result, snowmobiles raced freely through Flathead grizzly habitat all spring (Swan, "Judge" 3).

Litigation began anew in the summer. In July of 2009, Judge Molloy ruled FWS in contempt of court for allowing snowmobiling when brown bears had freshly emerged from winter dens. However, the attorney general needed to file a motion against the Forest Service in order to enforce this order of contempt, effectively delaying enforcement. In reality, the order was a mere slap on the wrist—completely ineffectual in protecting brown bears. Once again, a federal agency was able to skirt ESA regulations. I was quickly learning how underhanded government agencies/employees can be when it comes to threatened species.

Molloy's Mistakes—The Rule Rather than the Exception

The next stage of this legal battle showed me how U.S. courts enable federal agencies to pursue illegal activities, permitting them to blatantly ignore wildlife protections. Even though U.S. District Judge Donald Molloy reinstated the injunction (denying the snowmobile plan based on the old BiOp), he failed to scrutinize the new BiOp, which was essentially the same as the old one. Unfortunately, in this instance, Judge Molloy simply reversed his earlier decision, allowing snowmobiling as late as May 31 on some 52,000 acres of protected brown bear habitat in Flathead National Forest. This gross oversight permitted snowmobiles to tear through the entirety of the Flathead brown bear's otherwise quiet home, bringing gun-wielding poachers at a time when female grizzlies were emerging with young, hungry and weak from a winter of hibernation. Once outside their dens, dark against the bright snow, grizzlies are easy targets even when they run for their lives, pursued by gas-powered machines toting high-powered weapons (Swan, "Absurdity" 5).

Why did Molloy fail in his duty to scrutinize the new BiOp? Judges too often defer to government agencies/employees without properly analyzing the information at hand. Judge Molloy's decision to allow snowmobiles at this time, in this area, was based on his uncritical acceptance of a self-serving FWS BiOp claiming that brown bear deaths resulting from this additional snowmobile allowance would not "jeopardize the continued existence of the species," thereby satisfying the demands of the ESA.

What is perhaps more alarming is that Judge Molloy also overturned previously established forest plan standards that mandated very specific road closures for access roads. Molloy determined that these closures were nonobligatory for the agency: The Forest Service was not required to complete the required road closures to protect grizzly habitat as previously determined by law.

Judge Molloy neglected his duty in two important respects. First, unlike some land management plans, the standards of the Flathead National Forest Plan are both mandatory and highly specific—they are not just a general statement of priorities designed to be easily subverted or ignored. This is extremely important because forest plan standards are designed to force government agencies to comply with laws. If an agency can simply ignore these standards at a later date, forest plan provisions are entirely meaningless, in which case such plans fail to comply with and support federal law, including the ESA.

Additionally, Molloy had no business ignoring previous road closure provisions. The Forest Service had *already* made the decision to close specific roads. Therefore, any legal motion to enforce these existing decisions was consistent with the agency's *legal obligations*, and should not have required time-consuming litigation. Judge Molloy's decision effectively rendered forest plan mandates meaningless: the Forest Service offered a conciliatory plan based on the court's demands, then failed to follow through with these plans. Molloy then failed to enforce previously established legal requirements. In real terms, all of this legal maneuvering boiled down to more dead bears.

Of course there was a legal precedent behind Molloy's shady decision: "*SUWA*"—*Norton v. Southern Utah Wilderness Alliance*. The court in *SUWA* ruled that the Administrative Procedure Act only allows courts to examine the failure of government agencies to meet specific statutory requirements, and many agency planning document provisions are unenforceable. In essence, this decision destroyed the courts' power to examine agency decisions—to judge specific statutory and regulatory compliance. The *SUWA* ruling reflected a concern over "injecting the judge into day-to-day agency management." In the *SUWA* case, the Supreme Court ruled that land management plans can merely provide a statement of priorities (as opposed to mandatory obligations). However, the Supreme Court also noted that specific forest plan actions may be mandatory if *already obligated* (*Norton* 71). For example, the Forest Service had already acknowledged that Flathead road closure standards created a binding commitment—road closures were thereby added in the original litigation *in order to be in compliance with the law.*

In addition, Judge Molloy (and other courts) ruled that the ESA does not require government agencies to promote the recovery of an endangered or threatened species, highlighting a more general ignorance of ESA requirements and allowing federal agencies to dodge ESA mandates (Swan, "Absurdity" 5). It is easy for agencies such as Fish and Wildlife to convince uninformed judges that they "know best" regarding the science of forestry and species populations, and then use this leverage to avoid legal scrutiny. Because most judges erroneously assume that FWS has the best interests of threatened species in mind, and that the forest service engages in extensive studies and data accumulation on behalf of threatened and endangered species, FWS BiOps and other legal documents, as well as the agency's word in court, are often accepted without scrutiny. For example, FWS can argue that access roads and snowmobiles may not *benefit* a species, but these concessions will not *jeopardize* the species to the point of threatening extinction. How can a judge argue with the Forest Service on such highly scientific issues involving wildlife and forest access? Needless to say, it is extremely rare for the FWS to determine that any of their policies or actions are likely to jeopardize threatened or endangered species (Rohlf 115). Courts are likely to trust agency judgments, and quickly move on to the next case. But the willingness of many U.S. judges to trust federal agencies/employees to know and care about wildlife has led species to the brink of extinction.

As a naïve and idealistic law student it was difficult for me to understand this complicated, ingrained system of deceit and special interests. Why did it take so much money and time to convince federal agencies (charged with protecting threatened species) and courts (charged with enforcing laws that protect endangered wildlife) to do what they were *supposed* to be doing? The lives of individual bears lay at the heart of these courtroom battles, bears who would ultimately suffer from the corruption of our federal agencies and the ignorance and apathy of our courts. With each new road created to appease loggers, snowmobilers, and hunters, more and more bears would fall victim to poaching, hunting, and collisions with snowmobiles and autos.

I entered law school under the misconception that justice for nonhuman animals simply required lawyers to present convincing, logical arguments demonstrating how extant policies fail to comply with laws protecting species (such as the grizzly), and the necessary changes would be required and duly enforced. In reality, while laws such as the Endangered Species Act are designed to protect endangered wildlife, the federal agencies entrusted with enforcing this law—entrusted with the survival of endangered species—often cater to vocal special interest groups, such as hunters and snowmobilers. These powerful interest groups invest considerable time and money lobbying for their cause, and because they purchase licenses from federal agencies to hunt and snowmobile, they are a favored clientele. This capitulation and corruption is facilitated by overburdened courts governed by judges who simply do not make it a priority to examine the actions and assertions of government employees.

The Appeal—Our Day in Court

In October of 2009, with my professor at the helm, we appealed to the Ninth Circuit Court of Appeals (Seattle, Washington) with one specific goal: Force the Forest Service to comply with its own forest plan standards and limit roads and motorized vehicles in brown bear habitat as previously agreed. The Forest Service's position, if it held sway, would render forest plans (designed to protect and preserve forests and wildlife) virtually meaningless across the country. The crux of the Forest Service's argument relied on the SUWA case: The accused agencies maintained that they reserved the right to refuse to implement previously agreed upon specific road closures because the forest plan lacked specific road closure *dates*.

After months of preparation, the court day finally arrived. I was very excited to be on a team backing brown bears. Our team consisted of two students (of which I was one) and our professor/supervising attorney (who happens to be the foremost expert on wildlife law and the ESA). I had total confidence in my professor. It seemed we could not lose. We had the weight of the law *and* the forest service plan behind us. And we were *very* well prepared.

Still, my nerves were on end as I walked into a U.S. court, quietly harboring a newly acquired lack of faith in U.S. courts. To make matters worse, the three judges sitting on the bench seemed staunchly conservative. Even if we made the best arguments in the world, would they rule in our favor in light of those who had appointed them to the bench?

I had little confidence in my ability to assist my professor, or appear professional and calm throughout the proceedings. Nonetheless, we two students sat up at counsel's table with our professor to help him prepare for rebuttal. Our professor did not disappoint—he presented arguments logically and clearly, and the judges' questions seemed to reflect a desire to understand more fully rather than to criticize. It looked hopeful. How could it not be? Was this not the world-renown U.S. legal system in action? I could tell that the judges were beginning to see through the government officials' self-serving arguments—beginning to see that these agencies were skirting basic legal requirements, both those of the Endangered Species Act and their own agency's guiding documents.

What was I to think, a young and hopeful law student, when the Ninth Circuit court affirmed Judge Molloy's decision, siding with the federal agencies despite our compelling arguments—offering less than three pages of discussion and explanation, much of which we could see had been copied and pasted from the defendant's brief? (The court's written decision even duplicated miscited cases from the Forest Service brief—further proof that they had given very little consideration to our arguments.) Obviously, the court was not interested in the critical issues we had raised—critical to brown bears, not humans.

The Aftermath

U.S. courts are chronically overextended. The Ninth Circuit's docket is perpetually flooded with cases, and courts therefore feel compelled to make decisions without too much delay. This is especially true if judges feel that a case at hand is comparatively unimportant. Because of backlogged courts, and a traditional reluctance to overturn decisions previously handed down by district courts, we—and the brown bears—never had much of a chance. As a consequence of the court's decision, a threatened species will face increased likelihood of injury and premature death.

Bears were not the only casualties of the court's ignorance and indifference. My expectations of what the U.S legal system could offer wildlife were crushed. Our case seemed so simple and straightforward: We cannot possibly protect threatened brown bears if the Forest Service continues to allow more and more roads through Flathead National Forest. Grizzlies are clearly threatened and require specific legal protections under the ESA. The court's blatant disregard for Flathead's threatened brown bears destroyed a newly fledged lawyer's hopes for protecting species through legal action.

Are U.S. Courts Capable of Understanding and Protecting Endangered Species?

Why do the very agencies charged with protecting lands and wildlife fight so hard to avoid laws that should empower them to do the tasks with which they have been entrusted? Why were the Forest Service and FWS so timid about enforcing their own plans in the face of an absurdly late-season snowmobiling proposal? Unfortunately, it is both more profitable and more popular to allow logging and snowmobiling on Forest Service lands than it is to restrict and limit these special-interest citizens. Federal agencies, when faced with budget cuts, can gain some revenue through logging, snowmobiling, and hunting activities. What do brown bears have to offer?

We must rethink our assumption that U.S. federal agencies such as the Forest Service can be trusted to advocate for the environment or wildlife. Forest plans provide the means for protecting grizzlies, but are largely designed as a blueprint for managing human activities that are likely to be damaging to bears (like snowmobiling and logging). These activities are managed *on behalf of people*. Federal agencies are financially supported by the very interests they should be limiting to protect fragile lands and endangered wildlife.

A key problem with the U.S. court system—and one reason why we lost our case—is that courts do not always reflect our American system of checks and balances: Agencies such as the Forest Service and FWS create and put forward their own evidence and forestry plans, and the courts merely assume that federal agencies/employees are acting with integrity. Too often, federal agencies are merely extensions of our society's tendency to view forests as places reserved for humans to "utilize" trees and wildlife. In the process, snowmobilers find worthy representation, while brown bears remain unprotected.

Judge Molloy and the Ninth Circuit Court of Appeals did not seriously examine accusations eloquently brought to the table by our professor because our courts do not consider endangered species to be a priority. Most U.S. courts and judges are not interested in mitigating even the most horrific threats facing nonhuman animals (if they were, factory farms, furriers, and animal labs would be out of business). We live under a legal system where human desires—any desires—outweigh even the most basic needs of nonhuman animals. Consequently, the miniscule numbers of people who wish to snowmobile without limit in Flathead National Forest—for fun—are more important than the brown bear's desperate struggle for survival.

U.S. courts reflect U.S. society, where humans and human-related issues often take priority over the needs and concerns of nonhuman animals.

Protecting endangered species is perceived as interfering with the American commitment to freedom, property ownership, and capital acquisition—the route to human happiness as conceived in our capitalistic society. Protecting wildlife and habitat would require us to rethink some of our most basic American assumptions, and to exchange a few of our treasured individual freedoms for a greater good—one that includes nonhuman animals.

In addition, one could argue that U.S. judges are not properly educated to defend the ESA. If U.S. courts don't—or won't—question state and federal employees, then they should not hear cases involving federal agencies. If our judges assume that federal agencies are doing what they are supposed to be doing—protecting wildlife and forests—then what is the point of challenging these agencies in court? Furthermore, if judges do not understand the requirements of "newer" environmental legislation such as the Endangered Species Act, how can they defend these laws? How can judges who are trained and generally practice in more traditional areas of law, such as family or tax law, offer an informed decision on cases such as the one put forward on behalf of Flathead brown bears? Our Flathead case might well have been the first exposure to the Endangered Species Act for all three judges—is that why they asked so many questions?

Many students entering law school imagine that they are destined to join a noble force of "police" prepared and determined to enforce justice. But on entering the legal system, we soon face reality, and must rethink what we are called to do. Looking back, the only hero in my Flathead court experience was my professor, who seemed to be the last remaining person truly interested in justice. But such valiant efforts were—and will remain—insufficient in the absence of stronger, more specific laws regulating federal agencies like the Forest Service and FWS.

Looking Back, Looking Forward

And so it was that I found myself caught in an ineffective U.S. legal system driven by ignorance and special-interests. Even at the time, on reflection, I could see how easy it might be for advocates to lose sight of key goals as they become entangled in a legal fray. In the litigious scuffling, I could see that grizzly bears became mere abstract ideas—words rather than entities, things rather than individuals. And this inherently abstract process was about to determine whether or not a mother grizzly emerging from her den after a dark, cold winter with a furry cub would be likely to be pursued by a snowmobile, and whether or not a pregnant bear ambling across a dusty road deep in the Flathead would be likely to be shot.

I learned a few key lessons from the Flathead case. First, neither the Forest Service nor FWS are seriously committed to habitat protection, or even to enforcing laws that are essential to protecting threatened populations. Their decisions are not motivated by bears or other threatened species. Second, FWS has generally acquiesced in Forest Service inaction and has consistently allowed the Forest Service to postpone and ignore habitat improvements. Indeed, ultimately the Forest Service prevailed in court by arguing that management plans impose no enforceable obligations on either agency. In other words, forest plans are essentially meaningless. Don't these documents need to have teeth to maintain credibility with the public *and* to protect brown bears and other threatened species? Can't Forest Service employees see that such shoddy management plans ultimately undermine their very purpose and existence in the eyes of the public?

Court decisions affect whether or not individuals live or die. Judges and Forest Service employees need to be more personally connected with grizzlies and spotted owls and bobcats and wolverines, and they must be educated regarding specific issues facing each of these species when dealing with laws designed to protect these species. Legal reform is essential if we are to preserve endangered species—not just grizzlies, but eagles and osprey and lynx and many, many others.

The Obama administration incorporated several new principles into the mechanisms of federal agencies, such as ecological restoration, interagency collaboration, stronger mandates for forest plans, and a consideration of the effects of climate change on forest health. These should require the Forest Service to involve the public in creating new plans, which could bring valuable input from a diversity of citizens. Time will tell—the proof will be in the implementation (Fears).

The Flathead case highlights interplay between people, politics, and laws: Agency policies (rather than the ESA) are often decisive where species survival is concerned. We must therefore protect endangered species not only by hauling agencies into court when they fail to comply with extant laws, but also by lobbying, outreach, education, direct action, and by setting an informed example with our lives: If we are going to save wildlife, we must understand the relationship between our consumer choices (such as supporting the cattle industry) and wild populations (like wolves), *and act accordingly*. My day in court taught me that an interdisciplinary, integrated approach is vital if we are to protect threatened species, and essential for the mental well-being of activists.

References

Defenders of Wildlife. "Grizzly Bear." Accessed 1 Feb., 2011. <www.defenders.org/wildlife_
    and_habitat/wildlife/grizzly_bear.php#>.

Fears, Darryl. "National Forests Plan would Expand Local Discretion over Wildlife
    Management." Feb. 11, 2011. Accessed 16 Feb., 2011. <www.washingtonpost.com/wp-
    dyn/content/article/2011/02/10/AR2011021007627.html>.

Freed, James. "U.S. Court Rules Yellowstone Grizzlies are Threatened." Sept. 22, 2009.
    Accessed1 Feb.,2011.<green.blogs.nytimes.com/2009/09/22/fedearl-court-rules-that-
    yellowstone-grizzlies-are-threatened/>.

Greater Yellowstone Coalition, Inc., v. USFWS. CV 07-134-M-DWM (Sept. 21, 2009).

McLellan, B.N., C. Servheen, and D. Huber, 2008. "Ursus Arctos." *IUCN 2010: IUCN Red List
    of Threatened Species.* Version 2010.3. Accessed 6 Oct., 2010. <www.iucnredlist.org>.

Norton v. Southern Utah Wilderness Alliance. 542 U.S. 55 at 67, 71 (2004).

Rohlf, Daniel J. "Jeopardy Under the Endangered Species Act: Playing A Game Protected
    Species Can't Win." Nov. 28, 2001. Accessed 1 Feb., 2011. <www.washburnlaw.edu/
    wlj/41-1/articles/rohlf-daniel.pdf>.

Sabalow, Ryan. "Herger pushes to take gray wolf off Endangered Species list." Dec. 8,
    2010. Accessed 7 Feb., 2011. <www.redding.com/news/2010/dec/08/keeping-the-gray-
    wolf-out-of-california/>.

Swan View Coalition. "The Absurdity of Late-Season Snowmobiling." Winter-Spring
    2010. Accessed 1 Feb., 2011. <www.swanview.org/Newsletters/Winter-Spring%202010%
    20e.pdf>.

Swan View Coalition. "Judge Rules Snowmobiling in Contempt of Court!" Summer 2009.
    Accessed 1 Feb., 2011. <www.swanview.org/Newsletters/Summer%202009%20e.pdf>.

Swan View Coalition. "Lawsuits Continue to Reap Benefits for Fish and Wildlife." Fall
    2009. Accessed 1 Feb., 2011. <www.swanview.org/Newsletters/Fall%202009%20e.pdf>.

Swan View Coalition. "Standards Limiting Motorized Vehicles." Winter 2008. Accessed
    1 Feb., 2011. <www.swanview.org/Newsletters/Winter%202008.pdf>.

Swan View Coalition v. Barbouletos. No. 06-73-M-DWM, 2008 WL 5682094, *25 (D. Mont.
    June 13, 2008).

U.S. Fish & Wildlife Service. "Section 7 Consultation Handbook" (March 1998): 4–22.
    Accessed 1 Feb., 2011. <www.fws.gov/endangered/esa-library/pdf/esa_section7_
    handbook.pdf>.

U.S. Fish & Wildlife Service. "Threatened/Endangered Wildlife in the U.S." Accessed 8
    Oct. 2010. <ecos.fws.gov/tess_public/pub/listedAnimals.jsp>.

CHAPTER 19

Panda Preservation 2.0: Shifting Gears to Save a Species

Anna Beech, Marc Brody

The giant panda is China's most beloved global icon, an international symbol of peace and conservation that has become a microcosm of China's struggle to balance development with conservation. This struggle has repercussions around the world because of China's size and rapidly growing economy. Accordingly, the path forward, the next step on China's journey to rescue giant pandas from the brink of extinction, is important for us all. China must restore the balance between human beings, development, and the natural world.

China is experiencing enormous change—socially, culturally, and environmentally. This change has huge consequences for human beings, flora, and fauna. As an emerging global leader, China is in a position to provide leadership and business models that embrace sustainability. These models must balance development and conservation, and in doing so, preserve what remains of China's wild places and wildlife, as well as restore degraded lands. If China fails in this important role, it is more likely that we fail collectively—China has the potential to tip the scales with regard to human pressure on the planet. Without proper planning to address the effects of climate change, preservation of critically endangered species such as the giant panda will be in serious jeopardy. Without concrete, decisive actions to restore the balance between humanity and nature, essential resources like water, food, and fuel will become so scarce that we will be unable to sustain our increasingly large population.

Short History of People and Pandas

From the earliest historical records, pandas have been regarded as mystical, legendary, noble, brave, fierce, mighty, peaceful ... and extremely rare. Pandas have long been held to embody an assortment of attributes. In some circles, ancient warriors were compared to pandas who, like tigers, were acknowledged for great strength. Other historical records reveal the panda as an "animal of justice," a gentle, peaceful, vegetarian that hurts no other animals—despite great strength. The lore and mystery of the solitary, elusive panda persisted through time in the absence of artistic representations, which were not created

© KONINKLIJKE BRILL NV, LEIDEN, 2015 | DOI 10.1163/9789004293090_021

until the 1900s. Interestingly, other bears were depicted in ancient Chinese art—only the panda remained unseen and mysterious.

Accordingly, the Western world was unaware of the giant panda until the late 1800s. In 1869, French zoologist and botanist Armand David discovered the pelt of a giant panda in a local market, and became the first European to call attention to this little known species. Though fascinated by such an "exotic" creature, Europeans failed to recognize the giant panda as a bear. Zoos were soon clamoring for a live specimen, and the first zoo (outside of China) to house giant pandas was Chicago's Lincoln Park Zoo, which took Su Lin in 1936. But with little to no understanding of the biological needs of pandas, these fragile novelties died young: Su Lin survived for just over a year.

In 1949, with the birth of the People's Republic of China (PRC), China's Central Government prohibited export of giant pandas. In 1953, China began breeding these bears in domestic zoos. In 1962 China turned a corner with regard to giant panda conservation, banning hunting of these increasingly scarce bears, and in 1963 founded the first giant panda reserves (northwest of Chengdu in Southwest China), including the critically important Wolong Nature Reserve (in Wolong, Sichuan's capital). Also in 1963, Beijing Zoo saw the first giant panda born in captivity, named Mingming.

"Panda diplomacy" has been central to the Chinese government's efforts to normalize relations with other countries, beginning with China's gift of two pandas to First Lady, Pat Nixon, immediately after President Richard Nixon's historic trip to China in 1972—he was the first U.S. president to visit PRC while in office, ending twenty-five years of isolation between the United States and China. The United Kingdom's Prime Minister Edward Heath then requested and was granted two pandas after his visit to China in 1974. "Panda diplomacy" has continued to build China's foreign relations, providing nations around the world with a chance to experience the wonder of the giant panda.

Captive Breeding

Panda diplomacy was only possible because of China's domestic captive breeding programs. Over the last 30 years, China's captive breeding programs have been tremendously successful. Two different panda centers manage 80 percent of China's captive pandas: Chengdu Research Base (affiliated with the China zoo system) and China Conservation and Research Centre (affiliated with Wolong Nature Reserve and State Forestry Administration). While both centers are in Sichuan, their reach is worldwide, connecting panda conservation with nations around the world. Veterinary care and reproductive research is the focus of China's panda centers—especially with regard to breeding and raising pandas in captivity. As of late 2012, PRC's research, veterinary care, and breeding programs have built a captive population of roughly 320 pandas, demonstrating the Chinese government's commitment and competence with regard to preserving captive giant pandas.

Recently a new panda conservation chapter has been opened: reintroduction. In this practice, captive bred pandas are released in nature reserves in Sichuan Province. Reintroduction training (rehabilitation) started at the Wolong Nature Reserve, where pandas are learning necessary skills for survival in the wild, including how to mark territory, forage, build "nests" for napping, recognize and escape predators (such as leopards), and how to cope with parasites, including ticks and mites.

The first giant panda released into the wild, Xiang Xiang, was released in 2006 at just 22 months of age. Unfortunately, young Xiang Xiang was unable to find and defend his own territory. Just a few months after release, Xiang Xiang was found dead, mortally injured in conflicts with stronger male pandas. In the fall of 2012, a second young male, Tao Tao, was released in the Liziping Nature Reserve. This reserve, which has very few remaining pandas, is approximately 200 kilometers southwest of the place where Tao Tao was raised (a large natural mountain-side enclosure at Wolong, called Hetaoping). Initial reports indicate that Tao Tao is doing well in the wild. In 2013 a group of four pandas (all one year younger than Tao Tao), who are now being rehabilitated at Hetaoping, will be released into onto panda reserves.

Habitat Conservation

While a tremendous effort has been put into captive breeding programs over the last 30 years, much less has been done to protect China's wild pandas. In light of climate change and ongoing environmental degradation from human population sprawl and economic growth, wild giant pandas are at great risk of extinction. They are listed as endangered by CITES, by the International Union for Conservation of Nature (IUCN Red List of Threatened Species), and as a Class 1 Protected Animal in China. Under PRC's Protection of Wildlife, passed into law in 1989, Class 1 species are protected by the Central Government.

Why has so little been done to protect wild giant pandas and their habitat? People can connect with captive pandas. They can see them and even touch pandas—for a fee. With large heads, woolly coats, and stark colors, giant pandas are eye-catching—downright adorable. There is a reassuring and well-defined sense of success when dealing with the breeding of captive pandas.

In contrast, wild pandas are elusive, far from the human eye—let alone the human hand. There are also numerous complexities and uncertainties involved with preserving sufficiently large areas of forest to maintain wild panda's populations. People are generally more supportive of breeding programs that carry tangible perks than they are of hard-to-quantify, long-term habitat protection. Fundamentally, captive breeding—with all those fuzzy little black and white cubs—is much easier to sell to the public, governments, and NGOs than the long-term task of protecting habitat.

Consequently, preserving habitat has been understaffed and underfunded. But looking ahead, the next step—Panda Preservation 2.0—requires restoring and protecting panda habitat.

The historical range of giant pandas (over the last 2,000 years) extended into northern Vietnam and Burma (Myanmar), and far to the east, into the plains of central China. Today, remaining habitat is only found in the geographical transition area between the Tibetan Himalayan plateau to the west and agrarian China to the east. This remaining, very narrow crescent of fragmented panda habitat stretches from southwest to northwest Sichuan, continuing north just into Gansu, then east to the Qinling Mountains of Shanxi. Once every 10 years China conducts a census of wild panda populations. The last census (completed in 2004) indicated that there are only 1,600 remaining wild pandas. A new census was just completed in early 2015. The latest census data shows wild panda populations have increased to 1,864, though there are growing threats from continued degradation and habitat fragmentation due to increasing human pressures.

Fortunately, the Chinese government is already moving toward habitat restoration and protection. In the last 50 years, more than 50 reserves have been set aside for giant pandas, largely in Sichuan Province, where more than 75 percent of the world's pandas live, with one primary panda reserve in the northeast—Wanglang Nature Reserve in Shanxi Province. The largest contiguous block of giant panda habitat is Sichuan's Giant Panda Sanctuaries (The Sanctuary), a World Heritage Site since 2006, composed of 16 protected areas, home to more than 30 percent of the world's wild giant pandas. The most prominent and significant protected area within The Sanctuary is Wolong Nature Reserve, home to nearly 10 percent of the world's wild pandas and home to the China Conservation and Research Center for the Giant Panda—China's leading captive panda center, caring for more than 180 giant pandas. Outside of the world's tropical rainforests, The Sanctuary's protected areas are among the most biologically diverse lands on the planet, supporting up to 6,000 plant species that provide refuge for a handful of critically endangered species, including red pandas, snow leopards, clouded leopards, and of course giant pandas.

Prime panda habitat lies between 2,000 and 3,000 meters (around 6,600 to 10,000ft.), where the panda's critical food source, bamboo (especially umbrella and arrow bamboo) grows in abundance. To date, restriction zones have not sufficiently protected panda habitat, and recent research indicates that climate change is likely to threaten bamboo forests. Scientists have recently provided comprehensive forecasts predicting how climate change is likely to affect China's common bamboo species. Even the most optimistic scenarios predict that bamboo die-offs will destroy panda habitat by the end of this century. Other threats to panda habitat include unsustainable livelihoods, highway development, a lack of wildlife corridors, and the devastating Sichuan earthquake of May 2008—the epicenter for the largest natural disaster in modern China was just a few kilometers from the Wolong Nature Reserve. In the aftermath of the earthquake, impoverished villagers have turned to grazing farmed animals, who destroy natural flora along with the land's ability to rejuvenate. Furthermore, Wolong is ill-prepared for the large influx of tourists expected when reconstruction is complete, presenting new challenges for maintaining the integrity of wild lands for pandas.

Panda Preservation 2.0

In order to save the giant panda, habitat must be well protected. Like other developing nations, China walks a tightrope between economic development and conservation. With knowledge, foresight, planning and patience, both can grow and prosper.

A promising panda habitat conservation program is unfolding in the Wolong Nature Reserve—Panda Mountain (funded by U.S.-China Environmental Fund, an international conservation NGO). Panda Mountain works with indigenous communities within the reserve to restore degraded lands on behalf of giant pandas. This helps local communities, giant pandas, and a host of native flora and fauna.

At Wolong, where Panda Mountain is located, a new habitat conservation initiative for a long-term native forest restoration program has just begun. Fifty years ago, Sichuan foresters planted Japanese larch (*Larix kaempferi*, a fast growing, invasive, non-native tree) in the hope of quickly providing forest cover for logged Wolong lands. Decades later, Sichuan scientists have noted that these non-native monoculture stands inhibit natural forest regeneration—extremely dense larch stands out-compete all other vegetation. Furthermore, these trees dump a thick layer of needles on the forest floor each fall, causing an adverse effect on soil structure and chemistry, preventing germination of native seeds.

With strong support from the Wolong Nature Reserve Administration, Panda Mountain is building a team of Sichuan foresters, ecologist, and scientists, and is engaging local communities, to enhance and expand giant panda habitat. The first step is to replace mono-culture larch stands with local biodiversity, an ecological restoration project that employs (and trains) local villagers, who will grow and supply native plants for the project, especially trees. Local communities will also benefit from the sale of Japanese larch timber. By employing and training indigenous people, Panda Mountain has created local stewards for protected areas, helping them maintain their traditional connection to the land while offering sustainable livelihoods, restoring balance between people and nature. At Panda Mountain local villagers are critical to the long-term success of Panda Preservation 2.0.

Remediation and Restoration

Restated, the best way to save giant pandas (Panda Preservation 2.0) is the road less traveled—restoration ecology. Historically, reduce, reuse, recycle (three "r"s) symbolize mainstream environmentalism. A fourth and a fifth "r"—remediation and restoration—must be added to this list if we are to effectively bring change. After decades of industrialization—from factory farming and trawling to the spread of DDT and mercury—it is time for environmental remediation. Sustainable forest ecosystems also require restoration—not only for giant pandas, but for health of ecosystems around the world.

It is particularly important for restoration to create corridors between fragmented, endangered wildlife populations. Corridors help pandas (and other wildlife) to navigate roads, human settlements, and rivers, reducing the chance that isolated populations will interbreed and ultimately die out. Corridors allow otherwise isolated sub-populations to mingle, enriching their gene pool, increasing chances of long-term survival. They also help pandas to avoid human activities, and to increase their chances of finding forage in habitat likely to be significantly, negatively affected in the near future by climate change.

Conclusion

In 2013, the Wolong Nature Reserve, home to the largest population of giant pandas anywhere in the world, will celebrate a historic 50th anniversary. With high-profile international recognition as an International Biosphere Reserve and World Heritage Site, Wolong can—and must—serve as a showcase for what is possible on behalf of endangered species.

In the world of bears, the giant panda has been relatively lucky—they are not forced to do tricks, they are not farmed for bile, and they are protected from guns by laws backed by the death penalty. Despite all of this, the giant panda is in serious trouble. Their habitat has been continually diminished because growth-oriented humanity has been unable (or unwilling) to balance conservation with economic development. Perhaps the desperate plight of China's giant panda, much loved by people around the world, can provide motivation to heal our relationship with the world around us.

As we move toward Panda Preservation 2.0, we must look beyond giant pandas to re-examine the interface between humans and nature. We need new solutions, different approaches, and concerted efforts to change our relationship with the natural world so we can coexist with other species. If we are to save giant pandas and their habitat, nature can no longer be viewed as something separate from humanity. This breadth of vision will require financial investment, international participation, commitment to sustainability, knowledge transfer, and most fundamentally, a shift in how we view our relationship with the natural world. To save giant pandas, we must first restore the balance between people and nature.

PART IV

Bears and Beyond

∴

CHAPTER 20

Canary in the Arctic

Lisa Kemmerer

In some ways, our plight with regard to bears is like that of early coal miners who descended deeper and deeper into the earth, down longer and longer shafts that penetrated the earth's crusty surface. As miners descended, it became more critical—and more challenging—to maintain life-assuring oxygen. Canaries also require oxygen, but are more sensitive to methane and carbon monoxide than are human beings: Before human lungs are affected by "bad" air, canaries sway on their perches, fall to the cage floor, and perish. Miners exploited the canary's oxygen-sensitivity, toting bright yellow birds into dark mine shafts to serve as early warning signs for noxious gases. They understood that a dead canary was their first and final warning: Get out of the mine shaft before it is too late. Similarly, the world's disappearing bears warn us that we must change our course of action quickly if we are to mitigate the worst effects of past indulgences, and avoid yet more problems in the near future.

Polar Bears and Ice

Polar bears are well adapted to their cold, slippery habitat, and cannot survive without ice. They are more thoroughly covered with fur than any other bear—they even have thick fur on the bottoms of their feet (G. Brown 64, 127). Each hollow, transparent hair absorbs UV light (Amstrup 588). The difference between the temperature of a polar bear's body and the surrounding environment can be as great as 80 C (175 F) (Wood 31). Polar bears are not merely adapted to icy conditions—they require ice to survive. They need ice to hunt, and they quickly overheat in warmer temperatures. The polar bear's range is determined by sea ice (G. Brown 30; "*Ursus*").

Fossils and DNA evidence indicate that polar bears evolved from European brown bears less than 100,000 years ago (Macdonald 580). Most likely, glaciers forced a large group of brown bears onto sea ice during the last ice-age, where they learned to hunt seals and began an independent evolutionary path (Domico 5, 65). Polar bears hunt from the ice, quietly waiting at air holes for prey to surface—sometimes for fourteen hours (Domico 74). Ringed seals are their most important staple, followed by bearded seals. When an unlucky seal comes up for air, a bear swats the pinniped with powerful forepaws, or seizes the head with strong jaws, pulling the slippery seal ashore. When a polar bear detects sleeping seals, the bear swims swiftly to the surface, bursts from the water, and dashes across the ice to seize a seal before the whole group disappears under-water. They also hunt on ice by sliding on their underbellies, their hind legs pushing them quietly toward their prey. When close enough—within 100 feet (30 meters)—the bear leaps up and charges the seal (Wood 66).

Ideally, polar bears secure a seal every five or six days (Domico 74). If they are able to catch enough seals, they eat only the blubber, which they digest more easily than protein, leaving the rest for less successful hunters and for those who are unable to pull seals from the water, such as arctic foxes (Amstrup 592). (This is one of the many ways that polar bears are important to larger ecosystems.) When bears are unable to secure food their metabolism drops, just as it does for other bear species when they den. This can happen at any time of year, allowing polar bears to live on fat reserves in the hope that food will soon become available (Domico 75). This ability is unique among bears—indeed, this "ability could make polar bears the most advanced of all mammals when it comes to dealing with food and water deprivation" (Amstrup 598).

Snow and ice are also critical for polar bear reproduction. Generally, polar bears only den if pregnant (Domico 75). Expectant mothers dig cozy dens deep in the snow, sometimes crawling under 3 meters (10 feet) of ice and snow to give birth. Their dens are about 2 meters (6 feet) long and one meter (3 feet) wide and high, with a 3–4.5 meter (10–15 foot) entrance tunnel. Den openings are just large enough (about a foot across—30 cm) for the mother to squeeze through, provid-ing a safe haven for cubs, who sometimes return to the den to rest when they begin to explore the outside world (Wood 47, 35; Domico 76). Dens can be 20 C (36 F) warmer than the outside world, and seldom dip below zero (32 F), giving offspring a better chance of survival (Stonehouse 24; Wood 51; G. Brown 157).

Polar bears depend on ice for their food source, as well as for denning and birthing. Climate change is melting the polar bear's essential, icy habitat: In the last 25 years, northern sea-ice has dropped from 12.5 to 11.5 million km^2, and if these declines continue—and there is every indication that sea-ice will decline more rapidly in the near future—reductions in polar bear habitat are likely to threaten the polar bear's survival (Amstrup 605).

Eating Ice: GHGE[1]

The plight of ice-dependent bears in a rapidly thawing Arctic seems to strike many people as just one more environmental nightmare relentlessly unfolding

---

1   For more information on environment and animal agriculture, see *Eating Earth*, Kemmerer, 2015.

on our watch—one of many problems that is out of sight, out of mind, and beyond our control. This is not the case—there is something critical that each one of us can do to help preserve and protect polar bears.

Today's accelerated climate change is caused largely by humanity's greenhouse gas emissions (GHGE). More specifically, Arctic warming is caused by human activities that pour carbon dioxide, methane, and nitrous oxide into the earth's atmosphere, creating a greenhouse effect: The sun's warming rays enter the earth's atmosphere, and are held there by thick layers of pollution—by greenhouse gas emissions (GHGE). This retained heat is warming the planet and melting Arctic ice. I learned about GHGE in grade school thirty years ago, but only recently has the relationship between climate change and animal agriculture been brought to light.

Worldwide, animal agriculture contributes more carbon dioxide to the atmosphere (through the use of fossil fuels) than any other single source (Goodland and Anhang 11): Animal agriculture "creates more global warming" than all the world's cars, trucks, trains, boats, and planes combined (Oppenlander 16). Producing animal products pumps *at least* 32,564 million tons of carbon dioxide into the atmosphere every year, creating more than half of the earth's annual greenhouse gas emissions (Goodland and Anhang 11).

Choosing to consume animal products greatly increases our GHGE footprint; beef is likely the greatest offender. The United States and Brazil are the world's leading beef producers—the U.S. consumes about 26 billion pounds (12 billion kg) of beef each year, supporting an industry with a retail value of about $80 billion. The U.S. exports some 3 billion pounds (1.3 billion kg) of beef every year, bringing in more than $5 billion ("Cattle and Beef"). All this even though

· producing just one protein calorie in feedlot bovines requires nearly 80 calories of fossil fuels, while one protein calorie from soybeans requires just 2 calories of fossil fuels (Schwartz 86);
· one serving of beef creates the atmospheric warming potential of 80 pounds (36 kg) of carbon dioxide—as much as an ordinary car driving three hours to travel 155 miles (250 km) (Fanelli);
· industrially produced flesh has an energy input-to-output ratio of 35:1 (Cassuto 4).

Any one of these statistics ought to lead serious environmentalist to replace meat balls and cold cuts with more environmentally friendly options, but with regard to diet and the environment, the most important statistic is this: 70 percent of U.S. grains and 60 percent of EU grains are fed to farmed animals (Oppenlander 12; *Livestock's* 272). Worldwide, farmed animals consume more than 700 million tons of "cereals" each year ("Top"). Every year in the U.S., cattle alone consume roughly 110 billion pounds (50 billion kg) of grain: Producing one pound (.45 kg) of beef requires an estimated 16 pounds (7.3 kg) of grain (Dawn 280).

Feeding grain to cattle causes much more environmental damage than we would cause if we ate grains directly. Fossil fuels are burned to prepare the land, plant the crops, fertilize the soil, weed and cull crops, and to harvest and transport seeds, fertilizer, equipment, green waste, and grains. Additionally, fossil fuels are burned at every facility that breeds, feeds, and maintains cattle (or other farmed animals), as well as for slaughter, processing, and transportation. Humans create as much as 41 million tons of CO_2 just to produce chemical fertilizers for feedcrops ("Greenhouse").

Consuming dairy products also increases our environmental footprint tremendously. Cows raised for milk require and consume many more calories than do cattle raised for flesh because they must create and birth offspring and produce milk. Some lactating cows consume more than four percent of their body weight, or a whopping 54 pounds (24.5 kg) of grain daily (Grant and Kononoff). Preparing the soil, planting, tending, and harvesting so many tons of grain to feed cattle (and other farmed animals) wastes fossil fuels while greatly increasing GHGE.

In light of the fact that feeding grains to farmed animals wastes more calories than are ultimately produced, no additional grain production is needed as humans transition to a plant based diet. In fact, we can grow considerably less grain, cutting back on fossil fuel use, as well as our use of freshwater, pesticides, chemical fertilizers, and so on. Consuming animal products creates ten times as many fossil fuel emissions *per calorie* as does consuming plant foods directly (Oppenlander 18). We can feed ourselves much more efficiently—and therefore with a much lower environmental footprint—if we replace flesh and dairy with fruits, vegetables, and grains.

After fossil fuels, methane (CH_4) is our second largest—and much more potent—GHGE. Methane remains in the atmosphere for 9–15 years, and in that time traps solar radiation 25 times more effectively than does carbon dioxide (Goodland and Anhang 13). This means that methane holds 72 times more heat than carbon dioxide when calculated across just twenty years (*Livestock's* 82; Oppenlander 6; "Methane"). The decomposition of manure and the digestive process of ruminants (cud-chewing animals such as cattle, sheep, and goats—called enteric fermentation) are responsible for 80 percent of the methane stemming from agriculture. Ruminants exhale about 8.5 million tons of methane annually (*Livestock's* 112). Due to methane's potency, this provides the GHGE equivalent of 18 million tons of carbon dioxide (Cassuto 5; *Livestock's*

96). "Globally, ruminant livestock emit about 80 million metric tons of methane annually, accounting for 28 percent of global methane emissions from human-related activities" ("Entric"). Animal agriculture is the largest human induced (anthropogenic) source of methane, responsible for a whopping 40 percent of global methane (Oppenlander 6; *Livestock's* 82, 95, 112).

Grass-fed beef results in even more methane emissions than standard beef. It takes longer to fatten grass-fed calves for slaughter. Grass is more difficult to digest, so grass-fed cattle emit 50–60 percent more methane than grain-fed cattle (Oppenlander 125). Plants do not emit methane (Oppenlander 18). Dairy products also are linked with enormous amounts of methane. A 10,000-cow dairy farm (larger dairy farms contain more than 15,000 cows) emits 33,092 pounds of methane every day (along with 3,575 pounds of ammonia and 409 pounds of nitrous oxide) (Hawthorne 37; "Changes" 2). The U.K.'s 10 million cows produce 25–30 percent of Britain's methane pollution ("Future").

Nitrous oxide (N_2O) traps solar radiation 300 times more effectively than does carbon dioxide, and stays in the atmosphere "for an average of 120 years" ("Nitrous"). Nitrous oxide is the largest anthropogenic source of GHGE ("NOAA"). Worldwide, agriculture produces a startling 65 percent of human-induced nitrous oxide (Oppenlander 6; *Livestock's* 114). Animal agriculture is responsible for 75 percent of these emissions, resulting in the CO_2 equivalent of 2.2 billion tons of GHGE ("The Role"). Artificial soil fertilization (nitrogen, when added to the soil, emits nitrous oxide), fossil fuel combustion, and manure (oxygen combines with nitrogen as manure decomposes, emitting nitrous oxide) create 96 percent of the earth's nitrous oxide, and animal agriculture is the primary cause of each ("Nitrous"; Gluckman; "What"). All told, U.S. animal agriculture produces almost 1.5 million tons of nitrous oxide every year, providing the GHGE equivalent of more than 41 million tons of carbon dioxide (Cassuto 5).

Animal agriculture is by far the most significant single source of earth-warming GHGE. Our food choices are creating a steady drip in the polar bear's essential, icy habitat.

Eating Forests: Deforestation

Just as surely as polar bears depend on ice, most bears depend on forests, and the biggest immediate threat to bears around the world is deforestation, which robs bears of their homes, their sustenance, and their protective cover (Craighead 42, 123). Climate change and deforestation are inextricably linked. For Yellowstone grizzlies, fatty whitebark pine seeds are an essential source of sustenance, but winters are no longer cold enough to prevent whitebark pine beetles from marching northward, consuming Yellowstone's whitebark pines and robbing grizzlies of this rich source of fat (Van Noppen 4). The giant panda's bamboo supply is also feeling the heat, and these distinctive bears will not survive in the absence of the temperature-sensitive bamboo, on which they feed almost exclusively. Andean bears, South America's only bear species, are vulnerable to extinction due to "the expansion of the agricultural frontier" (*"Tremarctos"*). Not only is their habitat destroyed, but when they seek food outside of their vanishing forest home, farmers and ranchers kill bears to protect their property.

A section of rainforest roughly the size of 20 football fields (22 soccer/football fields) is destroyed pretty much every minute of every day. As with GHGE, animal agriculture is the most significant force behind deforestation. For the sake of grazing and feed crops, one fifth of the world's rainforests were destroyed between 1960 and 1990. Between 1985 and 1990, 210 million acres of forest were turned to pasture, "an area nearly the size of Texas and Oklahoma" (Kaufman and Braun 18). In "the Amazon, cattle ranching is now the primary reason for deforestation" (*Livestock's* 272). In just 50 years, 50 percent of Costa Rica's forests disappeared—60 percent were cleared for cattle ("Deforestation in Costa"); only 13 percent of Costa Rica's original rainforests remain, and remaining forests are "highly fragmented and degraded" (Reynolds 11).

South America suffers most acutely from deforestation, with Brazil leading the pack (by a considerable margin). Agriculture is responsible for roughly 98 percent of this deforestation, with cattle ranchers directly responsible for 65–70 percent of Brazil's loss of rainforests ("Causes"). There were about 10 million cattle in Brazil in 1980; there are now upwards of 55 million ("Deforestation: The Leading"). Both the U.S. and the EU are implicated: the U.S. imports some 80 million pounds of Brazilian beef every year: 85 percent of EU beef originates in Brazil. All this ecological devastation yields a mere spot of flesh—55 feet (17 meters) of tropical forests yield just a quarter pound (120 grams) of hamburger. If we continue to consume animal products as we are today, primary forests will be altogether gone by 2050 (Hawthorne 39, Pimm 844).

Those who consume any animal products—turkeys, pigs, chickens, cattle, eggs, cheese, sour cream, butter, mayonnaise, cottage cheese, yogurt, and so on—are implicated in the disappearance of the earth's forests. The primary reason for deforestation is conversion of woodlands to agriculture—for grazing and feed crops. The primary feed crop is now soybeans; 80 percent of the world's soybean crop is fed to farmed animals (Reynolds 13). Land is converted from forests to agriculture in Latin American countries largely to feed farmed animals, "notably soybeans and maize" (*Livestock's* 12). Those who accuse soy-eaters of destroying forests have missed a vital point: 80 percent of the earth's soybeans are raised for chickens, turkeys, pigs, and cattle, implicating those who eat cheese and chicken, not those who eat tofu (Reynolds 13).

Fragmentation and loss of habitat are the most immediate threat to bears around the world (Craighead 42, 123). Omnivorous consumers who buy animal products are chewing habitat—and bears—into oblivion.

Bringing Change

Human beings have brought much harm to other animals and the earth. The canary in the coal mine unwittingly served as a critical warning for miners: When a canary died, miners knew they needed to act quickly to survive. Similarly, the disappearance of bears warns that we must act quickly if we are to save innumerable dwindling species—especially species that are dependent on large expanses of fast-disappearing ice flows and forests.

Polar bears are threatened by climate change and Andean bears are threatened by deforestation. Both problems stem most prominently from human consumption patterns in comparatively wealthy nations—from animal agriculture. If we want to protect endangered species, we must change what we eat and inform others regarding climate change, habitat, endangered wildlife, and dietary choice. We must also encourage senators and representatives to:

- create/support policies that require industries and consumers to pay the full cost of production (including environmental costs) for all goods consumed;
- alter policies that create or maintain subsidies to artificially lower the cost of meat, milk, eggs, or feedstock grains;
- create/support policies that ban the importation of animal agriculture products from nations experiencing high levels of deforestation;
- ratify the Kyoto Protocol, which will commit the U.S. to follow international guidelines reducing GHGE;
- create policies that require the U.S. Government to provide nutritional information (especially in grade school texts) informed solely by international scientific research (excluding influence from powerful lobbies such as the meat and dairy industries).

Humans have taken over the planet, leaving little room for other animals. We have captured, caged, and shot bears; we have stolen their lands and forests, their gall bladders, paws, and fur coats. Bears around the world face exploitation, extermination, extirpation, and/or extinction. We are not at our leisure to waste time blaming and lamenting—we must pinpoint key threats, figure out what can be done on behalf of the world's bears, and do it.

Forests will not grow back overnight; previous GHGE will linger for many years to come, but we are not helpless. The fate of bears from the Arctic ice to tropical rainforests is not yet sealed. We have the power to bring change. Apathy, rather than climate change and deforestation, is our most dangerous enemy. Like miners watching a canary sway on her perch, we must heed the clear (and unnerving) warning signs: We can and must change our ways—starting with our diet.

References

Amstrup, Steven C. "Polar Bear: *Ursus maritimus.*" *Wild Mammals of North America: Biology, Management, and Conservation,* 2nd edition. Ed. George A Feldhamer, Bruce C. Thompson, and Joseph A. Chapman. Baltimore: Johns Hopkins U.P., 2003. 587–610.

Brown, Gary. *Great Bear Almanac.* CT: Lyons Press, 1993.

Cassuto, David N. "The CAFO Hothouse: Climate Change, Industrial Agriculture, and the Law." Ann Arbor: Animals and Society Institute, 2010.

"Changes in the Size and Location of U.S. Dairy Farms." *Profits, Costs, and the Changing Structure of Dairy Farming / ERR-47.* Economic Research Service/USDA. 2–4. Accessed Feb. 20, 2012. <http://www.ers.usda.gov/publications/err47/err47b.pdf>.

Comerford, John W., George L. Greaser, H. Louis Moore, and Jayson K. Harper. "Agricultural Alternatives: Feeding Beef Cattle." Pennsylvania State University. 2001. Accessed 26 Dec. 2011. <http://agalternatives.aers.psu.edu/Publications/feeding_beef_cattle.pdf>.

Craighead, Lance. *Bears of the World.* Stillwater MN: Voyageur, 2000.

Dawn, Karen. *Thanking the Monkey.* NY: William Morrow, 2008.

Domico, Terry. *Bears of the World.* NY: Facts on File, 1988.

"Entric Fermentation Mitigation." *Center for Climate and Energy Solutions: Working Together for the Environment and for the Economy.* Accessed April 13, 2013. <http://www.c2es.org/technology/factsheet/EntericFermentation>.

Fanelli, Daniele. "Meat is Murder on the Environment." *New Scientist.* July 18, 2007.

"Future Technology." *Future Electro Tech.* Blogspot.com. 23 Oct. 2008. Accessed 28 Dec. 2011. <http://futureelectrotech.blogspot.com/>.

Gluckman, Matt. "EPA Regional CAFO Waste Issues." *Epa.gov.* Accessed 27 Dec. 2011. <http://www.epa.gov/ncer/publications/workshop/pdf/gluckman_region582007.pdf>.

Goodland, Robert and Jeff Anhang. *Livestock and Climate Change.* Worldwatch.org Nov./Dec. 2009. Accessed 27 December 2011. <http://www.worldwatch.org/files/pdf/Livestock%20and%20Climate%20Change.pdf3>.

Grant, Rick and Paul J. Kononoff. University of Nebraska-Lincoln. "Feeding to Maximize Milk Protein and Fat Yields." Feb. 2007. Accessed 28 Dec. 2011. <http://elkhorn.unl.edu/epublic/live/g1358/build/#target2>.

Hawthorne, Mark. "Planet in Peril." *VegNews.* March-April 2012. 34–41.

Kaufman, Stephen R. and Nathan Braun. *Good News for All Creation: Vegetarianism as Christian Stewardship.* Cleveland: Vegetarian Advocates Press, 2004.

Kemmerer, *Lisa. Eating Earth: Dietary Choice and Planetary Health.* Oxford: Oxford U. Press, 2014.

Livestock's Long Shadow: Environmental Issues and Options. Food and Agriculture Organization of the United Nations. Rome: Food and Agriculture Organization, 2006.

Macdonald, David W., ed. *The Encyclopedia of Mammals.* Oxford U. Press, 2009. 574–588.

"Methane vs. CO2 Global Warming Potential." *Global Warning Forecasts.* N.d. Accessed 28 Dec. 2011. <http://www.global-warming-forecasts.com/methane-carbon-dioxide.php>.

"Nitrous Oxide Emissions: Greenhouse Gas Emissions." *EPA United States Environmental Protection Agency: Climate Change.* Accessed Jan. 31, 2013. <http://epa.gov/climat-echange/ghgemissions/gases/n2o.html>.

"NOAA Study Shows Nitrous Oxide Now Top Ozone-Depleting Emission." *NOAA National Oceanic and Atmospheric Administration United States Department of Commerce.* Aug. 27, 2009. Accessed Jan. 31, 2013. <http://www.noaanews.noaa.gov/stories2009/20090827_ozone.html>.

Oppenlander, Richard A. *Comfortably Unaware: Global Depletion and Food Responsibility ... What You Choose to Eat is Killing our Planet.* Minneapolis: Langdon Street, 2011.

Pimm, Stuart L. and Peter Raven. "Extinction by Numbers." *Nature* 403 (24 Feb. 2000): 843–845.

"Rainforest Facts." Raintree.com. 20 Mar. 2010. Accessed 28 Dec. 2011. <http://www.rain-tree.com/facts.htm>.

Reynolds, Laura and Danielle Nierenberg. *Worldwatdch Report 188: Innovations in Sustainable Agriculture: Supporting Climate-Friendly Food Production.* Washington, DC: Worldwatch Institute, 2012.

"The Role of Livestock in Climate Change." *Food and Agriculture Organization of the United Nations: Livestock, Environment, and Development.* Accessed May 27, 2013. <http://www.fao.org/agriculture/lead/themeso/climate/en/>.

Schwartz, Richard H. *Judaism and Vegetarianism.* New York: Lantern, 2001.

Stonehouse, Bernard. *A Visual Introduction to Bears.* NY: Checkmark, 1998.

"Top 5 of Anything: Farming & Agriculture Statistics." The Top 5 Most Common Types of Livestock Feed Used Worldwide. Accessed Nov. 15, 2012. <http://top5ofanything.com/index.php?h=2aadbfa5>.

"Tremarctos ornatus Andean Bear." IUCN Red List of Threatened Species. Accessed Aug. 22, 2013. <http://liveassets.iucn.getunik.net/downloads/andean_bear.pdf>.

"Ursus maritimus." The IUCN Red List of Endangered Species. Accessed Aug. 15, 2013. <http://www.iucnredlist.org/details/22823/0>.

Van Noppen, Trip. "A Bad Climate for Grizzlies." *EarthJustice* (Summer 2012): 4.

"What are the Main Sources of Nitrous Oxide (N2O) Emissions?" *What's your impact on climate change? Use our calculator and learn how to help!.* Accessed 28 Dec. 2011. <http://www.whatsyourimpact.eu.org/n2o-sources.php>.

Wood, Daniel. *Bears.* Vancouver, Canada: Whitecap, 2005.

CHAPTER 21

Bears, Birds, and Human Hubris: Imagining Bears in the Andes

Thomas Regele

In 1782 the bald eagle was specifically chosen as the national symbol of the United States at the Second Continental Congress. The eagle was assumed to be an appropriate image to represent our fledgling nation, and the bird's admirable attributes were again extolled in 2004 in the *American Bald Eagle Recovery and National Emblem Commemorative Coin Act of 2004*, which lists reasons for preserving the bald eagle:

1. The bald eagle is the greatest visible symbol of the spirit of freedom and democracy in the world.
2. The bald eagle is unique to North America and represents the American values and attributes of freedom, courage, strength, spirit, loyalty, justice, equality, democracy, quality, and excellence.
3. The bald eagle's image and symbolism have influenced American art, music, history, literature, commerce, and culture since the founding of our Nation (American Bald Eagle Recovery Act of 2004. 108–486, 118).

While the graceful bald eagle was deemed *the* image that best reflected our rising nation, this raptor soon proved to be a scavenger—even a nuisance—and was killed like any other "pest" to the point of near extinction. According to the U.S. Fish and Wildlife Service, the eagle was killed because these great birds occasionally preyed on small domestic animals (young sheep, newborn calves, and so on). Eagles were shot for their feathers, and also "in an effort to eliminate a perceived threat" to animal agricultural profits (U.S. FWS 1). In Alaska, the Territorial Legislature placed a bounty on eagles in 1917 on behalf of fisherman, again to eliminate a perceived threat to human profits based on the erroneous idea that eagles compete with fishermen for salmon, claims that were eventually discredited. Nonetheless, the bounty remained until 1953, when Alaska became a state, at which time these eagles were taken in under the protected canopy of the federal *Bald Eagle Protection Act* of 1940. Between 1917 and 1953 more than 120,000 eagles were killed in Alaska on behalf of the fishing industry (*Bald Eagle. Species Profile*). In 1973, the bald eagle received further protection under the nation's Endangered Species Act (Endangered Species Act of 1973—16 USC 1531–1544).

© KONINKLIJKE BRILL NV, LEIDEN, 2015 | DOI 10.1163/9789004293090_023

What changed between early U.S. celebration of the bald eagle and the near extinction of the same bird? Certainly not the eagle, nor the bird's role in North-American ecosystems. What shifted was our perception of the eagle, and consequently the bird's cultural role in the U.S.

In many ways the turning fate of the Andean bear (also known as *oso front-ino, oso andino, oso de anteojos, el salvaje, jucumari,* and *mashiramo*) parallels the plight of the American bald eagle, except that the future of the Andean (or spectacled) bear remains tenuous. This essay explores the underlying motives and processes by which an icon—the Andean bear in this case—becomes an unwanted pest perilously close to eradication.

Andean Bears in the Indigenous Worldview

The Andean bear has been central to the cultures of various peoples of South America for centuries. The Andean bear has great religious and historical importance: "In any society, there are particular ways of envisioning the sur-rounding reality ... [A]nimals and plants have played an important role in the thoughts of the Andean inhabitants" (Torres).

This is certainly true for the Andean bear in South America. The bear is sometimes viewed as a threat, a sacrificial victim, "kin" to humans, or in the case of the Yukpas in Colombia, as embodying the protective spirit of Mashiramo, and in fact they have named the bear Mashiramo in their native language. The bear's connection to strength and virility is widespread: Pre-Inca tribes wor-shipped the bear, as did the Tomebamba in Ecuador, and there are ceremonial sites and textual references demonstrating the bear's sacred nature among numerous indigenous peoples throughout Peru (Paisley 250). In a legend from the U'wa culture in Columbia, the bear is regarded as an "older brother" who watches over the people, and thus, it is forbidden to kill the bear, who is under-stood to be the favorite son of Sira, the creator (Torres). The Inca understood the Andean bear to be a link between Earth and gods. In parts of Peru, evil people—"condemned souls" (bosses who exploited natives, corrupt priests, the incestuous, those disrespectful towards their parents)—"may only gain access to the afterlife if they have been killed by the bear" (Torres). Quechua beliefs, despite the infusion of Christianity (*sincretismo*), hold bears to be mediators "between the upper world (the gods) and the inferior world (human)," and to signify salvation for souls—even if these souls belong to people who "committed a mortal sin" (Torres). Within the Quechua worldview, the bear remains an agent of redemption. The bear is also believed to be endowed with the ability to "maintain order when chaos emerges" and is viewed as humanity's benefactor in chaotic times (Torres).

Moreover, the Andean bear is endowed with a wide range of attributes in native cultures, and is connected to many beliefs from different areas of the Andes, where the bear may be seen as:

· dangerous, requiring extermination (held by certain groups of rural peoples of mixed racial ancestry);
· a victim of ritual hunts (by Yukpas from the Perij Mountain Chain, Venezuela, who have many rituals and taboos that accompany the Andean bear);
· an ancestor (Colombian U'wa legends hold that human beings descended from bears);
· a human being transformed into a bear (the legend of "Uncle Tom" comes from the Bolivian Andes and tells of a black slave from colonial times who flees to the mountains and changes into a bear);
· a protector spirit of the forest (The Yukpas from the Perija mountains of Colombia relate the bear to the spirit of Mashiramo, the protector of the forest);
· a divine-human inter-mediator (the belief originates among the Quechuas in Peru);
· an element from the native natural calendar (among the Quechuas in Peru, whose mythology teaches that the bear is an indicator of the passage of time);
· a symbol of strength, knowledge, virility, and conservation (throughout Peru, Bolivia, and Venezuela) (Torres);
· kin, able to hold relations with human beings (in Venezuela and across the Andes, as in the widespread myth of "El Salvaje," included below).

The legend of "Juan Salvaje" (John the wild-man) demonstrates the kin-like relationship envisioned between bears and humans. In this vivid story, a bear kidnaps a woman while she is washing clothes on the edge of a river. The bear takes the woman out to a cave, brings her inside, then blocks the entrance with a large stone. He supplies her with food, and they live together for many years. Eventually they have a son; mother and child are very close. As the boy grows, he becomes strong enough to move the rock, allowing mother and son to escape to a nearby town. When the bear returns to the cave and finds his family gone, he approaches the town and is subsequently killed. As for the mother and son, no one in the town ever learns of their past, and the boy (who is half bear) is seamlessly assimilated into the human community (Herrera 154–155). A later version of this legend, affected by the introduction of Christianity, includes a portion where the boy tells his mother that he will only remove the rock from the entrance to the cave if she promises to have him baptized when they return to human civilization. The mother agrees. Again, no one is able to distinguish the boy (now a man) from any other human being, except by reference to his incredible strength, which he maintains long into old age (Torres 1).

In this myth we see that the bear and the human are viewed as similar enough to share a life, breed and have children, and that children produced from human-bear unions are indistinguishable from any other human being.

Europeans in the Andes—Shifting Indigenous Worldviews

The first recorded shift in the bear's cultural status came via Europeans. For newly-arrived Spaniards, the Andean bear was a reminder of the European brown bear, feared and hunted to near extinction in the past several centuries. Their fears were transferred to Andean bears, which subsequently began to suffer a similar fate. Moreover, because the Spanish Conquest included religious and cultural "re-education," bears were demonized as a living symbol of indigenous South American religion.

With the arrival of Europeans and subsequent *mestization* (mixing of indigenous and European blood and cultures), traditional indigenous religious practices received an overlay of Christian beliefs and attitudes. Most importantly, the people of the Andes were handed a view of humanity as standing in opposition to nature, and this antagonistic relationship with the natural world slowly overshadowed and replaced previous beliefs and understandings.

Christian conquerors re-constructed nature as menacing and dangerous (requiring domination and/or eradication). The "mechanical model" replaced a "magical tradition" and its accompanying concept of "mother nature" as alive and intertwined with human activity (Merchant 111). While these changes began in Europe prior to 1492, the "discovery" of the New World fostered a re-articulation and re-enactment of the Western world's distaste for and alienation from nature as a whole. On arrival in the Americas, Christian conquerors re-cast nature as disorder and chaos, requiring it to be "subdued and controlled" (Merchant 127). The organic, holistic indigenous view of the earth shifted in the sixteenth century thanks to European influence.

The demonization and persecution of the Andean bear is but one outcome of this larger process of shifting attitudes as the Western worldview took root in South America. For example, in both Europe and the Americas, women, like the bear, were associated with the untamed, threatening, natural world, and were likewise "re-cast" and demonized. The fanatical persecution of women in early modernity (under the guise of extirpating "witches") is an example of this Western worldview. The witch, like the bear, who was assumed to hold an intimate connection with Nature, became a "symbol of the violence of nature"—it is she who "raised storms, caused illness, destroyed crops, obstructed generation, and killed infants. Disorderly woman, like chaotic nature, needed to be controlled" (Merchant 127). Compounding the problem, the inhospitable wilderness was placed in opposition to the "bountiful, fruitful Garden of Eden" (Merchant 131), and thus both woman (Eve) and nature (hostile) were re-cast as "evil." The Andean bear, like woman-turned-witch, was deemed "pagan," a sinister and threatening beast to be extirpated.

Pathological Arrogance

While indigenous peoples tended to hold bears in high esteem—powerful, kin, and as an intermediary between humans and the divine—Christians viewed the Andean bear as just another dangerous and annoying aspect of nature, best eradicated. The Andean bear was yet another threat to human happiness, to manifest destiny, and to the rightful reign of humans—of Western Christians—over the earth and all that dwells therein. These European religious and cultural views eclipsed traditional Andean beliefs in the bear's divine or "supernatural" powers, and provided a *theological* vilification of Nature generally, and bears specifically.

Humanity's domination of nature is ultimately self-defeating, since "domination of nature involves domination of man"—"domination becomes 'internalized' for domination's sake" (Horkheimer 93). The "reason" employed in order to dominate nature is a form of sickness (Horkheimer 176). Similar "reasoning" has led us to believe that economic benefits (for example, from extracting resources) eclipse all else—including the earth itself. This faulty reasoning holds that economics eclipses "irrational" aspects of life such as religious beliefs, traditions, trees, hillsides, and bears. This view, in which economics supersedes all, overtly rejects spiritual, sacred, "irrational" indigenous traditions. (Despite the fact that Western humanity has continued to propagate Christian beliefs, the spiritual and sacred are viewed as comparatively irrelevant, and human beings are seen as apart from and above the rest of the animal kingdom to support an economic model.)

Christian conquerors in South America demonized and dominated nature, establishing human superiority, and plundered the wealth of the region—a process which many people now recognize as pathological, even deadly.

Conclusion

We project human attitudes and feelings onto nonhuman animals, and thereby assess which species are worthy of our esteem—and protection—and which are not. The American bald eagle and the Andean bear have both been privileged and victimized by this primitive human tendency.

Perhaps changing views of bears and eagles embody humanity's sincere desire to understand our relationship with the rest of nature, and our place in the universe. But our willingness to behave as if our changing attitudes embody some larger truth results in a very narrow and self-centered assessment of other species. Our willingness to determine the fate of species based on super-ficial human attitudes and feelings obscures the fact that each individual ani-mal exists in his or her own right, possesses inherent value as the center of his or her own world, and exists independent of our fickle, subjective, self-serving valuations. Our perceptions of eagles, turkeys, and bears are just that—our perceptions. What if early settlers in North America had chosen the turkey instead of the eagle as our national bird? Would we eat the bald eagle and call the turkey a "visible symbol of the spirit of freedom and democracy"?

In 1973 the Andean bear was listed as endangered and thus belatedly pro-tected (Naves 1277), but as of 2008 they are still in decline, and this species' future remains tenuous (IUCN List of Threatened Species). Just as the *American Bald Eagle Recovery and National Emblem Commemorative Coin Act of 2004* reminded Americans of how and why their ancestors esteemed these unique birds, it is critical that those living in Andean bear habitat reexamine their attitudes towards this fast-disappearing species. If locals can rediscover all that their ancestors admired and respected in this shy and increasingly scarce neighbor, they will likely also rediscover ways to live peacefully with Andean bears.

References

"United States. 2889—108th Congress: American Bald Eagle Recovery and National Emblem Commemorative Coin Act." www.GovTrack.us. Oct. 2004. Accessed March 3, 2013. <http://www.govtrack.us/congress/bills/108/s2889>.

"United States Bald Eagle: *Haliaeetus leucocephalus*." *U.S. Fish and Wildlife Service.* Nov. 2010. Accessed July, 14, 2012. <http://www.fws.gov/migratorybirds/BaldEagle.htm>.

"United States Bald Eagle Protection Act of 1940 (16 U.S.C. 668-668d, 54 Stat. 250)." *Digest of Federal Resource Laws of Interest to the U.S. Fish and Wildlife Service.* Jan. 2013. Accessed Feb. 8, 2013. <http://www.fws.gov/laws/lawsdigest/BALDEGL.HTML>.

"State of Alaska Bald Eagle. Species Profile." *Alaska Department of Fish and Game.* 2013. Accessed March 17, 2013. <http://www.adfg.alaska.gov/index.cfm?adfg=baldeagle.main>.

"United States Endangered Species Act of 1973—16 USC 1531–1544." *U.S. Fish and Wildlife Service: Office of Law Enforcement.* Jan. 2013. Accessed Feb. 8, 2013. <http://www.fws.gov/le/USStatutes/ESA.pdf>.

Garshelis, Dave. "A Glimpse Back 200 Years." *International Bear News* 20:3 (Aug. 2011): . Accessed July, 2012. <http://www.andeanbear.org/IBN2011Aug.pdf>.

Herrera, Anne-Marie et al. "The Spectacled Bear in the Sierra Nevada National Park of Venezuela." *International Conference on Bear Research and Management* 9:1 (Aug. 1994): 149–156. Accessed July, 2012. <http://www.carnivoreconservation.org/portal/p_detail.php?recordid=1651>.

Horkheimer, Max. *Eclipse of Reason.* New York: Oxford Press, 1974.

Goldstein, Velez-Liendo et al. "IUCN List of Threatened Species." Accessed Feb. 23, 2013. <http://www.iucnredlist.org/details/22066/0>.

Merchant, Carolyn. *The Death of Nature. Women, Ecology and the Scientific Revolution.* New York: Harper and Rowe, 1983.

Naves, Javier et al. "Endangered Species Constrained by Natural and Human Factors: the Case of Brown Bears in Northern Spain." *Conservation Biology* 17:5, Oct. 2003. 1276–1289.

Paisley, Susanna and Nicholas J. Saunders. "A God Forsaken: The Sacred Bear in Andean Iconography and Cosmology." *World Archaeology* 42: 2 (April, 2010): 245–260. Accessed Sept. 12, 2012. <http://www.kent.ac.uk/dice/publications/Paisley_and_Saunders_World_Archaeology.pdf>.

Torres, Denis Alexander. "Spectacled Bear and Culture." *Centro Nacional de Cálculo científico Universidad de los Andes.* 2001. Accessed May 4, 2012. <http://www.cecalc.ula.ve/bioinformatica/oso/culture_cont.htm>.

CHAPTER 22

The Damage and Hope of Total Institutions: Visiting a Bear Sanctuary in Cambodia

Lisa Kemmerer, Daniel Kirjner

There is something about the eyes. They are the first place we look for expression when words fail. Looking into the eyes of a big sun bear, we could see that he was looking back at us. A wall and a cage stood between us. We felt safe—in an uncomfortable sort of a way. This wonderful creature was in *our* world: A world of electric fences. We were naked. Not literally, but as every animal always is. Maybe it makes no sense to feel naked in front of a bear—their eyes likely don't even recognize nakedness. Still, that is how we felt. Derrida notes that the gaze of the non-human doesn't hold the complicated nonsense of a human look. Other animals are not mired in human concepts, values, traditions, and discourse often intent on creating a species barrier (Derrida). We could see in the bear's eyes that he knew us in a way that we would likely never know ourselves.

Though we gazed at one another, locked in our worlds, we were free to leave, but he was not. We had traveled to Cambodia to visit Free the Bears, an animal sanctuary dedicated largely to bears. The sanctuary also houses tigers, pythons, gibbons, crocodiles, elephants, and other displaced wildlife—all victims of human greed, indifference, and ignorance. We had never been to a bear sanctuary before. But there we were, naked looking at naked bears among bushes, buildings, trees, walls, fences and contradictions. The sanctuary walls kept these previously exploited bears safe from the exploitive hands of humanity, safe from slavery, torment, and premature death, but it still felt like a prison. Not in the sense of restraining the liberty of criminals and catering to society's thirst for punishment, but in the sense of protecting those locked inside from an outside world that is simply not safe for them.

An uninformed visitor might mistake this sanctuary for a zoo. But only if uninformed. In zoos, individuals such as bears, giraffes and cobras are turned into a human spectacle. Their freedom is lost for the sake of human profit, interest, and pleasure. They are kidnapped or bred to be curiosities, pleasantries, points of education, and/or matters of scientific importance to a few powerful human beings. Sanctuaries provide a safe-haven for displaced beings—they are fundamentally about those *inside* the walls.

Free the Bears speaks the truth. Visitors wending their way between bear enclosures learn of the heartbreaking stories of human exploitation, cruelty, and stupidity, as well as heartwarming stories about the courage and recovery

© KONINKLIJKE BRILL NV, LEIDEN, 2015 | DOI 10.1163/9789004293090_024

of bears. Each resident has his or her own tale to tell: Some were trafficked as "exotic" pets, others lost their habitat to human enterprise, still others were starved in zoos or displayed as circus slaves; many were slated to have their body parts—paws, gall bladders, skins—sold for human consumption. Some of the bears were raised in captivity after watching the slaughter of their mothers; many were broken mentally, physically, or both. With their mothers killed or enslaved, their habitat destroyed, and their own bodies and minds damaged, these hapless individuals have nowhere to go—all are refugees, protected from the violence that surrounds them by fences, walls, and plexi-glass.

We noted signs of horrific suffering in the soulful eyes of the residents. We watched a sun bear perform a strange ritual behind her enclosure's plexi-glass window—stereotypical behavior brought on by stress and captivity. As soon as she saw us—humans—approaching, she bobbed her head frantically sideways, eyes fixed on our every move. Those naked eyes, again and again, spoke to us of fear as she performed her neurotic dance, a repetitive swaying that seemed to beg, "Please don't hurt me." Her body was healthy, but her mind was broken, too broken for life outside. Nearby, another sun bear padded through his pen on three paws. As a cub, he was caught in a snare. The good people who rescued him amputated his paw to save his life. Indeed, he looked very healthy, though his odd gait touched our hearts. The day he stepped into that snare, his life of freedom became a life sentence: he could no longer survive in the wild.

Free the Bears, like other bona fide sanctuaries around the world, was not created for education, amusement, or the scientific interests of a few old stuffed shirts. Sanctuaries are not designed to bring in profits or to make visitors feel happy or good about themselves. On the contrary, they are one of very few places where human beings are called to contemplate the consequences of their actions, one of very few places where we must face what we have done— what we do. That is why we felt naked in front of a crowd: We were forced to face the cruel legacy of our kind. Life is not only about a healthy, beating heart; life is a collection of choices, experiences, thoughts, and feelings that define and redefine who we are. Like never before, we understood the irreversible damage that humans bring to other animals.

We helped make "enrichments" for the bears, large, plastic balls and bamboo with food crammed or wedged inside. Enrichments are designed to elicit behaviors in bears that are "natural" (in this case foraging behavior), in order to provide physical and mental stimulation and prevent boredom and depression. Trapped in their little pens with no opportunity to do much, enrichments such as these encourage bears to at least make an effort while filling their bellies.

The bizarre spectacle of a host of sun bears gripping large hollow balls stuffed with greens, sweets, and dog food made us think of human children trapped in their modern video-game world, living on simulated experiences instead of the real adventures of life.

As we stood naked before the sun bears, we also pondered the life and death of Ota Benga. Ota Benga was an African Pigmy whose entire village was massacred by Belgian colonizers in the beginning of the 20th century. Bereft of community and family, he was taken from his homeland by Samuel Phillips Verner, a missionary and adventurer who bought Benga from the slave trade and took him to the United States. In 1904, Benga was displayed as an exhibit at the Saint Louis World Fair, where different "types" of humans were featured in cages. Because of Benga's black skin, small size, and sharp pointy teeth, Verner believed Benga would attract considerable attention.

Almost two years after the Saint Louis World Fair, Verner convinced the director of the Bronx Zoo, William Harnaday, to set up an exhibit featuring Benga. A committed social Darwinist, Harnaday placed the African man in an enclosure with orangutans, billing him as a human sub-species, closer to primates than self-proclaimed "more evolved" white Americans (Verner). Ota Benga spent most of 1906 in the Bronx Zoo. Like many bears, lions, and elephants imprisoned in circuses, he was forced to "put on a show" for visitors. He hunted imaginary animals with his spear and shot arrows from a little bow. When he grew weary of performing these unrealistic, stereotypical behaviors, passersby would throw things in the hope of provoking the captive to do something— anything—for their entertainment (Verner). Today, visitors to the zoo, especially children, throw things at thee captives–popcorn, peanuts, whatever might be found nearby–in the hope of provoking some more interesting behavior. As children—as humans—we don't usually think about how a caged animal feels, only about what we want. Children know that throwing popcorn is against the rules, but have no idea that such behavior is demeaning and oppressive. Zoos too often teach us to see displayed animals as subservient to our will, not as independent individuals.

Benga's exhibit created great controversy, and objections from important members of the community, most notably the Christian black community, eventually rallied public opinion against the zoo's racist exhibit, closing it down. But release from captivity could not bring happiness to Benga. He no longer had a place in the world. He was broken from deep loss, from exploitation—from *being* a racist exhibit. He moved about for some time, until he was adopted by a family in Virginia. Although they tried to offer him a better life, it was too little, too late. He was still forced to be a dependent, under the care of others, subject to their lifestyle and rules. Moreover, he remained in a white, racist society that viewed his being, his culture, and his identity as "primitive," as "sub-human." Captivity had transformed him, leaving scars from which he could not recover, and there was no sanctuary to which he might retreat. Ota Benga shot himself in the heart at the age of 32 (Verner).

The poacher's grandson, Phillips Verner Bradford, wrote Benga's biography. One of the most moving stories in Verner's book took place at the Saint Louis World Fair, where Benga was exhibited alongside Geronimo, hero of Native American resistance. Despite remarkable differences (including a language barrier), the two men became friends. They had much in common: Both had been overpowered and broken, and were now caged as an "exhibit" by their oppressors for the amusement (and supposed edification) of a society where white men ruled, and where all others were considered lesser—much lesser. Similarly, those interred at Free the Bears had lost their families and their homes. They were exploited by their captors in various ways, usually for "education" and entertainment, but also for body parts.

The absurdity and misery of caged and broken individuals recalls an Erwing Goffman article, "On the Characteristics of Total Institutions" (expanded into a book in 1961, *Asylums: Essays on the Social Situation of Mental Patients and Other Inmates*), where Goffman coined the term and popularized the concept of "Total Institutions." In modern society, Goffman wrote,

> we tend to sleep, play and work in different places, in each case with a different set of coparticipants, under a different authority, and without an overall rational plan. The central feature of total institutions can be described as a breakdown of the kinds of barriers ordinarily separating these three spheres of life. First, all aspects of life are conducted in the same place and under the same single authority. Second, each phase of the member's daily activity will be carried out in the immediate company of a large batch of others, all of whom are treated alike and required to do the same thing together. Third, all phases of the day's activities are tightly scheduled, with one activity leading at a prearranged time into the next, the whole circle of activities being imposed from above through a system of explicit formal rulings and a body of officials. Finally, the contents of the various enforced activities are brought together as parts of a single overall rational plan purportedly designed to fulfill the official aims of the institution. (Goffman 45)

Total Institutions have an important defining characteristic for Goffman: For those inside, being in this type of a facility is mandatory. Inmates have no

other option, and while present, they must adhere to a strict routine determined by a centralized power. Additionally, those trapped inside are subject to
the principles, objectives, and desires of those in charge. Inmates are forced to
adopt the values and goals of the institution that holds them. In sum, a Total
Institution, forcibly removes individuals from complex social, biological, and
psychological contexts and places them in institutions where they are reduced
to pieces of a very large machine.

Goffman focused on prisons and mental health institutions, but his observations also apply to zoos, circuses, aquariums, marine mammal parks, animal
labs, factory farms, feedlots, puppy mills, slaughterhouses, and other forms of
animal exploitation. Animals in these institutions eat, play, and sleep in the
same place. They remain in the company of others under a single authority.
Despite their individuality, they are all treated in the same way, and they are
required to act collectively. Their lives are scheduled, their behaviors are determined by explicit rules and both are enforced by those who hold power. One
might argue that nonhuman animals do not grasp the moral importance of
central control and deprivation, and that these institutions are therefore not
analogous, but to disqualify animal facilities as Total Institutions on this ground
is to miss the point: Total Institutions standardize behaviors and repress individuality in the process of controlling those within. At the end of the day, it
doesn't matter whether or not inmates understand the institutions—let alone
agree with policies and procedures—so long as they perform their duties as
part of this larger complex. The machine matters, they don't. Pieces of the
machine are expendable and replaceable—what matters is that the machine
persists. Zoos, circuses, aquariums, marine mammal parks, animal labs, factory
farms, feedlots, puppy mills, and slaughterhouses are, in this way, the same.
And those so interred are damaged permanently. As Goffman puts it with
regard to human beings in Total Institutions: "Not only is [a prisoner's] relative
social position within the walls radically different from what it was on the
outside, but, as he comes to learn, if and when he gets out, his social position on
the outside will never again be quite what it was prior to entrance" (Goffman 53).
When animals—including humans—are institutionalized, they are usually
damaged physically and mentally such that they are unable to regain their full
autonomy, freedom, and independence.

In other words, Total Institutions beget Total Institutions. Those leaving
prison often require a halfway house to help them reintegrate into society, inas-
much as they are able to reintegrate back into society. Similarly, nonhuman
animals forced into servitude at zoos, puppy mills, and other Total Institutions—
if they survive—require sanctuaries. In the process of being exploited as mere
means to human ends—profit most fundamentally, entertainment and science

secondarily—they are damaged, and most of them can never be freed into their natural habitat (if their habitat remains). As a result, people who care about these exploited beings create sanctuaries as a means of damage control. The difference between legitimate sanctuaries and places of exploitation (such as circuses, zoos, private petting zoos, factory farms, laboratories, and so on) is that legitimate sanctuaries are *designed for those in need and not for human purposes*. Nonetheless, sanctuaries are Total Institutions—prisons designed for animals who cannot survive outside these firm but gentle walls. Free the Bears is a Total Institution. The bears who live there cannot leave. All that they have and all that they do is tightly controlled by humans. Some were born in captivity, and don't know how to live in a jungle or forest; others were captured long ago and their behaviors are now shaped by strict human routines—created by exploitative outsiders, strangers...a different species. Before they came to live at a sanctuary, many suffered, year after year, from lack of space, malnutrition and starvation, long-term torment, and/or irreparable physical injuries. Though they are bears, they no longer belong to the world of bears. Our selfishness, indifference, and ignorance has robbed them of full bearness. The vast majority of residents at Free the Bears can never be freed. Whether born and raised in captivity or captured, residents have been forever changed by the exploitative hand of humanity. At Free the Bears, we were forced to see that freedom can only be realized in the company of a certain wholeness, in the company of learned skills and socialization. When bears are born into and/or broken by Total Institutions, they can no longer function in their natural environment, and are thereby forced to remain in captivity. Sanctuaries, though they are Total Institutions, are the most humane way that we have found to protect and care for such exploited, damaged beings. Consequently, we are well-advised to share our wealth and our time to support Free the Bears and other genuine sanctuaries (designed for the animals inside, and not for humanity), and encourage others to do the same. We must also insist that sanctuaries include a prominent, accessible educational platform, teaching humanity to leave other animals alone, to respect their habitat, their communities, and their independence—as Free the Bears does.

Perhaps animal advocates focus too much on eliminating suffering at the expense of fighting for total liberation. Maybe the intent of this focus is to create empathy, or perhaps it is a natural outcome of Peter Singer's groundbreaking book, *Animal Liberation*, which focuses on sentience. Whatever the reason may be, our visit to Free the Bears clarified for us the fact that animal advocacy requires more than release from suffering—respect is essential, and respect requires total liberation. While exploited and damaged nonhuman animals find safe-haven at sanctuaries—farm sanctuaries, wildlife sanctuaries, dog and cat sanctuaries, bird sanctuaries, and laboratory animal sanctuaries—their freedom, autonomy, individuality, and full potential are forever denied at these facilities. This cannot rightfully be an end in itself. Moreover, those who advocate on behalf of oppressed human beings do not generally seek to soften suffering—they fight for emancipation. Nelson Mandela encouraged those liberated to "live in a way that respects and enhances the freedom of others" (Mandela 751).

It makes no sense to offer pain relief and enrichments to exploited, damaged nonhumans while failing to attack the structures of oppression that lead to such exploitation and damage. Sanctuaries—Total Institutions complete with electric fences, walls, cages, enrichments, and dedicated caregivers—are not the ultimate solution, but only a measure of restitution for wrongs done. A full and lasting solution requires a change in how we see ourselves in relation to others, in this case nonhumans. We must come to see that we are not superior, and that even if we were, it would still be wrong to exploit other individuals. And we must work to stop the cycle of misery: We must prevent humans from exploiting bears and chickens and seals and chimpanzees in Total Institutions such as zoos and feedlots and aquariums and dairies and labs and breeding facilities. To break the chain of exploitation that traps individuals in Total Institutions in perpetuity, we must recognize our nakedness—not only when we are confronted with the gaze of a sunbear, but also when we are alone in our office or kitchen, or jostled by the masses on a busy city street.

References

Bradford, Phillips Verner. *Ota Benga: The Pygmy in the Zoo*. 1st edition. New York: St Martins Pr, 1992.

Derrida, Jacques. *The Animal that Therefore I Am*. Fordham Univ Press, 2009.

Goffman, Erving. *Asylums: Essays on the Social Situation of Mental Patients and Other Inmates*. Harmondsworth, Eng.; New York: Penguin Books, Limited, 1991.

Mandela, Nelson. *Long Walk to Freedom: The Autobiography of Nelson Mandela*. Little, Brown, 2008. Singer, Peter. *Animal Liberation: A New Ethics for Our Treatment of Animals*. 1st ed. New York: Random House, 1975.

———. *Practical Ethics*. 2 edition. Cambridge: Cambridge University Press, 1999.

CHAPTER 23

Bear Naked: Compassion and Wilderness

Dana Medoro

> The world is gone, lost; I must carry you, bear you.
> —PAUL CELAN

One of the most moving and harrowing works of twentieth-century literature is a short story by William Faulkner titled "The Bear." In it, we learn about Old Ben, a legendary bear who inhabits the Mississippi wilderness of the late 1800s and who has eluded hunters from time out of mind. The young male narrator of "The Bear" trails Old Ben for several years, learning from Sam, a Chickasaw elder, how to navigate the woods without gun or compass. What Faulkner explores through this narrator is a boyhood very different from the one marked by the key ritual of white masculinity in his culture—bagging a bear. He is ultimately forced, however, to watch someone else hunt and kill Old Ben. Significantly, the slaughter coincides with the Chickasaw elder's death, or rather precipitates it.

Borrowing from Chickasaw mythology, Faulkner indicates their entwined spiritual existence and destinies. As they both die—the bear's blood streaming out, the old man lying "motionless ... in the trampled mud"—so too does the spirit of the forest. On the one hand, the scene is mystical and incomprehensible to the white characters; on the other, it is pretty clear-cut. The men's determination to kill Old Ben intensifies and succeeds, and Sam sees the writing on the wall. The story closes with a logging company laying train tracks through the ash trees and a young bear running for cover.

While "The Bear" unfolds through this plotline, it widens into reflections on the conquest of the New World by such a ruthless culture, described as men who exhausted the "last fragments" and "snarled over the gnawed bones of the old world's worthless evening until an accidental egg discovered to them a new hemisphere" (Faulkner 247). The voraciousness that propelled Columbus (that accidental egg) across the sea extends the tale's pervading grief, but it isn't the only system of thinking that survives. The narrator buries Old Ben and Sam, together with the dog used and maimed in the hunt, and recalls what Sam taught him: We are not in the earth or on it, but rather "of earth, myriad yet undiffused of every myriad part, leaf and twig and particle and air ..." (313).

This "myriad yet undiffused of every myriad particle" constitutes a pushing beyond the polarity that would otherwise separate Sam and Old Ben, life and death, compassion and fear, human and wilderness. It is a reformulation of a Chickasaw lesson in a boy's memory, one who repudiates the hunt and its awful trophies of skins and severed paws. What Faulkner explores in his fictional mourning for a bear compares intriguingly with the kind of philosophical inquiry that French philosopher Jacques Derrida undertakes in his essay, "The Animal that Therefore I am," specifically when he illuminates the human/animal polarity at the basis of western thinking. As Derrida attempts to undo this violent division, he makes compassion for other animals central to philosophical inquiry.

Looking back on the past few centuries, Derrida discerns two significant trends running parallel to each other: the philosopher's insistence on defining what is human in relation to what other animals lack; and the increasingly systematized cruelty of human institutions toward other species and their essential habitats. What might philosophers say, he asks, about human meaning in the face of the rapid extinction of wild animals, the overproduction of farm animals, and the interminable torture of laboratory animals—all taking place on a planet that cannot sustain this activity very much longer?

An enduring metaphysics of Man and Animal—oppositional and patriarchal—has produced an abyss into which compassion has fallen. On the one side stands Man alone, dominant and superior and elusive. On the other side stand all manner of entities, from bees to bears, "corralled" (as Derrida cleverly puts it) into Animal. This categorical separation is a crime, he asserts unapologetically, a fault-line and a "wrong ... committed long ago, with long-term consequences" (Derrida 399). To regard the ongoing Western philosophical enterprise as preserving this fault-line is also to see what is at stake for other animals too—"living, dying, speaking, being, and world"—and to see this with new urgency (380). The Earth's ecosystems are dying, even as Man continues to speak in the same voice of separation and superiority.

We've heard it for a long time. It is a voice, for instance, that Faulkner recognized as having ushered in the nuclear era. As he set its sound against an apocalyptic background in his Nobel Prize acceptance speech in 1950, he announced: "It is easy enough to say that man is immortal simply because he will endure: that when the last dingdong of doom has clanged and faded from the last worthless rock hanging tideless in the last red and dying evening, that even then there will still be one more sound: that of his puny inexhaustible voice, still talking." Tackling this notion of immortality as precisely that which divides humans from other animals, he continued: "I refuse to accept this. I believe that man is [...] immortal, not because he alone among creatures has an inexhaustible voice, but because he has a soul, a spirit capable of compassion and sacrifice and endurance." Thus, quickly shifting from the possession of a soul to the capability for compassion as that which matters, Faulkner searches for something that might undo the damage on the edge of a "dying evening."

Derrida's essay turns precisely to our capacity for compassion, likewise searching for voices that include other animals in the creation of meaning; and through such utterances he imagines a potential reversal and the possibility of hope. These voices may yet emerge from the margins of discourse into which they have been forced across time. Moreover, at about the midpoint of "The Animal that Therefore I am," Derrida quotes Jeremy Bentham, asserting that Bentham's question, "Can they suffer?" is a protocol that "changes everything" (396). In other words, the groundwork for starting from a new place has already been laid even within the Western philosophical tradition. With Bentham, as with other philosophers who have followed or preceded him, the ability to suffer is understood as a "shared vulnerability" and as an "obligation with respect to the living in general" (Derrida 395).

This requirement is carried in the word's Latin roots, "com" (with) and "passion" (suffering), which level the Western tendencies toward hierarchy and the removes the central focus placed on human reason. According to Derrida, in light of compassion, everything must be shifted from the abyss between Man and Animal to the ground of "suffering with" other animals in a "heterogeneous multiplicity of the living" (399). Not that this is an easy or self-evident task, but compassion must be redefined from within a philosophical tradition that has long viewed human suffering as uniquely meaningful. "Work, worry, toil and trouble are indeed the lot of almost all men their whole life long," Arthur Schopenhauer aptly laments, "yet if every desire were satisfied as soon as it arose how would men occupy their lives?" He continues, asking us to imagine "a Utopia where everything grows of its own accord and turkeys fly around ready-roasted, where lovers find one another without any delay" (5). In such a Utopia, where turkeys are ready-roasted, lovers are surely all straight. Ways of being and appetites are subtly presupposed and thus the age-old chasm between Man and Animal also yawns wide between Man and everyone else: woman, queer, child, and so on. Each is quarry or quarantined according to Man's point of view.

Indeed, Derrida remarks on the thresholds that appear over the abyss, where the duality of sexual difference might be reconfigured as a multiplicity of sexual differences (in the plural), and where Man recognizes a "shared vulnerability" across all of these folds. He introduces the fault-line of sexual difference right at the beginning of the essay, when he describes his cat following him into the bathroom. Returning again and again to the scene, humorously noting that just as his cat follows him into the bathroom she ("other"—female and animal) immediately wants out. As this female cat (nameless) articulates something to the human male (Jacques Derrida, the great philosopher), she sets into motion a multitude of thoughts about compassion and control: inside and outside, entrapment and belonging, human corporeal shame and human intellectual pride. Though he does not delineate these possibilities, the scene that describes his naked self in the bathroom with his cat is staged in order to call attention to what it might mean to contemplate other animals recognizing our naked vulnerability, stripped of human clothing and other trappings of civilization. In the process, he exposes "human" as a kind of armor that we place between ourselves and the rest of the world.

Derrida's bathroom scene likely alludes to psychoanalyst Jacques Lacan's sketch of sexual difference in *Écrits*, in which he uses the image of bathroom doors to illustrate the power of symbolization over human bodies. Powerfully, two doors are depicted on the page as simple rectangles in order to insure the clarity of their visualization. Human language, Lacan argues, inscribes us into male and female; it functions like the symbol on a bathroom door and compels us to identify with one or the other. Lacan indicates that being human in the Western world is an experience of division—of being cut off from all other living beings and the earth itself.

What does it mean for a cat to follow you through one of those doors? What does it mean that she is admitted? In the bathroom, Derrida breaches the border that Lacan tries to secure. That is to say, whatever "human" may be, it is not inevitably or eternally split into a sexed identity, and neither is "human" cut off from other animals. As we pass through the bathroom door with Derrida, all capitalized polarities unravel—Human/Animal, Man/Woman, Straight/Gay— and we begin to recognize the optical, political, linguistic, mythic devices that sustain these false divisions. Even so, our capacity for recognition does not necessarily override our capacity for disavowal: Our powerful ability to deny that we are animals.

The question of compassion is thus a difficult one, for it is bigger than discovering our capacity for sympathy or vulnerability. As a species, we also have a remarkable capacity for repression, and this further complicates our ability to foster compassion across artificial barriers; we can see suffering, then immediately push it into the far recesses of our minds. Additionally, we manipulate the concept of compassion into yet another arrogantly distorted mirror of self-identification. The last thing the world needs is a framework of compassion in which people weep a little over a system of oppression that they endorse, sometimes termed the "Walrus and the Carpenter Syndrome," weeping while you devour the one you pity references a scene in Lewis Carroll's *Alice in Wonderland*:

The Walrus and the Carpenter
Walked on a mile or so,
And then they rested on a rock
Conveniently low:
And all the little Oysters stood
And waited in a row.
"The time has come," the Walrus said,
"To talk of many things:
Of shoes—and ships—and sealing-wax—
Of cabbages—and kings—
And why the sea is boiling hot—
And whether pigs have wings."
"But wait a bit," the Oysters cried,
"Before we have our chat;
For some of us are out of breath,
And all of us are fat!"
"No hurry!" said the Carpenter.
They thanked him much for that.
"A loaf of bread," the Walrus said,
"Is what we chiefly need:
Pepper and vinegar besides
Are very good indeed—
Now if you're ready, Oysters dear,
We can begin to feed."
"But not on us!" the Oysters cried,
Turning a little blue.
"After such kindness, that would be
A dismal thing to do!"
"The night is fine," the Walrus said.
"Do you admire the view?
"It was so kind of you to come!
And you are very nice!"
The Carpenter said nothing but
"Cut us another slice:
I wish you were not quite so deaf—
I've had to ask you twice!"
"It seems a shame," the Walrus said,
"To play them such a trick,
After we've brought them out so far,
And made them trot so quick!"

The Carpenter said nothing but
"The butter's spread too thick!"
"I weep for you," the Walrus said:
"I deeply sympathize."
With sobs and tears he sorted out
Those of the largest size,
Holding his pocket-handkerchief
Before his streaming eyes.
"Oysters," said the Carpenter,
"You've had a pleasant run!
Shall we be trotting home again?'
But answer came there none
And this was scarcely odd, because
They'd eaten every one.
         CARROLL 138

The ending is unexpected, leaving the reader engulfed in silence. Somewhere in the spaces between the last stanzas, the walrus and the carpenter have gobbled up the oysters. Readers probably knew it was going to happen all along, but the last line's finality captures the strangeness of their rapid consumption, the unconscious nature of destroying something that we know, somewhere in the deep recesses of our minds, that we should not destroy. The Walrus and the Carpenter hit the end without realizing it—or without wanting to realize it—even as their tears fall.

Derrida in fact finds in Lewis Carroll's strange animals an imaginative route into philosophical inquiry. The Cheshire Cat particularly fascinates him, for there is something momentous in the Cat's declaration: "'We're all mad here. I'm mad. You're mad" (quoted in Derrida 378). It seems that starting with madness, rather than rationality—and with compassion, rather than division and hierarchy—is one way forward. Is it not madness, for example, to lay waste the planet on which we depend? When the Walrus and the Carpenter emerge from their voraciousness to discover that the oysters have been consumed, their realization comes too late. This is the recognition upon which the meaning of extinction rests: it is too late.

This is also the Anthropocene, in which human activity has affected every aspect of Earth: climate, ecosystems, and species everywhere. All forms of life are increasingly endangered; everything from soil to sea is disrupted by our incursions. We have arrived at a place where it has become urgent to turn back toward compassion, toward suffering with, and to address our own madness evidenced in foundations of seemingly sane human institutions. We must dismantle false and divisive polarities, perhaps starting with the polarity that separates Civilization from Wilderness, even as the former encroaches unendingly on the latter, allowing us to view everything that exists in the natural world as a resource to satisfy human wants. Historically, the Western world has seen the natural world as something to be feared, conquered, and plundered. But there are many alterative models for human interactions with the natural world offered through myth and religion, math and physics, biology and animal studies, down through history and around the world.

Myths, for instance, tend to tell a different story, a story of interwoven webs of correspondence and vulnerability. In North America, before Europeans invaded, earlier peoples developed conceptual systems in which the land, animals, and natural forces were part of the human community, rather than lesser, waiting to be vanquished. Consider this: while Jacques Derrida's domestic house cat is the creature before whom he stands naked in Paris, contemplating co-existence with other creatures, Native Americans negotiated shared spaces with other animals who might eat them for dinner. Jacques Derrida, while contemplating his animal nature, does not gaze into the eyes of a grizzly bear. That would not be advisable. Myths of aboriginal cultures present humans and other animals in complex ways, unique and democratic, in comparison with those that predominate in Western philosophy. These myths do not indicate a radical separation between Man and Animal, as Faulkner's "The Bear" so carefully attempts to show. For example, this compelling excerpt from a myth of origin among the Modoc people of North America illuminates an entwined genealogy of humans in the so-called wilderness:

> Now the grizzlies possessed all the wood and all the land even down to the sea at that time, and they were very numerous and powerful. They were not exactly beasts then, although they were covered with hair, lived in caves and had sharp claws; but they walked on two legs, talked, and used clubs to fight with instead of their teeth and claws as they do today. At this time there was a family of grizzlies living close up to the snow. The father found this child, red like fire, hid under a fir bush, and took her to the old mother who said she would rear her with the other children. When their eldest son was grown up he married her and many children were born to them. But, being part of the Great Spirit and part of the grizzly bear, these children did not resemble either parent, but partook somewhat of the nature and likeness of both. Thus the red man was created, for these children were the first Indians.
>
> MODOC MYTHS

This Modoc myth paints co-existence as something that humans and bears worked out early on, stressing "being part of" rather than separation and hierarchy.

Their myth of human origins is also a genealogy of bears, in which bears are "not exactly beasts," indicating that human and grizzly are not necessarily in separate categories. In this worldview, human and bear are pulled together in a mystery of being and belonging. These long memories of bears and forests— describing how to be myriad, as Faulkner puts it, or compassionate, as Derrida defines it—have a chance to show the way forward, if we are looking for a path that might preserve what is left of the world.

References

Carrol, Lewis. *Alice's Adventures in Wonderland and Through the Looking Glass.* 1871. New York: Jackson Mahr Press, 2010.

Derrida, Jacques. "The Animal that Therefore I am (more to follow)." *Critical Inquiry* 28.2. Winter 2002. 369–418.

Faulkner, William. "The Bear." *Go Down, Moses.* New York: Vintage International, 1990.

———. Nobel Prize Acceptance Speech (1950). <www.nobelprize.org>. Accessed 1 April 2013.

"Modoc Myths and Legends and Other Stories." *Klamath County Museums: Research Resources.* Mount Shasta, from Diller, Mt. Shasta National Geographic Monograph 1895. Accessed 1 April, 2013. <www.co.klamath.or.us/museum/modocmyths.htm>.

Schopenhauer, Arthur. *On the Suffering of the World. Penguin's Great Ideas Series #14.* London: Penguin, 2005.

Index

www.ingramcontent.com/pod-product-compliance
Lightning Source LLC
Chambersburg PA
CBHW050415280326

41932CB00013BA/1865